CHAIN OF GOLD

Chain of Gold

Greek Rhetoric in the Roman Empire

Susan C. Jarratt

Southern Illinois University Press
Carbondale

Southern Illinois University Press
www.siupress.com

Printed in the United States of America

22 21 20 19   4 3 2 1

Cover illustration: *The Course of Empire: The Consummation of Empire*, 1836, by Thomas Cole (cropped). NEW-YORK HISTORICAL SOCIETY; CREATIVE COMMONS.

Library of Congress Cataloging-in-Publication Data
Names: Jarratt, Susan Carole Funderburgh, author.
Title: Chain of gold : Greek rhetoric in the Roman empire / Susan C. Jarratt.
Description: Carbondale : Southern Illinois University Press, 2019. | Includes bibliographical references and index.
Identifiers: LCCN 2019011044 | ISBN 9780809337538 (pbk.) | ISBN 9780809337545 (e-book)
Subjects: LCSH: Rhetoric, Ancient. | Greek literature—History and criticism.
Classification: LCC PA3265 .J36 2019 | DDC 808/.00938—dc23 LC record available at https://lccn.loc.gov/2019011044

Printed on recycled paper ♲

In memory of James L. Kinneavy

CONTENTS

ILLUSTRATIONS

ACKNOWLEDGMENTS

What a great pleasure it has been to call to mind and express my gratitude to the many people and institutions that have played a part in the development of this project. It began with a National Endowment for the Humanities University Fellowship awarded for a book about rhetoric and the public sphere across a number of historical periods. I'm very grateful for this award, although the resulting publications took quite a different shape from what I originally proposed. The fellowship year gave me time for archival work that found its way into journal articles but also provided space for reflection about the larger endeavor, which metamorphosed from a pan-historical enterprise into a focused study of Greek rhetoric in the postclassical period. Susan Wells was a strong supporter of this project in its initial iteration and has been an invaluable touchstone over the years for all things rhetorical, professional, political, and familial. Miami University, where I taught at the time, gave me research leave, for which I'm grateful. There I experienced my first-ever writing group; with Alice Adams, Lori Merish, and Victoria Smith, I learned so much about process, imperfection, and persistence. I was fortunate to have a number of fine graduate students then who helped me think through publics theory and many other rhetorical and political issues, especially Scott Lyons, Gwendolyn Pough, and Jill Swiencicki. It's been a great pleasure to follow their impressive careers in the years since. I also appreciate continuing conversations with Peter W. Rose, a comrade from Miami days who has read and commented on chapter drafts and whose own work on rhetoric and imperialism has led to many stimulating exchanges.

When I moved to the University of California, Irvine, I found an institutional home in the vibrant and eclectic Department of Comparative Literature, whose faculty welcomed a historian of rhetoric into their midst. Jane O. Newman and John H. Smith have been especially encouraging over the years, prodding me to keep going on this project when it seemed overwhelming. I thank the department and the School of Humanities at UCI for various forms of support for this work. A thoroughgoing Hellenophile, I slowly came to see that a project so solidly grounded in the Roman imperial context needed a finer attunement to that world. Thus I was honored when Eleanor Leach and Eve D'Ambra included me in an NEH Summer Seminar called Identity and Self-Representation in the Subcultures of Ancient Rome, held at the American Academy in Rome in 2008. The experience of reading, viewing, studying, and living amid the beauties of the Roman world with fifteen talented, energetic, generous, and fun participants in that seminar was a gift of the gods. I thank them all—gods and participants—for introducing me to the wonder and delight of encountering art and architecture in situ, and for the opportunity to see Roman art, history, and culture through the eyes of such fine scholars. I learned so much from my congenial and creative flatmates Sonia Sabnis and Livia Tenser. A few years later, a grant from the Borchard Foundation allowed me to draw on the expertise of French specialists in second sophistic rhetoric. I'm extremely thankful for this opportunity to have had conversations with Barbara Cassin, Estelle Oudot, and especially with Laurent Pernot, who generously shared his deep knowledge of the period and offered encouragement for my project.

On this side of the Atlantic, I appreciate those dedicated to the American Society for the History of Rhetoric for keeping our field alive and growing, and for their support of my work. I'm thinking especially of Ira James Allen, Michele Kennerly, Kathleen Lamp, Ned O'Gorman, Scott Stroud, and Dave Tell. Janet Atwill has been a valued interlocutor on many topics, including ancient Greek rhetoric and language. I owe her many thanks for arranging our travel to the beautiful ruins at Ephesus, Aphrodisias, and Hieropolis, and for a long and intellectually stimulating friendship. Other rhetoric scholars who haven't been directly engaged with this project but are valued fellow travelers in the history of rhetoric include Michelle Ballif, Barbara Biesecker, Rosa Eberly, Michael Halloran, Ekaterina Haskins, Debra Hawhee, Andrea Lunsford, Carolyn R. Miller, Arthur Walzer, and Victor Vitanza. My work, whatever its worth, would be impossible without the innovative and inspiring scholarship of Jeffrey Walker.

I'm grateful for having had opportunities to share portions of the book while in progress, including invitations from the graduate student rhetoric group at the University of Nevada, Reno, and the English graduate student conference organizers at California State University, Northridge. I also thank colleagues at the University of Wisconsin, Madison; Portland State University; the University of Strasbourg; and the American Comparative Literature Association for invitations to present my work. Here at UCI, it was a special honor to present a keynote address on the conclusion of my book at a local conference on persuasion organized by Jonathan Alexander and Jens Lloyd on the occasion of my retirement.

I also thank those who have solicited and published earlier versions of several chapters. Material in chapter 1 on Libanius' encomium of Antioch appeared as "Libanius' Antioch: A Rhetorical Construction of the Greek (Cosmo)Polis" in *Polis and Cosmopolis: Problems of the Global Era*, edited by K. Boudouris (Ionia Publications, 2003) and also in "The Prospects for the Public Work of Rhetoric: A Coda on Codes" in *The Public Work of Rhetoric*, edited by John Ackerman and David Coogan (University of South Carolina Press, 2010). An earlier version of chapter 2 on Dio Chrysostom was published in a special issue of *Advances in the History of Rhetoric* (2011), edited by Ned O'Gorman. I thank Laurent Pernot for inviting me to contribute my study of Aristides' *Roman Oration* (chapter 3) to *Aelius Aristide Écrivain* (Brepols Publishers, 2016), and Cheryl Glenn and Roxanne Mountford, editors of *Rhetoric and Writing Studies in the New Century: Historiography, Pedagogy, and Politics* (Southern Illinois University Press, 2017) for including a version of my work on Julia Domna and Philostratus (chapter 4).

Karl Kageff, former acquisitions editor at Southern Illinois University Press, offered encouragement for this project year after year. Many thanks for his gentle persistence and optimism. Since Karl's retirement, Kristine Priddy and her colleagues have been very supportive. The two anonymous readers of the manuscript were thoughtful and generous; I very much appreciate their contributions to the work.

Closer to home, the faculty and graduate students in the rhetoric group at UCI and across Southern California have forged a lively and sustaining community through our quarterly reading groups, road trips, local conferences, and many other adventures. Jonathan Alexander, Ian Barnard, Daniel Gross, Stephen Mailloux, Vorris Nunley, Ellen Quandahl, and Aniel Rallin show up and keep the conversation going. Our astute and agreeable graduate students ask hard questions and lead us into new rhetorical terrain. My warmest thanks for their intelligence, wit, and rhetorical energy to Katherine Mack, Abraham Romney, Alexandra Sartor, Libby Catchings, Jasmine Lee, Jens Lloyd, Maureen Fitzsimmons, and Allison Dziuba. The latest brainstorm in the West Coast rhetoric world brought forth SCRAWL, the Southern California Rhetoric and Writers' League. For the genesis of the chapter on curation, I thank fellow SCRAWLers Jasmine Lee and Alexandra Cavallaro.

Friends and family sweeten the labor and knit up the raveled ends of thoughts and days. Nasrin Rahimieh has become a stalwart companion. It's a rare friend with whom you can sort out institutional politics, trade fashion tips, and share bottomless cat love. Jonathan Alexander has been more than a supportive colleague: over the years our writing collaborations, conversations about journal editing, edgy opera adventures, and music-making have been life-sustaining. And at last, my special thanks to Ellen Quandahl—brilliant scholar of Greek, collaborator on our Anna project, fellow protest marcher, and listening ear over years of drama and angst as this project has slowly crawled to its completion. How fortunate that we ended up in the same corner of the world. My families know who they are: the Millers in Portland, the two best brothers imaginable, the Houston family unit, and the Easter County Texans. Thanks for dutifully asking about my studies of the ancient world over all these years and, much more so, for giving me here-and-now worlds of love and joy.

My final expression of gratitude comes in the dedication. James L. Kinneavy was a professor in the English department at the University of Texas at Austin when I entered the PhD program in 1981. He welcomed me into the rhetoric and composition group, although, as a writing teacher with an MA in English literature, I knew almost nothing about rhetoric, history, theory, ancient languages, or the demands of scholarly inquiry. I cannot imagine a better mentor and exemplar. Kinneavy brought together deep learning in ancient rhetoric, a mind for contemporary theory, and a passion for teaching composition, with a lightness of spirit, even irreverence, that leavened all these weighty enterprises. There's a bit of sophistry in that mix, though I don't think he would have embraced the label. I'm still thankful that he suggested the sophists to me as an area of study, and I hope this book honors his memory.

PREFACE

For of all who have ever gained empire you alone rule over men who are free.

—Aelius Aristides, *Roman Oration* (144 CE), ¶36

Empires speak to each other across time. The post-cold-war era created a kairotic resonance for this study when advocates of US global supremacy began referring to a *pax Americana* on analogy with *pax Romana* (Roman peace), a phrase inaugurated during the reign of Augustus at the turn of the first millennium to describe, praise, and promote Roman imperialism.[1] Proponents, both ancient and contemporary, endorse imperial projects because of their supposed benefits: political stability, technological advance, and the spread of "freedom." But scholars from classics, political theory, and rhetoric studies as well as journalists expose the *pax* labels as ideological constructs covering over harsh realities of continuing war abroad and various forms of violence perpetuated by and within the state.[2] As Greg Woolf writes, "Roman peace may be seen as simply a component of wider patterns of violence, a concomitant of other structures of domination" ("Roman Peace" 172). The quotation above from Greek rhetor Aristides' encomium of the city of Rome subtly prefigures this insight: How much and what kinds of freedom are possible in these "peaceful" empires? Today in the US we can easily access vigorous public discourses of critique and resistance, but what was it possible to say or write in the face of the *pax Romana*? Histories always serve present needs, and for our time, there is a need to recognize empire not only as an empirical historical fact but also as an analytic frame for rhetorical study, and to put ancient and contemporary discourses in critical contact with each other.[3]

Thomas Cole's eerily beautiful painting *The Consummation of Empire*, a section of which appears on the cover of this book, visually enacts such contact. Cole, born in England in 1801, immigrated as a child with his family to the US and began to create a singularly American body of work. Inspired by the natural beauty of American landscapes, Cole's paintings "mapped the grand possibilities of a still barely known continent" (J. Jones). In the 1830s, he traveled back to England and then toured ancient ruins in Italy. On his return to the US, he produced five large canvases in an allegorical series titled *The Course of Empire* (1833–1836). The sequence begins with a pristine American scene that evolves gradually into the elegant city depicted in *Consummation* (the third painting in the series) and then falls into an ugly, brutal ruin brought about by war. Neither Cole's moralistic message about the corrupting force of civilization nor his investment in a rise-and-fall theory of history is relevant here. But his vision of America as the next great empire on analogy with those of the ancient Mediterranean sets a suggestive tone. The Greekness of the Roman scene—with its pedimental architecture, caryatids, and sacrificial fires—layers one empire atop another. An air of decadence washes over the painting, the dreamy pastels embellished with touches (if not yet chains) of gold. A busy harbor occupies the center of the scene, but the action seems stilled somehow by the calm reflections in the bay. And the figures in the military triumph moving across the foreground—the emperor or general in red—are so tiny that we can barely make out the spoils of war and the enslaved victims of conquest that, historically, would have been part of such a procession.

These enticing optics of empire are evocative of themes and tensions, aesthetics and interpretive puzzles, characteristic of Greek rhetoric in the first four centuries of the Common Era. Considering the second sophists, as these Greek rhetors are known, as colonial subjects, this study attempts to bring to light the perilous political conditions within which Greek rhetorical performance under the Roman empire took shape: the world it mediated and re-presented, and in which it sought to intervene. For those unfamiliar with the period, this book will serve as an introduction, but my purpose is less a comprehensive overview and more a focused analysis of rhetorical practices within specific historical contexts. The chapters to follow highlight the power relations constantly impinging upon Greek rhetors in the imperial world and the tactics with which those rhetors acknowledged, figured, and negotiated that imperial power.

Concerning texts and translations, I use Loeb Classical Library editions of the ancient Greek when they are available. Other editions and translations are listed in "Works Cited and Consulted," and my own translations of key terms and passages are indicated in the text. Where Greek terms are given, I use transliteration, and for ease of reference I've preserved inflections from the original contexts. Translations from the French are my own.

CHAIN OF GOLD

CHAPTER 1

Rhetorical Possibilities under Empire: Captivity, Complicity

[Under empire] a tide of horror lapped close to the feet of all educated persons . . .

—Peter Brown, *Power and Persuasion in Late Antiquity*

The contemporary imperial context is a provocation and field of reception for this project: an exploration of Greek rhetoric during the period of the Roman empire. That the rhetoric of this period has undergone a recent revival of scholarly interest may have something to do with the changing fortunes of empires across the globe since the mid-twentieth century. B. P. Reardon, in his introduction to new translations of the ancient Greek novels, points to the significance of imperialism in changing assessments of literary/rhetorical value: "In the nineteenth and early twentieth centuries the imperial nations of the West . . . took it for granted that what was important about the early centuries of our era was the immensely impressive political fact of the Roman Empire; it naturally had the sympathy of people who themselves ruled empires, or aspired to do so, and the Greek world of the imperial period attracted less attention" (13). Now, observes Reardon, in an era of postcolonial consciousness, we can look "behind the Roman Empire" to the Greeks of the imperial period (14). Tim Whitmarsh signals this shift in his survey of the second sophists: "The Greek literary culture of the first three centuries of our era is no longer viewed as an embarrassing epilogue. . . . [T]hat Greeks of the period were under Roman occupation is now more likely to inspire sympathetic analyses of colonial politics than dismissive sniffs at a weak and decadent culture" (*Second Sophistic* 1).[1] The older view that rhetorical activity and quality declined in this era has been eloquently refuted in a dynamic and growing body of scholarship by (among others)

British classicists Simon Goldhill and Tim Whitmarsh, French rhetoric scholars Barbara Cassin and Laurent Pernot, and by US rhetorician Jeffrey Walker, who asserts that the Greek *paideia*, the encyclopedic course of study with rhetoric at its center, flourished not only as a scholarly enterprise but as a political instrument: it "gave the rhetorically skilled, well-educated provincial a means of countering and to some extent reducing the inequities of power when dealing with imperial authority" (*Rhetoric and Poetics* 88).

In the modern period, the successful overthrow of European imperial control by former colonies in India, the Middle East, Africa, and Latin America has given rise to a rich rhetorical and theoretical legacy: the impressive body of postcolonial thinking from writers such as Homi Bhabha, Franz Fanon, Edward Said, and Gayatri Spivak. It is tempting to turn to this body of work as a framework for analysis for the earlier period, and a few classicists have done so. D. J. Mattingly, for example, in his introduction to an edited collection titled *Dialogues in Roman Imperialism: Power, Discourse, and Discrepant Experience in the Roman Empire*, notes a tendency for contemporary scholars reading ancient texts (in this case visual art) to emphasize emulation of dominant forms and to neglect or overlook multiple readings for encoded resistance (11).[2] Mattingly recommends that classicists "show more awareness that the ancient sources available to us are part of an imperial discourse of extraordinary inequality, and that our own reading of these written sources is made within the framework of value systems and ideological baggage of the modern imperial age" (14). Though Mattingly uses the language of resistance, neither he nor the contributors seek to find or presuppose a unified resistant stance and instead adopt Edward Said's "discrepant experience" as a guide (*Culture and Imperialism* 31–43).

But other scholars find even such qualified terms too blunt an instrument to account for the second sophistic phenomenon. Pernot writes of Aristides, "It is neither a matter of frontal attacks, nor of being 'pro-Roman' or 'anti-Roman.' We are not speaking of opposition or dissidence" ("Aelius Aristides" 177). In another case, we find Ian Henderson in "The Second Sophistic and Non-elite Speakers" using Homi Bhabha's concept of mimicry to identify a group of "pseudo-sophists" at various degrees of remove from the most secure elite status of second sophist. Noting comments about rusticity or vulgarity in Philostratus' extensive catalogue, Henderson observes ambiguities in Favorinus' cultural, sexual, and political identities; proposes certain Christian authors as sophistic imitators in "centres of cultural *métissage* such as Alexandria and Corinth"; and speculates about the reason Lucian—the most virtuosic and daring of literary artists in this era—was not a successful sophist. This is fascinating work that breaks up the clustering of second sophists identified by Philostratus (*Lives*) and draws on the postcolonial theorist with the subtlest address to rhetoric. But these scholars are the exception in finding critical resonances with contemporary postcolonial theory. Differences between the Roman imperial situation and modern empires, it would seem, are dramatic enough to demand distinctive modes of analysis calibrated to the particular character of the Roman empire.

Historians such as P. A. Brunt (*Roman Imperial Themes*) and Fergus Millar (*Emperor*) detail the distinctive character of the Roman imperial project in contrast both with ancient Greek empires (Athenian and Macedonian) and with modern empires.[3] In contrast with the Hellenizing practices of Athens in the archaic and classical periods and later of Alexander, as well as with the settler colonialism of modern empires, Rome was relatively uninterested in cultural imposition. Where local control was concerned in the eastern provinces, Rome relied on indigenous elites for administrative expertise. Of course the extraction of resources—tribute—is a common element in all imperial relations, as is the violence attendant on conquest and the maintenance of rule. Investigating the particular situation of Greek intellectuals within this system is the aim of this chapter and of the whole project, but a crucial starting point is the observation that, unlike other premodern and modern colonized subjects whose differences are marked by language, economic deprivation, and racialization, Greek rhetors under Roman empire spoke both from within and without simultaneously.[4]

Like colonized speakers and writers of every era, they engaged *topoi* of geographic displacement, cultural memory, and tactical political agency, constructing not merely beautiful, trivial distractions of a smoothly assimilated elite but intricate negotiations with *imperium*. But notwithstanding their status and rhetorical accomplishments, the second sophists were subject to the vicissitudes of imperial force. In his recent overview Andrew Erskine notes that, despite the Roman disinclination to interrupt the local customs of their colonies, "Roman authorities never lost their appreciation of the value of terror" (*Roman Imperialism* 69). As Peter Brown observes in the epigraph above, imperial violence—potential or immediate, material or symbolic—was the unavoidable backdrop for every rhetorical act: a reality perhaps too easily forgotten or disregarded by scholars of ancient rhetoric in imperial settings. The Roman conquest of Greek cities and territories, already subjugated by the Macedonian and Seleucid empires after Alexander's death, occurred over a period from the mid-third century BCE up to the razing of Corinth in 146 BCE. The subject of a massive, and massively influential history by Achaean Polybius (200–118 BCE), Roman imperial dominance over Greece may seem less brutal than it was because of Polybius' purportedly pro-Roman outlook. But more recent assessments of this first Greek historian under Rome are beginning to emphasize his status as hostage and the shift in perspective in the later books, after the violent destruction of Corinth (Erskine, "Polybius"; J. Henderson; Jarratt, "Historiographical Trauma"). Another broad assumption—that Roman violence abated after the establishment of empire under Augustus—likewise deserves closer scrutiny. While armed conflict moved for the most part to the far reaches of empire during the first through fourth centuries, and a series of more moderate emperors from Trajan through Marcus Aurelius reigned during the period, "state-sponsored violence [was] rarely far from the surface in the Roman world, a truth evident to all ages and all levels of society" (Erskine, *Roman Imperialism* 69).[5] Against this backdrop then, we apprehend the rhetorical phenomenon of the second sophistic.

Second sophists: Greek captives, cultural captors

> Now ancient sophistic, even when it propounded philosophical themes, used to discuss them diffusely and at length; for it discoursed on courage . . . justice, . . . heroes and gods, and how the universe has been fashioned into its present shape. But the sophistic that followed it, which we must not call "new," for it is old, but rather "second," sketched the types of the poor man and the rich, of princes and tyrants, and handled arguments that are concerned with definite and special themes for which history shows the way. Gorgias of Leontini founded the older type in Thessaly, and Aeschines, son of Atrometus, founded the second, after he had been exiled from political life at Athens.
>
> —Philostratus, *Lives of the Sophists*, ¶481

Histories of rhetoric are replete with lost geographies, not only those pockets of populations excluded from public life, but also terrains present in the record but previously unreadable.[6] The culturally Greek intelligentsia from the eastern provinces of the Roman empire inhabited some of those geographies—not completely lost but temporarily misplaced in rhetoric's history.

Until recently encased within a narrative of decline into "literariness" on account of the diminished opportunities for deliberative rhetoric with the decisive arrival of empire (Kennedy, *Classical Rhetoric*), these rhetors—many of whom are gathered under the term *second sophistic* by Philostratus, one of their number—flourished and struggled in the first through fourth centuries of the Common Era.[7] An older view of this period, taking its cue from some contemporaneous assessments of the era itself, dismissed Greek rhetoric in Roman imperial times as impotent and trivial, merely decorative, or sometimes as decadent, diseased, or corrupt (Gibbon; Saintsbury). It is the case that the writings of these figures sometimes have qualities unexpected by contemporary readers: uncontained fancy, digressiveness, excessiveness, a kind of compulsion for reworking classical themes and references, strange ways of representing bodies, an obsession with visual representation. But scholars in the past two decades have begun to reconsider this period, arriving at a dramatic counterstatement to centuries-old historiography: that public rhetoric did not die out in the era of Roman empire; that opportunities for imagining, performing, and arguing for the collective good for subjects of empire did not disappear but in fact persisted, though coded within an array of unfamiliar genres. Located at a unique nexus of rhetorical expertise and Roman imperial power, Greek rhetors in the first four centuries of the Common Era not only advanced the pedagogical project of Greek rhetoric, and their own fortunes, but also addressed their circumstances as subjects of empire. Whereas older studies viewed culturally Greek rhetors scattered across the empire as staid and conservative (or even decadent) for dwelling continuously in the fossilized world of classics in the interest of preserving their positions in an intelligentsia after the rise of the Roman empire, a new wave of scholarship has radically revised this orientation by elaborating on observations such as Laurent Pernot's that the cultural phenomenon of the second sophistic was not contained within the walls of the schoolroom but intervened in the life of the city, the province, and, in some cases, the emperor ("Rhétorique de l'Empire" 138).

We get the name for Greek rhetors who lived after the end of Athenian democracy from the member of their group who described them: Flavius Philostratus (170–244 CE). His *Lives of the Sophists* constitutes the fullest record of Greek rhetoricians of the period in the form of an informal biographical list and account.[8] Most historians of rhetoric comment on the arbitrary nature of Philostratus' time line and categorizing: Aeschines, fourth-century BCE antagonist of Demosthenes, is counted among the ten Attic orators of the classical period (Pernot, *Rhetoric* 36–38), while the other forty-odd second sophists in Philostratus' *Lives* lived in the Roman imperial era. Pernot terms Aeschines a "forefather" (186); perhaps his exile foreshadowed the circumstances of the later sophists because he was displaced from the crucible of democratic political life. The second sophists shared characteristics of their fifth- and fourth-century BCE predecessors: they were traveling orators, ambassadors, and educators, each associated with a provincial city and some occupying chairs of rhetoric, offering the equivalent of advanced degrees in the subject. And, as in the case of the first sophistic, the figures grouped as second sophists did not affiliate formally with each other in a self-conscious program but rather gave evidence to others of having a "common spirit, a shared educational and intellectual practice" (Pernot, *Rhetoric* 187).[9] At the outset of his work, Philostratus contrasts the more philosophical and ethically oriented project of the first sophists with the preoccupations of the later ones who offered character types from declamation exercises (the rich, the poor, the tyrant) and concrete historical cases.[10] But as crucial a reference as it is, Philostratus' work has its limitations. In the view of Maud W. Gleason, "The praises left on marble and in the pages of Philostratus give to lives of outstanding rhetorical accomplishment a triumphant sheen that seems almost designed to distract our attention from questions about what cultural forces were at work beneath the surface" ("Greek Cities" 245). Thus not too much weight should be put on Philostratus' section-opening epigraph as a defining statement, but the categories of rich, poor, and tyrant do predict the potential for social critique in second sophistic oratory. At the same time they call to mind the *paideia*, a general course of study offered by Greek rhetors and assumed as common cultural capital among both Roman and Greek elite. Getting a fuller sense of the second sophistic demands that attention be paid to the special status of Greeks and their culture for the Roman conquerors.

Romans drew on Greek culture from the beginning, as, according to Horace, Hellenism "took its fierce captor captive" (*Graecia capta ferum victorem cepit*) (Epistle 2.1.156; qtd. in G. Anderson, *Second Sophistic* 7; on this passage, see also Whitmarsh, *Greek Literature* 11–12). There was a persistent valuing of Greek language and culture in the Greek-Roman connection and a "strong sense of continuing Hellenic identity" (G. Anderson, *Second Sophistic* 3). Indeed, the Greeks, with their own history of empire, shared an identity as conquerors. A central aspect of the cultural interaction was their mutual interest in Greek traditions. According to Graham Anderson, "the very fact of the Greek past as a past invested [the new Roman empire] with a veneer of antique wisdom at the outset. The tendency of Greeks to persevere in the preservation of things Greek would have provoked admiration from those in search of a complex of historical and legendary traditions longer and more illustrious than their own" (7). Anderson gives an example of this reverence from a letter by Pliny the Younger to one Maximus, soon to become governor of Achaea; several generations after Polybius' time there, Pliny represents Greece as a land "real and pure, where civilisation and letters . . . originated." Pliny advises respect for ancient glory, for "sheer antiquity," and advises against detracting from his subjects' dignity: "Remember that this is the land which gave us rights and provided us with laws, not as conquered subjects, but at our own request" (Pliny, Epistle 8.24.2ff.; qtd. in Anderson 102). Pliny's euphemism is not echoed in the advice of Plutarch, a first-century Greek intellectual who became a Roman citizen, to an aspiring Greek military man: he was advised to model himself after Pericles but not to forget about the Roman boot just above his head (*Praecepta gerendae reipublicae* 813D; qtd. in Anderson 102). From the razing of Corinth through the civil wars at the end of the first century BCE to the installation of Octavian Caesar as Augustus in 27 BCE and beyond, Greek cities were pillaged for art and intellectuals, denied freedom, and suffered economic decline.[11] The almost-schizophrenic differences in attitudes on the part of both conquering Romans and conquered Greeks telegraphed above must be factored into an understanding of rhetorical activity in the period. Contemporary postcolonial theory has generated a range of approaches to rhetorics of the colonized, and yet no modern imperial relationship quite replicates the complex entanglement of Romans and Greeks.[12] This special relationship requires its own terms of rhetorical analysis.

Greek rhetorics under empire

Free speech and public space would seem to be rhetorical casualties of the shift from democracy to monarchy and empire. Political rhetoric in the classical period—say, a speech of Demosthenes against Philip of Macedon or a forensic address by Lysias such as *Against Eratosthenes*—appears to offer a clear example of the free speech made possible by democracy and characteristic of the public sphere as it was theorized in the twentieth century: the confrontation of enfranchised speakers in clear and direct terms in a space of equal access on issues of collective interest. And yet, as numerous scholars of ancient Greek rhetoric in the classical period (fifth and fourth centuries

BCE) have pointed out, these conditions almost never obtained: access was severely constrained, political arguments were actually delivered through legal or epideictic genres, and face-to-face confrontation was the exception, with written texts of uneven circulation more the norm.[13] Our post-Enlightenment rhetorical culture places a high value on the heroic act of speaking truth to power, often with disregard for effectiveness or consequences to the speaker (Hauser, *Prisoners*). It's possible to bring the rhetorical assumptions of critical truth-telling to such scenes: an anti-rhetoric of plain speaking and straight talking.[14] Immersion in the world of Greco-Roman rhetoric, however, brings forward a different attitude in the Burkean sense (see *Rhetoric* 50 passim): a reconfigured articulation of power, stance, and rhetorical art.

To speak openly and truthfully to those in power or to cloak your ideas and opinions in artful allusions—these were the terms of a rhetorical debate during a period when arbitrary violence was a constant possibility, in the city itself, in the provinces, and even against members of the elite classes.[15] From the conquest of Philip of Macedon over Greece at the end of democracy, to the imperial sweep of Alexander, the rise of Rome as a conquering power in the third and second centuries BCE, and finally to the declaration of empire by Augustus in 27 CE, public exchange took place "in the suspicious atmosphere of a court society, where people tend to assume a demeanour conformable to the pleasure of the ruler" (Konstan, *Emotions* 31). What Brown termed a "tide of horror" lapped continually at the feet of those in proximity to an emperor or his proxies, requiring carefully crafted communications. Yet the textual tradition in Greek, from the very beginning, records examples of historical actors as well as literary characters risking violent retribution to break through the censorious barrier to speak uncomfortable truths. From "ugly Thersites who spoke back to Agamemnon in book 2 of the *Iliad* to Antigone's rebuke to Creon in Sophocles' tragedy, the free-speaker had a noticeable presence before the advent of democracy.[16] The word *parrhēsia*, "freespokenness," appeared first in Euripides' *Hippolytus* (l.422), where the disgraced Phaedra expresses the hope that, despite her shame, her sons "may live in glorious Athens as free men, free of speech" (trans. Kovacs). Considerable attention has been paid to the concept of free speech in recent years by critical theorists after the publication in French and subsequent English translations of Michel Foucault's late lectures.[17] In a project he styles a "history of thought," Foucault traces the origins and history of *parrhēsia*, outlining its distinctive parameters as a speech practice: the free-speaker "make[s] it manifestly clear and obvious that what he says is his *own* opinion . . . us[ing] the most direct words and forms of expression he can find" (*Fearless Speech* 12; emphasis in original). Moreover, this free-speaker takes a risk, puts him- or herself in danger, by addressing someone in a position of power. The relationship to the interlocutor is a game but with risk to only one party; it is a game but also a duty.

In the Roman ethnic ideology, however, Greeks are rarely associated with the persona of the free-speaker and are more often characterized as slippery or devious. Gleason writes that the Romans viewed the Greeks as "poised somewhere between civilization and decadence" ("Greek Cities" 228). We see the dark side of this rhetorical stereotype illustrated in a letter from Cicero to his brother Quintus on the occasion of the latter taking a high provincial office in Asia. In an eerily modern-sounding orientalization, Cicero warns Quintus to be wary of provincial (Greek) rhetors: "[T]he nature of each and every one of them is wrapped in a fold of pretense and covered, as it were, in veils: their brow, eyes, and expression often lie, but their speech does so almost invariably" (qtd. in Konstan, *Emotions* 31).[18] Cicero puts us on the alert for rhetorics of the body in the imperial context.

Free speech lies at the heart of a rhetoric invented in classical Athens—an ideology at least partially realized in practice—with its law courts and deliberative assemblies. It is arguably such a rhetoric that undergirds most contemporary educational rationales for courses in writing and communications: the facility with language that enables public participation and assures the testing of ideas, knowledge, and policies in democratic forums. The persona most likely to deliver this speech is upright, honest, and straightforward, speaking earnestly in his or her own voice with nothing to hide.[19] For Foucault, "the touchstone of the good ruler is his ability to play the *parrhēsiatic* game" but what he means by this is an understanding between the free-speaker and the *good* king that the former will speak frankly, offering useful advice, and the latter will listen and accept criticism of his decisions (*Fearless Speech* 22–23). The trajectory of Foucault's analysis is the internalization of the discourse of truth, what he terms a postdemocratic practice, beginning with Socrates. This philosophical *parrhēsia* is concerned with "the nature of the relationships between truth and one's style of life, or truth and an ethics and aesthetics of the self" (106). It was not persuasive in a public sense but in a personal one, involving a change in "one's style of life, one's relation to others, and one's relation to oneself" (106).

Published almost simultaneously with Foucault's lectures, classicist Frederick Ahl's comprehensive article "The Art of Safe Criticism in Greece and

Rome" takes up a similar set of questions—What did free speech mean to ancient Greek and Roman intellectuals? How and when was it used and to what effect?—with reference to some of the same sources consulted by Foucault. The aim of Ahl's study, however, is to show how ancient rhetoricians, poets, and dramatists calculated the effects of choosing a rhetorical tactic in situations of threat or danger for maximum persuasive force given the circumstances. Unlike Foucault, Ahl finds a continuity of practice over the centuries—from Homeric epic through the classical period, into the Hellenistic era, and forward into Roman times.

Ahl's primary ancient sources are Demetrius, *On Style*, a Greek text of uncertain authorship and date but perhaps from the first century BCE, and book 9 of Quintilian's *Orator's Education*, the magnum opus of Rome's chief orator composed late in the first century CE. A third source used less by Ahl is a work of Greek rhetorical theory from the second or third century CE (or perhaps later) by Hermogenes, *On Invention* (4.13; see Kennedy, *Invention*). Although Quintilian's discussion is the fullest and most nuanced, as a Latin text it would not have been included in a second sophistic education.[20] An interesting aspect of Demetrius' treatment is his emphasis on the stylistic superiority of the forceful style (*deinotēs*) as opposed to the plain, or unfigured, style: "And (strange as it may seem) even obscurity is often a sort of forcefulness, since what is implied is more forceful, while what is openly stated is despised" (*On Style* ¶254). Some of his examples present lower-stakes situations involving decorum, occasions when using a figured or oblique discourse may give the speaker an advantage. But Demetrius is also quite clear about the usefulness of "allusive verbal innuendo" (¶287) in situations where power differentials are great: "in addressing a tyrant, or any other violent individual, if we wish to be censorious, we often need to be oblique out of necessity" (¶289). He later offers an example from Plato's experience with the tyrant Dionysius (¶290), an encounter of high risk. Hermogenes' text is more schematic, suggesting that the rhetor speak by implication (*emphasis*) "whenever we are not able to speak (*openly*) because hindered and lacking freedom of speech" (Kennedy, *Invention* 189; interpolation in original). Hermogenes categorizes types of figured speech, including (1) saying the opposite of what one means, (2) deflecting the issue, (3) using implication, and (4) speaking in the voice of another. The last of these would have been practiced in school through the exercise of *prosopopoeia*. These theoretical/critical treatments confirm that figured discourse had entered into the metadiscourse of rhetorical training and helpfully condense the practices of rhetors in their eras. As we will see in the chapters that follow, the employment of figured discourse by talented Greek rhetors exceeded in complexity and nuance the treatment offered in treatises.

Second sophistic rhetors, like their classical forebears, circulated the concept of free speech and on occasion adopted the stance of *parrhēsiastes*. But it was always understood *as* a figure or a stance, oscillating in relation to its other: figured discourse. Cloaking one's criticism in metaphors or, even better, lodging it within allusions to Greek history, myth, and literature was not only a safer path for the Greek rhetor in Roman imperial times but sometimes more effective because it was more impressive and artful. "Blunt speech gives way to oblique speech in situations where the speaker is (or feels) threatened or unsure of his audience," Frederick Ahl explains. "Many ancient poets, and all ancient rhetorical theorists, lived when overt criticism of the ruling powers was dangerous. They sensed the need for obliqueness. But they also sensed the greater persuasiveness of oblique suggestion" (184). He goes on to observe that "rhetorical theorists wanted to train students not in how to achieve martyrdom, which requires no special education, but in how to deal successfully with the powerful and even shape and direct their power" (203). A successfully figured message gives the listener—a ruler, but also the others present—the pleasure of solving a mystery, of realizing the power of their common education: the *paideia* shared by Roman, Greek, and provincial elites alike. As Gleason remarks, "the highly textured allusiveness of sophistic literary production made it possible to create texts that could be read . . . on multiple levels, not all of them favorable to Rome" ("Greek Cities" 245; see also C. Miller on concealment).

Postclassical dispositions

A fanciful anecdote recounted by Philostratus imagines the emperor Trajan seating the sophist Dio (called Chrysostom, or golden-mouthed) by his side on the golden chariot in which he rides in triumphal processions, turning to him and saying, "I don't understand what you say but I love you as I love myself" (Philostratus, *Lives* ¶488). This scene, no doubt apocryphal, dramatizes a relationship between rhetor and emperor organized around patronage and affiliation. Trajan, from a long-established Roman family that had emigrated to Spain (a fully Romanized province) in his grandfather's time, came up through the army, was "adopted" by the emperor Nerva in 97, and succeeded him as emperor without struggle in 98. Trajan stood as the second in a sequence of "good" emperors, following the violent and turbulent reigns of Domitian and Nero before him.[21] He was a mild-tempered, generous, and judicious ruler who enacted a number of policies benefiting children and launched utilitarian building projects. He achieved more renown and popular goodwill, however, for his military conquest of Dacia (modern-day Romania) and the elaborate gladiatorial games following thereon. He died in 117 while returning from an attack on Parthians in Armenia, an attempt to extend the eastern reach of the empire.

Dio (40–110 or 120), a native of Prusa, (now Bursa, on the Aegean coast of Turkey), chief city in the province of Bithynia, was born to wealthy parents who had been granted Roman citizenship. He was provided with a first-rate Greek education and, like many of the figures in this group, cultivated close relationships with powerful Romans, including the emperor Vespasian, early in his career. Dio's free speaking, however, provoked the ire of Domitian, who exiled him from his native province and from Italy in 82. Dio returned under Nerva in 96 and then formed a close relationship with Trajan, to whom he may have addressed his four discourses on kingship near the end of the century.

Why, in this made-up story, does the emperor say he doesn't understand what the sophist says?[22] In one interpretation, we can note the importance of the sophist's proximity, which perhaps overrides any particular position or piece of advice he may be offering; love, or *philia*—manly friendship—is what matters in the networks of power relations between rhetor and emperor.[23] On the level of rhetoric, the anecdote raises the question of how communication operated across cultural and power differences: not only what it was and was not possible to say but how it was possible to be heard. In fact, local elites were essential to the management of the empire: "Everywhere it was the Roman policy to win over, and to enfranchise, the local leaders" (Brunt, *Roman Imperial Themes* 268). In the East, Roman rule maintained existing civic institutions and relied on the indigenous property owners for crucial operations of the city. Some sophists nurtured these relationships not only in their own self-interest—by building status that would help them gain an official appointment (if one was available), avoiding heavy financial obligations to the city, and attracting students—but they also served as diplomats and power brokers for their cities.

So from the sophist's perspective, being heard *and* understood mattered a great deal, even though the historical distance and state of the archival record make linking any one sophistic discourse to a specific audience or outcome very difficult.[24] Public rhetors were concerned with the circulation of discourse—its call, its constituents, and the climate it created. These we can establish for the second sophistic, and they were, in many cases, powerfully oriented toward a vision of the democratic polis as a sustaining form of human organization; although polis was a Greek concept, some of its features translated into Roman republican ideology. Whether or not Trajan was influenced by Dio (or by Pliny, a Roman of the same era who composed an extensive panegyric to the emperor, at points arguing for the exercise of good government), the emperor could not have imagined or enacted his benevolent policies in the absence of a discourse outlining and supporting such actions. As Thomas M. Conley notes about epideictic rhetoric at imperial functions, a "perhaps more subtle side of such celebrations may be appreciated when one considers that what seems on the surface to be abject flattery may in fact be a reassertion of continuing standards of kingly or other virtue against which an emperor . . . might be compared and measured" (61; see also Pernot, *Epideictic Rhetoric*). This idea could also be understood in terms of legitimation. The Greek rhetors played a role, literally, in keeping alive the imagination and value of democratic rule, on the one hand, and the condemnation of tyrannical imperial behavior on the other. What Peter W. Rose identifies as the ideological work of Cicero's oratorical arguments is perhaps even more true of the epideictic discourses of the postclassical Greek rhetors: "An oration does more than propose a specific course of action: its persuasive function is aimed at constructing a vision of the real. . . . This vision of the real is the oration's enabling fiction."[25] Taking the risk of creating such visions in the performative public spaces available in this era involved elaborate rhetorical balancing acts, given the vicissitudes of fortune as emperors came and went. The status of a Greek rhetor under empire could be as precarious as being perched on the back of a chariot in a triumph.

Chain of gold

It's difficult to show figured discourse at work because the hidden message is embedded in culture and allusion; unearthing the message is a matter of historically informed speculation at such a distance.[26] What gets communicated through figured discourse is, most often, a stance, attitude, or posture, rather than a full-fledged argument (although there are examples of these from the imperial period). In the ceremonial contexts where Greek rhetors made their appearances, figured discourse ran against the grain of smooth, showy oratorical performance: it was the grain of sand in the oyster, the off-key note left echoing in the minds of the auditors—Roman, Greek, and all the others listening at such events—the sense, discomfiting or enlivening, depending on one's position, that all was not well in the political order.

The most characteristic examples are drawn from references to classical Greek mythology and literature. The prick comes when the educated listener, who would have brought to the occasion a deep familiarity with conventional impressions of characters and stories from Homer, the tragedians, and Greek mythology generally, hears a reference that subtly recasts the valences of the *paideia*. Consider the city encomium of Libanius (314–93), one of the imperial period's most prolific Greek rhetors: a native of Antioch, trained in Athens, called to serve in Constantinople by imperial command, and eventually allowed to return to his beloved city on the Orontes River as the official sophist of the city.[27] Libanius will be considered in more detail in chapter 7, but a preliminary sketch of his life will bring to light the perilous balance between violence and coercion on the one hand and beneficence on the other that determined the lives of Greek intellectuals in the imperial era. When Libanius was born in 314, his family was recovering from a disastrous punishment inflicted upon it a decade earlier by the emperor Diocletian. In a later incident, when the sophist returned to Antioch in 354, the entire city council, including Libanius' uncle, had been arrested by the Roman prefect whose policies had provoked riots. This prefect was soon replaced by a friendly and effective one, and at the time of the composition of Oration 11, *Antiochikos*, Libanius was safe, respected, and soon to enjoy a brief period of stimulating exchange with the emperor Julian.[28] From these few details in a long and eventful life, the extreme vicissitudes of fortune, along with the actual impact, for good or ill, of public rhetoric at this time, become clearer.

What did empire mean to the Greek sophists? Protection, employment, awe, threat, and the way things were. What was it possible for a Greek to say in the face of Roman imperial power? Libanius delivered his encomium of the city of Antioch in 356 on the occasion of an Olympic games, in the middle of his long career and at a hopeful moment in the course of his relations with emperors: the eve of the accession of Julian to the highest office. Two-thirds of the way through a richly detailed description of the history and physical beauties of this thriving metropolis, Libanius mentions the existence of Rome almost as an aside. When the "will of heaven" (*tēs en ouranōi boulēs*) decreed that post-Alexandrian rulers of Antioch were to be replaced, and the world was "girt with the golden chain of Rome" (*tē de Rhōmaiōn oion seirai chrusēi ta panta ezōnnu*) (Foerster, ¶129; trans. Norman), the transfer of power occurred with no violence or rancor, Libanius claims, and Romans simply added their customs to existing ones.[29] To a reader of today, Libanius may sound happily reconciled to the conditions of empire. If there are some constraints implied by the figure of a chain, material compensations, beauty, and technical artistry weigh against them, especially coming from a Greek intellectual who appears to have been faring reasonably well under imperial rule at the time.[30]

But the *pepaideumenoi*, the educated listeners, would have heard more. The Greek expression for "chain of gold," *seira chrusou*, comes from Ionian Greek—the Homeric dialect—and is used by Zeus in the *Iliad*, book 8, in an admonition to the lesser Olympian gods.[31] At this point in the epic narrative, frustrated with the interventions of gods and goddesses on either side of the Trojan War, Zeus harangues them, commanding that none of them help the Trojans or Achaeans in the conduct of the war and that they let it play itself out. The language of the passage is extremely violent; anyone who violates Zeus' order will be snatched up and hurled "down to the murk of Tartarus" (8.15). To get the fullest sense of the reference, we need to hear Zeus' declaration of his dare:

> Come, try me, immortals, so all of you can learn.
> Hang a great golden cable down from the heavens,
> lay hold of it, all you gods, all goddesses too:
> you can never drag me down from sky to earth,
> not Zeus, the highest, mightiest king of kings,
> not even if you worked yourselves to death.
> But whenever I'd set my mind to drag you up,
> in deadly earnest, I'd hoist you all with ease,
> you and the earth, you and the sea, all together,
> then loop that golden cable round a horn of Olympus,
> bind it fast and leave the whole world dangling in mid-air—
> that is how far I tower over the gods, I tower over men.
> (8.20–31; trans. Fagles)[32]

If the citizens of lovely and prosperous Antioch had been lulled through the first hundred paragraphs of Libanius' oration into feeling that Rome was far away, they were wrenched back by this reference to a vision of a violent power struggle—one that only the *autocrator*, the first among them, will win. With the ferocious power of the empire, he can drag even its most privileged members, "and the earth . . . and sea, all together," up with a golden cable and leave them "dangling in mid-air."[33]

Romans had a stake in appearing and acting in moderate ways. David S. Potter cites the *deditio in fidem*, a written text confirming the willing subordination of a conquered city to the Romans, as having "the rather curious effect of imposing an obligation upon the victorious power to behave decently toward the weaker" ("Unity" 17). He argues that "*fides* was built upon respect of reciprocal power relationships between victor and vanquished" (17). The ideology of benevolence at the center of *pax Romana* could not be sustained in complete contradiction, however, as the recent removal of the violent prefect in the case of Libanius' family had demonstrated. The city sophist's role required simultaneously speaking to his fellow Antiochenes and keeping the content of this ideology present to the mind and vision of the Roman rulers, both in its negative and positive aspects. Elsewhere in the speech, Libanius directly and eloquently defends practices of civic rhetorical deliberation (¶139–49), and thus we see the oscillation between figured discourse and *parrhēsia*. The council, Libanius asserts, has the wisdom and oratorical ability of a group of sophists in their prime, and "this ability compels the [Roman] governors to live up to their name, but not to go beyond it, and play the tyrant" (¶140). The mastery of deliberative oratory guarantees the independence of the council, providing it with a "magic" even greater than that of the governors (¶141). Libanius gives precise instructions to the Roman governor about how to conciliate the local population and succeed: "any governor who wins a fair reputation thinks that he gained the crown of virtue, not because he has overcome insubordination, but because he has gained his praises among free and intelligent men" (¶143). Finally, the rhetor names the art of unconcealment specifically: "It is not a case that some may speak and others may not; there is a freedom of speech in which all share" (¶145).[34] And here we rotate back into the realm of the wished-for or projected state of affairs.

Memory, space, genre

Libanius' coded evocation of the Homeric epic, along with a legendary ancestry associated with Heracles, in a fourth-century CE Greek sophistic oration could be read as yet another example of the Greek rhetor dwelling in the past. Greek rhetors in postclassical centuries were notoriously absorbed with their ancient and venerable heritage. So their rhetoric is not only grounded in ancient principles; it is also infused with references to archaic and classical epic, poetry, tragedy, history, and philosophy. What, if anything, does this well-known penchant for dwelling on the past have to do with the colonial condition? At one point in his influential *Power and Persuasion in Late Antiquity*, Peter Brown offers a relatively stable reading of rhetoric as a re-creation of the Greek city: "The rhetorical culture provided by a teacher such as Libanius amounted to nothing less than the patient re-creation, in every generation, of the 'collective memory' of the urban upper class. Through it, they relived, in a condensed, almost proverbial form, the religious, social, and political history of the Greek city" (40). Memory in second sophistic rhetoric, Brown writes, is "arthritic" and "eminently predictable" (42). Following this line of interpretation, George Kennedy in his *New History of Classical Rhetoric* makes a link between the second sophists' valuing of the literary and rhetorical style of the Attic orators and the former's political conservatism. Here is a passage:

> The older [first] sophists were the radicals of their time: they introduced new methods of teaching, questioned traditional values, and encouraged their students to do the same. The later sophists were conservatives, even reactionaries: they introduced no innovations in education, they did not generally encourage original thought on the part of their students, when they criticized contemporary society, it was generally for its failures to live up to past standards of conduct. (231)

Kennedy sees the second sophistic relationship to the past as a form of nostalgia; their figured and excessive rhetorical productions were a "literaturization" of classical genres, in effect, a falling away from the political power of their Golden Age predecessors.[35]

On my reading, the second sophists' uses of history may, on the contrary, be seen as varied and dynamic, rather than monologic and static, providing a politically protected way of "talking back" to empire. Postcolonial and race theorists have explored the significance of history and collective memory for subjugated peoples. The second sophistic habit of dwelling in the past may be interpreted along these lines. As Peter Brown puts it, the repeated themes and tropes from the past acted as a *paideia* that bound elite Greeks to their Roman rulers and provided the former with a subtle form of influence on the behavior of rulers who otherwise operated through impenetrable bureaucratic machinations or brute force (see also Whitmarsh on *paideia* in *Greek Literature* 17–20). Exalting and repeating the cultural accomplishments of the ancient Greeks provided postclassical Greeks with a multiform cultural lever in the highly nuanced contexts of colonial power relations. Later in *Power and Persuasion*, Brown writes eloquently about the great significance of rhetoric in the late empire as a check on the violence of emperors and governors (52).

The idea of democratic rhetoric—an imagined (or remembered) space and the agency possible within that space—took hold in the imperial era and was reiterated across a multitude of Greek rhetorical genres.[36] When read as critical memory rather than as nostalgia, re-creations of democratic scenes, including the numerous narratives about the decline of democratic rhetoric in the early imperial era, kept concepts of a deliberative civic space alive; reimagined publics were conceptualized under the constraints of empire.[37] The tensions between city and its other—city and country, city and surreal hypercity (Rome)—are activated through epideictic genres. In a sense, the rhetoric of Greeks under empire is concretely spatialized, as orations were delivered in theatres and odeons (figure 1.1) in Rome and provincial cities widespread across the empire, though the discourses have seemed to some critics to be lost in space and time because of their persistent reference to classical texts and contexts. The rhetoric of Greco-Roman rhetors plays with time and space, often operating through a kind of spatial-temporal time warp: speaking to current situations and concrete spaces but referencing the classical world of texts and times-out-of-mind. In so doing, they led audiences and lead readers to a kind of alienation effect—Where am I? What world am I in? Speaking from within the space of Rome, the cosmopolis—a space that is everywhere—the second sophist reimagines the concrete, inhabited, and defended spaces of the provincial city in ways useful for survival under empire.[38]

Representations of space played out differently in different genres: pedagogical texts, encomia, direct political addresses (within the context of the provincial or imperial court), and long prose fictions. One of the most recognizable of spatial imaginaries in ancient Greek rhetoric is captured by the pedagogical exercise of declamation. Consider D. A. Russell's delightful coinage for the imagined city in the *meletai*, or exercises, of the rhetorical curriculum: Sophistopolis. Suggesting generic links between declamation

Figure 1.1. Odeon at Aphrodisias, Turkey (late second to early third century CE). AUTHOR PHOTOGRAPH.

and the genres of New Comedy, mime, and fable, Russell implies that the imagining of an ideal city in the pedagogical exercise might have a satiric force of critique. But Russell is generally dismissive about the potential rhetorical force of the imagined city. He places a strong emphasis on the gap between the everyday life of the student and reality: "Sophistopolis is a city of the imagination, from which there is less to be learned about the realities of ancient life than about its characteristic fantasies" and the values and prejudices of teachers (22). The "sub-literature" of declamation, Russell writes, "its characteristic scenarios and attitudes [has] the same sort of interest as the world of the comic or the detective story—or for that matter, the world of the epic" (22). Even if they let him beg the question of the interpretive potential of popular culture objects like comics or detective stories, most contemporary scholars would pause at Russell's suggestion that the epic is not worth exploring for its ideological force. In fact, the unacknowledged question of ideology lingers over this whole discussion.

The world of the declamation is certainly stuffed with exaggerations, types, clichés, and wild improbabilities. Like the Greek novel, it does not benefit from a reading stance one brings to realism. One of the nonrealistic elements of the sophistic city in the Roman era is democratic government. Russell would place this convention in the same category as other classical trappings, along with the convention that cities in declamations are always at war. Here's what he says on this subject:

> Sophistopolis is usually at war with her neighbours, and her young men conscripted for service. . . . Yet for most of the time when the rhetors were composing and teaching these exercises, real Greek cities were locally at peace; the only wars that might affect them were conducted by the Roman power, either against barbarian enemies or when it was at loggerheads with itself. . . . [War was] hardly a reflection of any direct experience. (23)

Russell's word *reflection* offers a key to the limitation of his approach. The interpretive stance in *Chain of Gold* takes second sophistic texts as reflections neither of the identity or class of the speakers, nor of their real-world situations. The related visual process of refraction more adequately figures a mode of reading that locates cultural production within a system of power relations but does not assume that the outcome will be completely determined by such relations, any more than second sophistic works can be read totally in terms of their reproduction of rhetorical conventions. Recent scholarship on the ancient Greek concept of *phantasia* argues for the centrality of the imagination, of vision in rhetorical production, particularly in epideictic genres but in rhetoric generally as well. Ned O'Gorman's analysis of *phantasia*, "imagination" or "appearance" (and the related *phantasma*, "image") in Aristotle's *Rhetoric* and in *De Anima* emphasizes the productive capacity of visualization for deliberation (20–21).[39] A broad rather than narrow conceptualization of vision or imaging as "phantasmatic mental activity" counterbalances what O'Gorman calls the "heavily rationalistic" view of Aristotelian civic discourse (16). O'Gorman's analysis suggests that, when this capacity is taken to the realm of the political, it creates utopian possibilities.

The division between the world of the schoolroom and the realities of imperial city life is one of the frames of vision that contemporary scholarship on second sophistic rhetoric is radically readjusting. Greek cities may have been at peace, but their citizens were not free from violence, and the virtually perpetual warring of the empire on its borders put continual pressure on colonial populations, including their rhetoricians. Reimag(in) ing for Roman audiences the ideal of the democratic city (even if that ideal were never realized) served Greek rhetors, and the populations of colonial cities, as a bulwark against the excesses of Roman power. Visions of good government—responsible provincial city councils, indigenous council members who bore their burdens of financial commitment and service responsibly, governors who made grain available to citizens and kept excessive violence in check—appear repeatedly in the Greek rhetoric of the imperial era, sometimes in direct political tracts (Libanius, Oration 2) but more often in epideictic genres such as the city encomium, panegyric, and mixed-genre orations. Such visions are more than empty clichés, even though their effects cannot be easily gauged. We can read them as projections of possible futures. Putting the emphasis on the power of imagining rather than on historical realization or on disciplinary agon (philosophy versus rhetoric) enables a reevaluation of these epideictic rhetorics (see Pernot, *Epideictic Rhetoric*).

Even when a particular oration does not specifically project a vision of the city or of democratic rhetoric practice, second sophistic rhetoric bears some of the character of Arendt's *vita activa*. The speaker "shows who he is" by making an appearance but, in most cases, not as an intentional individual. The competitive and performative world of sophistic rhetoric produced rhetors whose names circulated, whose fame became a brand, and who risked their status and reputations through public performance, "disclosing and exposing [themselves]" (Arendt 186). They strove for the public notice Arendt describes: "Because of its inherent tendency to disclose the agent together with the act, action needs for its full appearance the shining brightness we once called glory, and which is possible only in the public realm" (180). The point of Arendtian action is in part the sustaining of a web of human relationships rather than a results-oriented instrumental rhetoric (184). This condition is particularly appropriate given the indirection required of Greek rhetoric in imperial times and the emphasis on display. The proliferation of speech and writing by intellectuals in these centuries (even given the fact that only a fragment of what must have been produced remains) gives evidence of the vitality animating the public that Arendt imagines in the classical era. The variety of rhetorical productions and the mobility of their creators make them present to us as rhetors "indissolubly tied to the living flux of acting and speaking" (187).

The proliferation of genres in the period makes another piece of a three-dimensional puzzle: the space of performance, the created space of the oration, and generic space are overlaid, all suspended at various relations of proximity or distance within the imperial setting. It now becomes possible to put some of these pieces together to propose a new critical vocabulary for postclassical Greek rhetoric: a rhetorical analytic of empire endemic, one might say, to the material itself. To Arendt's work on appearance and the focus of *phantasia* of numerous critics, we may add the interest in *enargeia*, the power of bringing-vividly-before-the-eyes so potent in the work of the second sophists (see Newman; Webb, *Ekphrasis*). Related concepts from French scholars include Barbara Cassin's idea of "sophistic effect," Estelle Oudot's work on Athens and Rome as visual fields, and Laurent Pernot's emphasis on sophistic rhetorical power as *rayonnement*: the power of influence as a kind of dissemination—a beautiful brilliance or radiance (*La rhétorique de l'éloge*, vol. 1, 55–56). Reaching beyond not only instrumentality and influence but perhaps even beyond representation to achieve a kind of ancient virtuality, this constellation of analytics could be termed an *optics of empire*. The chain of gold to which Libanius alluded in his encomium of Antioch shifts its figuration to become a glittering web of discourse flung out over its auditors—Roman and Greek.

Case studies

Each chapter of this book presents a reading of a major text by a second sophist, intended to highlight the genres and rhetorical strategies employed by highly trained and precariously placed colonial subjects, both enchained and empowered by Roman imperium. I've selected in most cases the best known—or a very well known—work by prominent figures from each of the first four centuries of the Common Era and have located each sophist geographically on the map of empire and politically in relation to the imperial conditions of the time. For some of the figures I treat, we have extensive bodies of work: such is true for Dio Chrysostom, Aristides, and Libanius. Where there are choices, I've set aside pedagogical, aesthetic, professional, and philosophical work in favor of a text that highlights the political (so, Aristides' grand encomium of the city of Rome in lieu of his "To Plato: In Defense of Oratory"). Further rationales for the selected texts appear in each chapter, and in chapter 7, I take up the issue of political subjectivity across the body of work. The figures appear in chronological order, although there is no possibility that a project covering so much ground could presume to summarize or synthesize the second sophistic in general.[40] Writing primarily for scholars and students of rhetoric, communications, writing, and media studies, I assume little background knowledge of these figures and their world. But at the same time, I hope that the quality of the analysis will be of interest to scholars in classics, comparative literature, and related fields. My readings of these genres of Greek rhetoric, which flourished under conditions of violence and across the displacements of violent times, constitute an inquiry into the politics of rhetorical form. Although all the texts were authored by men, issues of gender and sexuality arise at key points in most chapters. Skin color, ethnicity, social class, and religious difference all find their way into these rich discourses, opening windows onto colonial experience and presenting interpretive challenges.

The first text we encounter comes from Dio Chrysostom (ca. 40–120), about whom we heard briefly above. Inhabiting the persona of a wanderer, Dio builds into the *Euboean Discourse* generic color and complexity, combining a castaway's rural fable with the severe pronouncements of a censorious moralist. A classical city in northern Greece serves as the point of rescue for the storyteller, evoking a Golden Age resonance and projecting the utopian potential of the pastoral. But the fabular aura is shattered by economic distress and legal conflicts. Rhetorical practices are dramatized and land-based legal issues fictively adjudicated in this early example of the projected city-space of second sophistic rhetoric. The analytic questions addressed concern the potential for critical memory in the sophist's work with conventions, as well as the shifting postures of rhetor as storyteller and philosopher.

The next chapter takes us from the provinces to the heart of the empire. Aelius Aristides' grand encomium of Rome was delivered by the talented young rhetor from the Near East in 144 CE. It paints a disturbing vision of a city that cannot be seen. Probably delivered in an odeon adjacent to the monumental space of the new Temple of Venus and Rome Aeternae, the speech paradoxically dislocates listeners from the imposing physical presence of the Roman city, often thought of interchangeably with the empire itself. In chapter 3 I read the oration in the context of Longinus' *On the Sublime* (*Peri Hypsous*), perhaps composed close in time to Aristides' performance, and argue that Aristides' eerie description of Rome creates an anti-sublime through figured references to Homer's epic. What is the nature of praise as a rhetorical act under conditions of colonial force? How did Aristides' mixed audience hear his uncanny figuration of the imperial city? The result is an exposure of the failure of the name "Rome" and a bizarre rhetorical performance of absence.

In a rare report of a woman's participation in rhetorical life, Flavius Philostratus informs the readers of his intellectual biography, *Life of Apollonius of Tyana*, that the work was sponsored by Julia Domna, whom he describes as "a devoted admirer of all rhetorical exercises" (book 1, ¶3). Born in Syria to a highly placed priest, Julia Domna was married to the Roman emperor Severus and eventually established a circle of intellectual, rhetorical, and astrological activity including prominent members of the second sophistic. Drawing on contemporary historical references to the empress by historian Cassius Dio, chapter 4 explores the nexus of gender, power, cultural identity, and sophistic rhetoric as they emerge in the first philosophical biography. The chapter postulates that the mediation of a powerful empress—one with commitments to non-Roman religion and culture—enabled the sophist to construct in Apollonius a character who tested the boundaries of imperial power, as well as the links across magic, religious practice, and philosophical/rhetorical intellectual activity in an era of religious syncretism and extreme cultural diversity.

Philostratus comes on the scene again in chapter 5, where the sophist's relationship to Roman power is imagined as a scene of patronage and pedagogy. A Greek rhetor and art critic walks a Roman boy through his father's picture gallery in Naples: such is the narrative frame for an extensive collection of *ekphraseis*, brief descriptions of paintings with mythic and historical themes composed early in the third century CE by Philostratus. This curious work constitutes a tour de force in response to the question of how far a second sophist can take one of the rudimentary exercises from the *progymnasmata*, the sequence of exercises for rhetorical training. Building on recent analyses of rhetorical vision (Hawhee, "Looking"; Newman; O'Gorman; Webb, *Ekphrasis*), this chapter brings the perspective of colonial relations to bear in a rhetorical reading that finds Philostratus pressing the limits of the picture, and of representation itself, to stage guarded (and often humorous) commentaries on gender, ethnicity, language, and art as plunder. But a more comprehensive understanding of the pedagogical relation the sophist constructs is derived through recurating the entire collection.

Returning to an inquiry into the emperor's role in times of religious turbulence and transition, chapter 6 explores these themes in a fourth-century Greek novel: Heliodorus' *Aithiopika* (*Ethiopian Story*). Several scholars of ancient prose fiction find strong affiliations between the *paideia* of second sophistic rhetoric and these fanciful and (perhaps) popular narratives (Laird; Pernot, "Chariclée"; Whitmarsh, Introduction). Repositories of rhetorical materials (*progymnasmata* such as fables and descriptions, orations, laments, legalistic pleadings), the Greek novels also invite rhetorical interpretation at a broader level. Almost all the remaining examples of the genre offer sensational, episodic narratives starring a culturally Greek heterosexual couple—an innovation in Greek literature—whose adventures carry them over colonial territories: in this case, from Ethiopia to Greece to Egypt and back. With its strong female protagonist, Charikleia, whose white skin and Greek education belie her black Ethiopian origins, *Aithiopika* troubles every category of social, political, and geographic identification, not only gender, skin color, and ethnicity but even the human/animal distinction. All such distinctions come under pressure in the final book of the novel in which the protagonists are in danger of being offered up as human sacrifices in line with a traditional (invented) ritual of the Ethiopian state. Animal sacrifice and the surrounding ceremonies—staples of Greek religious cult—continued to be practiced in the fourth century and as such came into conflict with Christianity's imperial advocates. During his brief mid-fourth-century reign, the emperor Julian made a final effort to turn back Christianity and reinstate traditional Greek religion. The reading offered here proposes that Heliodorus was less interested in authorizing a particular religious position—even Julian's vigorous pagan revival—than in figuring a comic resolution to religious crises by staging a civic performance of modified traditional rites. Sacrifice, as a mediation between humans and gods, is preserved and celebrated but requires adaptation achieved through rhetorical tactics.

In the political orations of Libanius, the fourth-century Antiochene rhetor introduced above and the final subject of analysis, we find a direct address to the abuses of empire. *To Those Who Call Him Tiresome* offers an oddly contemporary-sounding defense of political patience. Responding to students and citizens of his beloved home city of Antioch (in contemporary Syria) who tire of hearing him prod them to live up to their civic responsibilities, Libanius lays out a pedagogy of emotional identification with suffering others, relying on Greek myth and tragedy for his examples. Here we move away from the figured discourse highlighted above in his city encomium and find an ancient corollary for the modern political subject seeking to persuade in a melodramatic mode. In chapter 7 we explore what might be called refractions of empire, locating sophists' rhetorical strategies at two ends of a spectrum: from highly intentional and crafted scenarios with designs, practical projects or reforms, and utopian visions of another way of living (Dio, Libanius) at the one end to movements away from representation toward virtuality (Aristides), aesthetic excess (Philostratus), and the limits of verbal communicability (Heliodorus) at the other.

With chapter 8 the study closes by posing questions that resonate between the old and new empires: What are the current conditions of possibility for *parrhēsia*? Do new global conditions of communication call for a *poikilos* (beautifully variegated) rhetorical practice? And if so, what are its outlines? Can, or should, it be taught? Are there political phantasms—utopian sophist-imagined cities—worth envisioning and speaking for today? The conclusion suggests directions for the field in response to these questions.

CHAPTER 2

Sophist in Exile: Dio Chrysostom's *Euboean Discourse*

In the first chapter we met Dio via Philostratus' improbable anecdote—the sophist perched on Trajan's chariot, murmuring in Greek to the uncomprehending emperor (*Lives* ¶488). A strikingly different impression comes from another scene Philostratus spins out: Dio has gone into exile—"not merely a traveller's tour"—wandering through various lands and supporting himself through menial labor.[1] When he learns of Domitian's assassination, he leaps onto a "high altar" and shows himself to be a "sage" (*sophos*) by quoting the scene from Homer's *Odyssey* where the epic wanderer, disguised as a beggar, strips off his own rags in a similar revelation (22.1–7). The sophist proceeds to deliver "a spirited and energetic indictment of the tyrant" and advises the Roman soldiers about to mutiny that they would be better off organizing themselves in accord with "the will of Roman people" (*Lives* ¶488). Here we have a dramatization of the second sophist as *parrhēsiastes*, an image Philostratus reinforces by offering abundant praise for Dio's habit of speaking to cities—rebuking their licentiousness, praising their good governance, and tempering his attacks with benevolence (*Lives* ¶487).

Philostratus groups Dio with those philosophers who were called sophists because they gained renown by articulating their philosophies so eloquently (*Lives* ¶484). And it was, presumably, this very talent and publicity that led Dio into a series of encounters with the first-century empire and its leaders.[2] Given the eighty orations that have come down to us, it helps to sort them out by their various ways of addressing the city.[3] Dio makes his first marks by speaking to his own city of Prusa. As a Greek from a prosperous family with Roman citizenship, he played an important role in his city's public life both before and after his exile. In Oration 46, for example, Dio confronts his townspeople at a time of distress. A grain crisis has led the people to riot; with violence in mind, they are converging on the house of Dio and those of other prominent city figures. Perhaps addressing a meeting of the city assembly, Dio describes the anger of the crowd and defends himself against accusations of grain hoarding (C. P. Jones, *Roman World* 19–25). This oration and other later ones known as the *Bithynian Discourses* offer striking examples of deliberative eloquence (Orations 38–51; Pernot, *Rhetoric in Antiquity* 174–75). Kennedy designates this group the "only surviving examples . . . of the day-to-day deliberative oratory of the Roman Empire" (*New History* 235).

In a second group, we can place orations presented to the colonial cities of Rhodes, Alexandria, Tarsus, and others to which Dio offers both praise and criticism (C. P. Jones, *Roman World* 26–114). Beginning in epideictic fashion by lauding the origins and physical properties of the city, the sophist often in these orations moves on to advising (and sometimes haranguing) Greek colonials to arrange their affairs so as to maximize their autonomy and well-being under Roman imperial rule. These works are notable for their direct address to problems at hand (C. P. Jones, *Roman World* 29). In them, Dio presents an earnest persona before audiences from colonial cities, urging *harmonia* (concord), *eutaxia* (discipline), and stability in the face of Roman rule (Salmeri 78). Were one to get the impression, however, that Dio was primarily a *parrhēsiastes*, a pragmatic free-speaker who brought hard truths to his countrymen under empire, they would be missing significant dimensions of Dio's rhetorical practice. These complexities appear throughout his oeuvre but especially in discourses addressing a third site of the city.

As a self-styled wanderer throughout the empire even before his exile, Dio probably encountered and possibly studied with the Stoic philosopher Musonias Rufus, perhaps in Rome. Not only did Stoic philosophy contribute to Dio's philosophical habits of living and thinking, but it may also have led him to embrace a more profound and challenging concept of the city. Ancient Greeks from Homer forward envisioned ideal polis orders, and the Stoic vision of a worldwide community of rational beings found expression in the language of a cosmic political order, or *cosmopolis* (Epictetus, Discourse 2.10.3). Stoicism's cosmopolis enabled intellectuals of the postclassical period to imagine belonging and humanity beyond the limits of the classical polis by using the "Stoic concept of the world itself as a kind of city" (Long 3). Not only a philosophical abstraction, the Stoic cosmopolis can be understood as a Hellenistic response to new geopolitical realities of Roman domination (E. Brown). Augustus' accession as *princeps* in 27 BCE and the publication of his *Res Gestae* present the Roman *imperium* not merely as a projection of political order but as "the [actual and ongoing] conquest and pacification" of the world, "henceforth enclosed in a harmonious and everlasting way" (Nicolet 15). In other words, Roman imperial ideology had its own investment in the idea of a cosmopolis, an idea and reality that provoked rhetorical responses from the second sophists. In Dio's case, one might consider the famous kingship discourses (Orations 1–4), which stage imagined encounters between a sage adviser and a world leader, in this light. They address the question, How should the cosmopolis be ruled? Other works fall into this category as well, including Dio's most distinctive oration (Oration 7), a genre-blending exile tale called the *Euboean Discourse*, a combination of figured and direct discourse. A return to the rhetorical practice of declamation will help to develop a reading strategy for this important work.

Rhetorics of the imagined city

As we saw in chapter 1, D. A. Russell cleverly identified the practice of imagining the city within Greek declamation exercises with his coinage "Sophistopolis." At several points throughout his useful study, Russell raises the question of word and world: "We are bound to ask whether the declaimers' obsession with tyrants and tyrannicide has any basis in the politics of their own time, or is simply a melodramatic element in their historical fiction" (32). He continues at that point to discuss local despots in Hellenic and Roman times and declamation themes related to tyranny, concluding that, despite the possibilities for "propaganda," the second sophists were natural allies of rich and powerful Romans and that their uses of the past are best understood as escapism (109). The division Russell makes between the world of the schoolroom and the realities of imperial city life gives his reading a reflectionist bent: because the details of government, character, and history in the declamations do not reflect Greek life under empire so far as it can be reconstructed through history, these rhetorical productions are best characterized as fantasy.

More recently, however, colonial relations under empire and the intricate imbrications of Greek and Roman culture and life have become more compelling frames of vision for contemporary scholarship on second sophistic rhetoric, as we saw in chapter 1. Simon Swain's comment from 2000 on changing critical paradigms is instructive: "In recent years students of classical Greece have come to recognize that the traditional way of dividing

Greek studies between 'history' and 'literature' is unproductive. Cultural activities in literature and art cannot be separated from politics, warfare, and the economic and religious background of society" (2).[4] As Swain suggests, a method of reading that places more emphasis on mediation than reflection would make somewhat different sense of the fantastic projections in declamation and in related sophistic discourses. For us, the most relevant of the "characteristic fantasies" of the imagined sophistic city in the Roman era is democratic government. "Most important," observes Russell, Sophistopolis is "a democracy, where the rhetorician—both politician and expert in oratory—is something of a hero"; "partisans of the *demos* are honest, the rich are cruel, potential tyrants are a constant danger" (22). For Russell, the point is most often rhetorical positioning: through these references, Greek sophists continually reestablish their links to the classical world. By repeatedly restaging conflicts between rich and poor, "in which the rich are always unjust and cruel and the poor are innocent victims," they play on the power of the "underdog" stance (27). But Russell offers an observation here that begins to bridge the distance between Sophistopolis and the imperial polis, especially where Dio is concerned: "to some degree the rhetor, because his power rested not on resources but on his personal skill, could represent himself as the voice of the oppressed" (27–28).[5] Russell's lively evocation of Sophistopolis gives us a vivid picture of how memories—and we could add, projections—of the democratic city entered into conventional Greek declamation. Putting the emphasis on the power of imagining rather than on a reflectionist reading stance enables an inquiry into the creative tactics through which second sophists as subjects of empire refracted difficult political realities.[6] In these refractions, the real and the imagined coexist in a balance between "idealization and realism and between fictionality and fact" (Moles 178).

The hybrid *Euboean Discourse* offers a fascinating example of a discourse operating on these levels. In this two-part oration, Dio takes us first into a pastoral setting—or more accurately, an impoverished but idyllic rural scene—a utopian pastoral interrupted by the harsh economies of a flawed city government. He shifts in the second part to a direct address to problems of cities with particular reference to Rome. Despite its literary style and the romanticization of the rural scene, the *Euboean Discourse* should not be read as a declamation—that, is, a performance piece designed primarily for entertainment purposes. Probably intended for a Roman audience (C. P. Jones, *Roman World* 56–16; Moles 178), the narrative offers an intriguing example of figured discourse. As with most of the cases I present in this book (with the exception of the novel by Heliodorus), the sophist, even while crafting a figured text, maintains an identifiable rhetorical persona. In Dio's case, a key factor is his stance as an exile. As several critics have noted, the experience of exile offers rhetorical leverage: Whitmarsh notes that the language of the exile serves as a tactic of "polemical engagement" (*Greek Literature* 141). Moles remarks that the narrative is "'authenticated' . . . by Dio's eyewitness testimony and personal experience [of exile]" (178). The complexity of the work emerging from these conditions, its charm, and the regard in which it is held by Dio scholars make Oration 7 an ideal subject of analysis.

Word and world in Dio's *Euboean Discourse*

The *Seventh Discourse*, or *Euboean Discourse*, one of Dio's "most admired works" (C. P. Jones, *Roman World* 50), features a charming narrative of a castaway and a hunter, paired with a section of explication and political commentary.[7] The oration was thought to have been delivered in Rome during the reign of Trajan, thus after Dio's "rehabilitation" (C. P. Jones dates it in 96). The oration begins like one of the long prose fictions (*plasmata*) just developing in this period, as the speaker, while on a trip across the Aegean from Chios to Euboea, is shipwrecked on the famously dangerous shoals of this northern Greek region.[8] A hunter comes to his aid and brings him to the humble home he shares with a cousin, their wives, and children. There the hunter relates the story of the two fathers' displacement from the land, to which they had been attached as tenant farmers, when the owner was robbed of his property and executed by a previous emperor (most take the reference to be to Domitian). As an outcome of bad land policy, the fathers and then their sons devolved from farmers to hunters but still live a happy, because simple and virtuous, pastoral life. The hunter then recounts a trip to the city, which came about when he was brought up on charges of land theft and tax evasion. The legal proceeding, conducted in a theatre, exonerated him. The hunter's story concludes with the wanderer observing the affection of a grown daughter for a son of the other family, and the first part of the discourse ends like a comedy with a joyful marriage scene. The speaker then draws moral and political conclusions from the narrative about the status of the poor in imperial cities, the moral superiority of poverty over materialism, and the evils of brothel-keeping (*pornoboskia*).[9]

In this work, we see the literariness—and utopian impulse—of the declamation's imagined world. But the picture of rural life drawn here accords with concrete problems "anchored in [the] reality" of the times (Moles 178): the dispossession of tenant farmers through the expansion of large country estates and the difficulty of surviving under a money economy for the poor who were driven to live in cities. Dio's achievement is the overlay of the idealistic vision of the Stoic citizen of a cosmopolis ordered by brotherly love onto the ragged and imperfect cities of the first-century empire. His concern throughout the discourse with creaturely survival under conditions of duress—what Giorgio Agamben (*Homo Sacer*) terms "bare life"—merges with the classical Greek rhetoric of citizenship, or political life: a transformation experienced by Dio himself as an exile returned to political viability. The narrative of the hunter brought into the city and then returned to the country doubles this movement.

Dio introduces the work in first person: "I shall now relate a personal experience of mine (*Tode mēn autos idōn . . . diēgēsomai*) (¶1). Referring to himself obliquely as a wanderer (*alētikon*), he says that he will "describe the character and manner of life of some people that [he] met," thus blending fictional expectations with a kind of ethnographic or realistic aim. Describing his own conditions of exile, Dio presents himself in the Cynic style as an impoverished sage:

> [After meeting the hunter,] I followed him gladly without fear of any treachery, since I had nothing but a shabby cloak. Now I had often found in other situations like this—for I was continually roaming about—and I certainly did in this one, that poverty is in reality a sacred and inviolable thing and no one wrongs you; yes, much less than they wrong those who carry the herald's wand [*ta kērukeia*]. (¶8–9)

Dio combines the stance of sage as free-speaker (*parrhēsiastes*) with that of storyteller. Evoking an epic world with reference to the "herald's wand" (*Iliad*, book 2), Dio classicizes the narrative, enacting the part of a philosopher whose exile and poverty offer him a kind of privileged insight into human affairs.

The utopian element in Dio's text enters early on when the narrator, shipwrecked and abandoned, encounters a hunter who shares his kill and invites the stranger home (¶3–7). The hunter describes the castaway as "a man from the city" (*tōn astikōn*) but also one who seems "to be suffering from some grievous infirmity of body" (*tina astheneian tou sōmatos*, ¶8). Through this language, political and apolitical identities are fused: the citizen has become a creature or body. The generosity of the hunter and his family, along with the beautiful description of the country, places the listener or reader momentarily in an idyll: an imagined world of the happy rural poor. But this scene is quickly disrupted by an intruder from the city demanding taxes for land use. When the hunter can't pay, he's dragged into the city: an unfamiliar place with walls, houses, and a chaotic public trial conducted in a theatre (¶21–22).

Direct attention to rhetoric comes in the trial scene, which takes up almost a third of the text (¶21–63) and features four speakers: a prosecutor, a defense "attorney," the hunter speaking in his own defense, and a citizen in the crowd who testifies to having benefited from the hunter's good graces in another shipwreck scenario. The prosecutor is referred to as a "rhetor" and is characterized in a completely negative way. He unjustly seeks to wrest away the virtuous hunter's land and meager possessions, misrepresenting him as a deceptive thief living on the benefaction of the city—on untaxed public land. Through the hunter's eyes, the scene of public deliberation is frightening at points, thunderous, chaotic, driven by anger, and producing fear: "Now at first the crowd deliberated on other matters for a considerable while, and they kept up a shouting, at one time in gentle fashion [*praiōs*] and all of them in cheerful mood, as they applauded certain speakers, but at other times with vehemence [*sphodra*] and in wrath [*orgilōs*]. This wrath [*orgēs*] of theirs was something terrible" (¶24–25). With some similarities to Russell's Sophistopolis (22–23), the scene of civic discourse here is uncivil, both in the conduct of the proceedings and in the motives of the forensic prosecutor, a corrupt Roman tax collector.[10] As Karadimas has noted, the Greek sophists of this period often denigrated forensic rhetoric: Libanius, for example, often rails against the shift in education to "Latin and law."[11] More broadly considered, this scenario effects a multilayered critique. The Greek city stands in for those of other provinces, including Prusa—colonial cities required to pay an annual tribute to Rome and lacking freedom, despite the functioning of local bodies with names from ancient Greek democracy (*ecclesia* and *boule*). Most pointedly, residents could not take charge of legal cases: "Prusans did not even have the privilege of litigating in their own city" (C. P. Jones, *Roman World* 5). The condemnation of the rhetor then calls attention to an absence of judicial participation and articulates a criticism of unjust land policies under the management of the Roman proconsul or his legate. The speaker defending the hunter says, "It is therefore surprising that orators trump up charges against the industrious people of Caphereus in the remote parts of Euboea" (¶38).

But the utopian possibilities of deliberation in the public space rise above the chaos.[12] The outcome of the hunter's trial is positive: justice carries the day and the opinion of the crowd through the efforts of speech. The hunter finds the speaker for the defense a "good kindly man," judging from his words and his appearance. He asks for silence, speaks quietly, and argues that those who had worked idle land in the countryside did no wrong, and even deserved commendation (¶33). The hunter himself is an exemplar of plain speech and articulates the classical ethos of hospitality.[13] He crosses the boundary of country and city—moving from pastoral naïf to civic subject—through his willingness to pay taxes and his assertion of citizenship across the generations of his family. Here he is quoting himself in the trial:

> "if you want everything, we are willing to give it to you voluntarily. There is no need for you to take it from us by force as though it belonged to foreigners or rogues; for, mark you, we are citizens too of this city, as I used to hear my father say[,] . . . raising our children to be your fellow-citizens, and should you ever need them, they will help you against brigands and foreign foes. Just now there is peace; but if ever such a crisis does arise, you will pray heaven that the majority be like ourselves." (¶48–49)[14]

One might read this moment as the happy fusion of utopia and declamatory rhetoric without examining the fiction in light of rural economies of the era. In fact, a number of scholars have addressed the accuracy of Dio's representation of rural poverty and Roman land policies in the narrative section of the oration. Brunt supports Dio as a political critic in this discourse, arguing that the social program the sophist envisions in the *Euboean Discourse* exceeds a merely conventional idealization of nature and simple rural people, a commonplace of the era ("Aspects"). Alcock is less convinced of the accuracy of Dio's critique: "Other sources of evidence for Euboea during this period fail to confirm Dio's grim account," but she acknowledges that the trend toward large estates may be an accurate reflection of imperial land economies of the era (3). C. P. Jones assumes the pertinence of the critique but posits that Dio was writing in conformity with and in support of agricultural reform plans already undertaken by Nerva and Trajan (*Roman World* 60). Finally, Ma cites Galen among others on the practice of cities confiscating grain from country dwellers in times of shortage, "leaving them to subsist off roots and vetches until the next crop" (115).

Despite their differences, all these critics recognize Dio's attempt to act rhetorically in relation to the material conditions of his era. Whatever elements of "declamatory unreality" (Ma 118) he produces through the narrative mediate this relationship. The city evoked in the narrative is defined by a scene of democratic deliberation, sketched in broad and typified strokes, full of color and humor. But the second section of the oration, including Dio's extensive justification for the length and nature of the work, breaks the frame of both utopian expectations and declamatory fiction. Setting out his aims directly, Dio writes, "we are not at present mapping out the form of government that would be best, or better than many, but we did set out to discuss poverty and to show that its case is not hopeless" (¶125).[15] Dio's pragmatic utopianism presents a phantasm of the good city, along with instructions for how to read it.

From narrative to argument

At the end of the story part, Dio takes pains to insist that he is not merely entertaining by remarking on the rhetorical status of his discourse and its purpose:

> Now I have not told this long story [*ton logon*] idly or, as some might perhaps infer, with the desire to spin a yarn [*adoleschein,* talk idly], but to present an illustration [*paradeigma*] of the manner of life that I adopted at the beginning and of the life of the poor—an illustration drawn from my own experience [*ho autos ēpistamēn*] for anyone who wishes to consider whether in words and deeds and in social intercourse the poor are at a disadvantage in comparison with the rich on account of their poverty. (¶81)

As Graham Anderson has pointed out, several of the *progymnasmata* are artfully combined in the *Euboean Discourse*: extended *diegesis*, *ekphrasis* of natural scenes, *syncrisis* on the rich and the poor, an *ethopoieia* of the slanderous demagogue, and most substantially, an argument on a thesis: Should the city poor be given land in the country to farm? (*Second Sophistic* 53). Wielding the craft of the sophist, Dio simultaneously keeps before the reader the fact that neither his nor his subjects' poverty and isolation were of their own making. He does this by continually breaking the frame of fictional construction, multiplying his roles in the discourse: castaway, narrator, and political commentator. Justifying his method, Dio argues that the long narrative was useful for shaping public policy (*pros politeian*, ¶127) and that "the speaker has not abandoned the real theme of the whole provided he treats of the matters that are essential and pertinent to philosophy" (¶128). In analogizing his method to that of the hunter, Dio implicitly links himself with the virtuous character of the hunter in his own narrative, but at the same time he may have led his educated listeners to remember the character of the Sophist in Plato's dialogue of that name. The allusion becomes more probable as Dio goes on to compare his own lengthy discourse with that of "a man who sets out to discuss the just man and justice," the city, and the state, setting out "very clearly and magnificently the features characteristic of each" (¶131). He refers here to Plato's *Republic* and, in so doing, suggests the utopian cast of his own project but also marks its difference. Noting with regret that it isn't possible to take "each member of the multitude aside and show him his error or to cross-question everybody in turn" (using Plato's term for Socratic questioning: *elenchein*, ¶100), the sophist stages his own hybrid discourse, one combining narrative, commentary, and extended classical reference of the type for which the second sophists were renowned.

In support of the point made both narratively and prosaically—that it is not a disadvantage to be poor and, in fact, the poor exceed the rich in hospitality—Dio draws on Homer. Contrasting the servant Eumaeus' unconditional welcome of Odysseus, just home from the Trojan War, with both Telemachus' and Penelope's more conditional and skeptical responses, Dio remarks that "Homer does not say that even she gave him a cloak as he sat beside her in a bare tunic" (¶84). Dio emphasizes the bargaining nature of their arrangement: only when Odysseus performs so as to verify his identity and banish the suitors does Penelope help him. Dio's conclusion is that "what seem to be acts of kindliness and favours turn out, when examined rightly, to be nothing more or less than accommodations and loans, and that too at a high rate of interest as a usual thing" (¶89). It does not take much to link the wandering epic hero returned to Ithaca with the formerly exiled sophist returned to favor under the new imperial dispensation.[16] Thus through the narrative of the hunters, and both plain and figured discourses in the commentary, the hospitality and gift economy of ancient times are idealized in contrast to the brutal money economy of the contemporary provincial city.

In a double move, Dio may been seen as seeking to secure his status as an intellectual essentially dependent on the largesse of the emperor—a position from which he can on occasion take the risk of plain speaking—and at the same time urging reforms of genuine benefit to the people far outside the realm of the Greek intelligentsia.

We might understand the hybrid genre of the work as an attempt to open the doors of interpretation for his listeners. He presents to them the pleasurable fiction of the conflict between city and country with its fictional resolution but goes on to demonstrate the political uses of rhetorical fictions. His discussion of the desirable occupations for the poor in the city (¶103–26) embeds the details of these instructions. In this section, Dio validates poverty as a "life and existence befitting free men" (*biou kai zōēs prepousēs andrasin eleutherois*) (¶103) and seeks occupations for them in the city that are not injurious to the body (¶110). Dio brings to light here the situation of the poor as city dwellers who are not citizens: they have "no other possession than their own bodies" (¶106). These "respectable poor" (¶108) may become rustics, but they may also, Dio argues, be accommodated into city life without harm and with the capacity to make a living. He goes into some detail concerning appropriate and inappropriate occupations for the poor in the city (¶109–27), emphasizing at the outset the importance of a healthy body attained through activity. He criticizes those who sneer at lowly jobs, such as hired service, harvesting, wet-nursing, or serving as a schoolmaster (¶115). Among the inappropriate occupations are listed acting in tragic or comic roles (¶119), drawing up contracts for pay, or becoming "learned and clever pettifogging lawyers" (¶123).[17] One might read this injunction against performative professions as an aristocrat denying the poor the capacity to participate in the role of "representer." They can *be*, but they cannot *seem* to be. Another reading would place less emphasis on an apparent class difference and note the value Dio gives to moderation, given the exploitative excesses of "tongue-craftsmen" (*glōssotechnas*) and "law-craftsmen" (*dikotechnas*) in the cities. Dio expresses here the Stoic respect for the natural human, one who has no need of artifice. This principle undergirds his condemnation of the "silly luxury of the cities," a familiar theme in cultural commentary, both Greek and Roman, throughout the imperial period, and one Dio addresses very directly in his Oration 13, *In Athens, about His Banishment*. Reporting on the opinions he disseminated after taking up the habits of the roaming, humble philosopher, Dio says that he advised the Romans "to despise gold and silver and ivory, yea, and rich food too and perfume and the lust of the flesh, [so that they] should thereafter live happy lives, and be masters first and foremost of themselves and afterwards of all other men as well. 'For only then,' I continued, 'will your city be great and strong and truly imperial'" (¶33–34).

In the *Euboean Discourse* as well, Dio addresses himself both to cities and to the city of Rome: to men who live in "the capital or some other city" (*peri tōn en astei kai kata polin*, ¶104). His polis is both the provincial city, with its population moving to and from surrounding rural areas, and the city that metonymically stands for the empire itself: Rome the cosmopolis. Dio speaks both from within and without: a onetime intellectual with credentials and citizenship who was later cast out, forced to consider and care for himself as a body or creature. This life history comes sharply to mind at the close of the work when Dio turns to the subject of the sexual slavery of women and children (¶133). Insisting on the need for rhetorical action in the face of injustice and rejecting a Stoic attitude of passivity, Dio finds that his duty is "to give some heed" to this condition and "under no condition to bear this mistreatment of outcast and enslaved creatures [*ta atima kai doula sōmata*] with calmness and indifference" (¶138). When Dio makes an analogy between the enslaved woman and the Greeks, "in former times almost free but now liv[ing] in bondage utter and complete," he figures the intersections of subjugation under Roman imperial rule.

Dio's fellow Stoic Epictetus advises that a man should be at the same time cautious and courageous (Discourse 2, ch. 1), and Dio uses strategies of second sophistic rhetoric to create city visions both cautious and courageous. Neither the charming narrative nor the seemingly straightforward pronouncements of a Stoic philosopher stand alone; the one permeates the other, weaving the complex strands of a colonial counterdiscourse. Dio brings a second sophistic vision of the polis into critical contact with the imperial cosmopolis, revealing the complexities of political subjectivity on the boundaries of city and country, Greek and Roman, exile and citizen, enfranchised and poverty-stricken, philosopher and sophist. And none leaves its other untouched.

Postscript: Speaking to the emperor

I chose to focus on Oration 7 in this chapter because it brings together Dio's artful staging of his exile persona with the direct and forceful arguments for which he is justifiably praised. The narrative of the city—a badly run colonial city with parallels to the corrupt city of Rome—offers a strong example of figured discourse. We have seen how exile was for Dio a lived experience—an exercise in survival—as well as a rhetorical stance, as previous scholars have noted. Desideri remarks on the value of wandering for building a philosophical ethos (101). What seems crucial to understand about this philosophical sophist who often adopts the position of free-speaker is that he is striking a pose "never less than when he signals the abandonment of artifice" (Whitmarsh, *Greek Literature* 161). While the focus here has been rhetoric addressed to cities, Dio's corpus also includes a striking set of discourses imagined as addresses to the emperor himself.

The four kingship discourses (Orations 1–4), composed after Dio's return from exile, presumably for the emperor Trajan, offer four different scenarios through which the topic of the true king (i.e., the good ruler, as opposed to the tyrant) is examined and tested by a pair of speakers in dialogue.[18] This rhetorical scenario—the philosophical advisor confronting a king (or tyrant or emperor)—appears in ancient Greek and Roman rhetoric from as early as the Homeric epic and gains fresh importance in the Roman imperial era when Greek intellectuals find inroads to influence. As we noted in chapter 1, Michel Foucault in his late work focused attention on the free-speaker in the Greco-Roman period, and on two occasions he worked closely with Dio's fourth kingship discourse (*Fearless Speech* 120–33; *Courage* 275–83). The extensive treatments of this fascinating corner of Dio's corpus by classicist Whitmarsh and continental theorist Foucault line up with a rhetorical reading on a crucial point: the variety of characters appearing in these four dialogues thwarts any attempt to identify free speech as the straightforward authorial voice of the rhetor. These characters include versions of Dio himself (Orations 1 and 3), Philip of Macedon and Alexander (Oration 2), and Alexander in conversation with the Cynic Diogenes (Oration 4)—the liveliest (or "spikiest," writes Whitmarsh, *Greek Literature* 204) of the four.[19] Figured discourse is obviously in play in Orations 2 and 4, with Alexander as a figure for Trajan. In Oration 2, Dio speaks through Philip, Alexander's father, and in Oration 4, as Diogenes (Whitmarsh, *Greek Literature* 202–03). My purposes in this postscript are to acknowledge these related studies of Dio's sophistic practice, to draw attention to the subgenre of addresses to the emperor—a motif that returns in the work of Aristides (chapter 3), Philostratus (*Life*, chapter 4), and Libanius (chapter 7)—and to suggest that Dio's Diogenes is, in fact, less Cynic-al than Neoplatonic.

In the dramatic scenario of the fourth discourse, Alexander comes to the Greek city of Corinth to receive Greek embassies and runs into Diogenes in an off moment. The Cynic, "having no court either great or small, nor house nor hearth of his own as the well-to-do have . . . made the cities his home and used to live there in the public buildings and in the shrines, which are dedicated to the gods, and took for his hearth-stone the wide world, which after all is man's common hearth and nourisher" (¶13–14). Here we see the enactment of a relationship between Cynic philosopher and the idealized city, polis as cosmopolis. After some banter in which the philosopher demonstrates his independence through impudent behavior, Alexander puts the following question to Diogenes: "How," asks he, "could one be the best king?" (¶24). The directness of the question diminishes the rhetorical drama, moving the work in the direction of a Platonic dialogue. Indeed, in his next move, Diogenes proposes a Platonic essence as the core of kingship: "no one can be a bad king any more than he can be a bad good man; for the king is the best one among men," supporting the point with reference to standard Platonic points of reference—the charioteer, the pilot, and the physician all know how to do their work by nature (¶24).

Diogenes seeks to convince Alexander that only through knowledge of the Greek *paideia*, as opposed to the false education of the sophists, will a king learn how best to rule. As it plays out, the "divine" education belongs to those who are noble by nature and manly, while the merely human kind—that purveyed by the "tricky sophist" (¶32)—"will wear him out by leading him hither and thither, dragging him now to the east and now to the west and now to the south, not knowing anything himself but merely guessing, after having been led far afield himself long before by impostors" (¶33). In fact, the sophist is no better than a "lecherous eunuch" (¶35). The Dio of this discourse has disavowed any identification with the (negatively sexualized) sophists. To what end is the elaborate dialogue directed? If this advice was directed toward Trajan, we might wonder how it would have been received.

The Diogenes character discourages Alexander from pursuing the conquest of new territories. With reference to the king of the Persians, Alexander asks, "But shall I not be a great king when once I have overthrown him?" "Yes, but not for that reason," Diogenes replies, "for not even when boys play the game to which the boys themselves give the name 'kings' is the winner really a king" (¶47). Discouraging an emperor from pursuing military exploits could conceivably put an advisor at risk. As Diogenes continues to deny the glory of battle, encouraging Alexander "to put his trust in well-doing and devotion to righteousness and not in arms," the young king, we are told, "came near hurling his spear" (¶64). Much more of Diogenes' advice, however, concerns the king's spiritual state than his behavior. Returning to the dualities of a Platonic repertoire, the philosopher urges the king to propitiate his "attendant spirit," making it "free-spirited and kingly, instead of, as in your present state, slavish, illiberal, and vicious" (¶75). At this point, the narrator reports Alexander's amazement at the "courage and fearlessness of the man" (¶76).

Given our lack of knowledge about the conditions of performance and circulation of the kingship discourses, it's difficult to assess to what extent Dio may have felt constrained by the chain of gold to "figure" or cloak his commentary on the emperor. The fact that we have four full discourses in this mode may suggest that Dio spoke with a degree of freedom at this stage in his life. That he crafts a "Diogenes" who is more Neoplatonist than Cynic in the fourth discourse may dull the cutting edge of his message. The character of the king in the drama announcing his amazement at the free-speaker's courage could be an author indulging in a bit of self-congratulation rather than putting himself out on a limb. As Whitmarsh notes, *parrhēsia* in the Trajanic era may have become a "token of imperial propaganda" (*Greek Literature* 161) and so no longer posed a rhetorical risk. Although Foucault reads the dialogue as a game played "at the limits of the parrhēsiastic contract" (*Fearless Speech* 127)—one conducted with "great aggressivity" (130)—he confines his reading to the fictional encounter between Alexander and Diogenes; that is, he never contemplates the situation of the sophist speaking in a figured way to the emperor (133).[20]

There's certainly more to be said about approaches to Dio's kingship discourses specifically and the many personae he adopted through his long life as a Greek sophist of a philosophical cast. This reading has set up some touch points for second sophistic practice in the era of Roman empire: physical mobility, generic hybridity, the figured use of Greek *paideia*, and flexibility of stance in precarious situations. We will see these features adopted and adapted by second sophists in the centuries to follow.

CHAPTER 3

An Imperial Anti-sublime: Aristides' *Roman Oration*

> Thus with good reason the present circumstances are satisfactory and expedient for both rich and poor, and no other way of life is left. And there has arisen a single harmonious government embracing all.
>
> —Aristides, *Roman Oration*, ¶66

With Aelius Aristides, born seventy years after Dio but also from Asia Minor, we have a rhetor with a decidedly different personality coming of age under changed political conditions. The Flavian emperors of the turn of the first century stabilized the empire and, as we have seen with Trajan, created a viable context for the sophistic activities of Dio. They were followed by a series of rulers of generally benign disposition, several of whom were favorably disposed to Greek culture and especially to sophists. The famously philhellenic Hadrian (117–138), Antoninus Pius (138–161), and the greatly admired Marcus Aurelius (161–180) ruled during Aristides' active professional years, thus smoothing the path for a culturally Greek colonial elite intent upon a rhetorical career.[1] Very well educated in the Athenian tradition, Aristides distinguished himself from the beginning of his career by his mastery of pure Attic Greek and unabashed admiration for classical predecessors such as Demosthenes and Isocrates (Philostratus, *Lives* ¶581–85; Swain, *Hellenism* 254–97). Of all the figures appearing in this book, Aristides perhaps bore the chain of gold most lightly. He had no interest in lower classes or political controversies, and he argued vigorously (and successfully) to be granted immunity from financial obligations to his city, Smyrna, on the basis of his status as a sophist. Pernot offers a telling contrast: "Unlike rebellious and philosophical types like Dio and Lucian,

Aristides outwardly resembled an applied panegyrist, the good student in the class" ("Aelius Aristides" 177). Concerning that key word *outwardly*, we have more to say later.

The good student's subject of choice was rhetoric, and he began well with a tour of Egypt, offering public declamations at several Greek sites as well as Alexandria.[2] But when he arrived at Rome at the age of twenty-six, he was stricken with an illness that would defy the diagnosis and treatments of doctors and remain with him for the next ten years. During that period, Aristides became a devotee of Asclepius, the god of healing, and spent considerable time as an *incubant* at Asclepius' shrine in Pergamum. Being an incubant meant sleeping in the shrine and receiving dreams that prescribed treatments. Aristides later brought together records he kept of his treatments and his dreams as communications with the god during that period and compiled them in a text titled *Sacred Tales*, a fascinating picture of medical and religious practices of the era, a window into his psyche, and a precious example of life writing. From these dream narratives, several scholars have derived a theory about Aristides' relationship to emperors (Behr; Pernot, "Aelius Aristides"; Swain, *Hellenism*). They propose that, although this seemingly fully assimilated Greek rhetor never openly challenged Roman power, he maintained a distance—"an attitude of reserve" (Pernot, "Aelius Aristides" 199)—by virtue of his status as a protégé of Asclepius. His intimate relationship with the god came before his association with emperors, thus diminishing the latter.

Although I do not take up *Sacred Tales* here, the insights derived from the text's staging of a confrontation between Greek rhetor and Roman emperor provide a provocative backdrop for a reading of Aristides' encomium of Rome, *Roman Oration*. No matter how accomplished a culturally Greek rhetor might have been, delivering a praise of the city, and thus implicitly the empire, that was responsible for conquering Greece must have posed a monumental challenge. In what follows, I read Aristides' discourse with a sensitivity to the historical context but by no means adopt what Whitmarsh terms, quoting Catherine Belsey, an "expressive realist" account (*Greek Literature* 30). With Aristides, and particularly in this encomium, it is not a matter of reading off an attitude; Whitmarsh warns that we can never "'know' how a 'Greek' 'felt' about 'Rome'" (*Greek Literature* 3).[3] But, as we shall see, not all readers have approached the discourse with the same cautions in mind.

History in the encomium

In his 1953 monumental study of Aristides' encomium of the city of Rome, James H. Oliver characterized the oration as "one precious literary document, which is relatively unread" (871).[4] Casting an essentially book-length edition, translation, and commentary of this single text as a study of "the ruling power," Oliver established, as no one had before, the significance of this second sophistic text—which, in terms of twenty-first-century disciplines, must be claimed as rhetorical as well as literary—as an essentially political act, crucial for gaining perspective on attitudes toward empire. Oliver sought to discover "how the Roman Empire looked, not to Italians, not to Roman senators, but to the educated people who sat or might have sat in the town councils of Greek cities during the second century after Christ" (871). Oliver didn't approach the text naively as a historical record: in his extensive discussion of evidence, he created subheadings for "what can be used" and "what can't be used" (cf. Swain, *Hellenism* 275n82). But he ultimately took Aristides' praise of Rome at face value: "Aristides may certainly be used as evidence for much satisfaction with Roman rule, or specifically with government by the emperor and the provincial officials of his time" (889).

Aristides' lengthy and seemingly detailed address to Rome, although clearly presenting itself within the rhetorical genre of encomium of a city, continues to spark historical curiosity and even comparisons with ancient historians of empire. Oliver, for example, contrasted Aristides with Tacitus and offers brief comments on Polybius.[5] A review of recent treatments by historians reveals that Aristides' *Roman Oration* continues to provoke comment because of the way it activates the instability of discourse and knowledge: rhetoric and history cannot be clearly divided. The oration gives us a view of the Roman empire, but through what angles of perception? A review of recent references to Aristides' *Roman Oration* provides a revealing map of interpretive stances: a guide of sorts to the range of possibilities for rhetorical analysis and of the predicament for the Greek sophist under empire. What can contemporary readers know about life under empire, and what is at stake for a subject of empire in speaking about it?

In a striking instance of the power of Aristides' text, we find historian Aldo Schiavone framing his entire project *The End of the Past* with Aristides' analysis of the empire in what Schiavone terms a late stage (3–15, 204). The aim of this unusual study is to argue that slavery was the primary cause of Rome's downfall, a narrative that echoes in tone, if not in logic and evidence, Edward Gibbon's notorious and profoundly persuasive Victorian-era analysis of the empire's decline and of Greek rhetors' role in that process. In his introduction to Aristides, Schiavone entertains the possibility that "an encomium of the empire delivered before the court by an ambitious author may not at first sight appear to be an example of moral independence and intellectual autonomy" (4). But Schiavone ultimately judges that Aristides was expressing a vision "largely shared by a significant number of his contemporaries . . . rooted much more solidly in the reality of his time than in a stereotype of the court" (8). Finding that "there was neither disjunction nor artificiality in [Aristides'] appraisal of the civilization of the empire," Schiavone writes that Aristides presents a "distillation" of the perspective of urban elites of the time, staging "a display of the fidelity and unconditional approbation that surrounded the power of Rome on all sides" (11). The *Roman Oration*, in Schiavone's view, is an "unequivocal legitimization of Rome's supremacy" (8–9). Further, Schiavone participates in Gibbon's psychologizing, describing Aristides the man as a "nocturnal" rather than a "diurnal" personality (11), one whose anxiety and malaise are signs of the frozen state of the empire; one who, like the empire, suffers from torpor and "indolence" (204). What do we make of this appropriation of Aristides? On the one hand, there is a strong recognition of the oration's significance in capturing a moment in Greco-Roman relations. On the other, one might ask why such an innovative and thoughtful historian as Schiavone reproduces the narrative of decline with the Greek orator playing the same role as he did in Gibbon's time.

Other contemporary historians refer to Aristides but without coming to Schiavone's dark conclusions. Colin Wells, a professor of classics, in the second edition of his erudite overview of the Roman empire, offers a more rhetorically astute reading. In a chapter titled "The Orderly Government of the Empire: Hadrian to Marcus Aurelius," Wells cites Aristides in support of the stability of the empire from Hadrian's time and continuing into the accession of Antoninus Pius in 138 (202–22). At one point, Wells ventriloquizes Aristides, projecting something of the Greek orator's tone into his own prose: "Happy are those who enjoy the *pax Romana*, wretched those outside the Empire who are denied its blessings" (215). Subtly telegraphing the rhetorical bind of a second sophist, Wells comments, "No doubt Aelius Aristides said what he knew his hearers would want to hear . . . but the climate of opinion where such a speech was welcome was not one to encourage innovation" (215). Here we see a recognition of the complexity of the rhetorical situation Aristides faced.

A third example of appropriation of Aristides by a historian takes us to a more dramatic claim on the plane of political analysis. In her sourcebook *The Government of the Roman Empire*, Barbara Levick cites three passages from the *Roman Oration* for quite different forms of evidence. In one case, she interprets an early section of the oration (¶30–33) as a verification of Greek subjects' loyalty to the emperor (126). Her reference to a passage on local festivals and *euergitism* (good works) makes the point that the empire failed to inspire patriotism (200). But in a third reference to Aristides, Levick sees evidence of resistance: "Further, all the common masses in the Empire need have no fear of the powerful man among them: they can have recourse to you; but if they venture to cause a disturbance swift is the anger and vengeance visited on them by you" (¶65). As we saw in chapter 1, few readers of second sophistic rhetoric name resistance as a political stance, but Levick's categorization is provocative. The passage she cites immediately precedes the one quoted as the epigraph for this chapter. Both, at a minimum, cast an ironic shadow on Aristides' characterization of imperial relations as grounded in good reason (they operate "reasonably"—*eíkotōs*; in Oliver's translation "naturally"—and as "satisfactory," *areskei*). The observation that "no other way of life is left" carries the listener from the space of safety within the comfortable embrace of *pax Romana* into a place of chilling inevitability.

Rhetorical and literary critics have moved in the direction suggested by Levick, and my reading follows that path, finding accord with Laurent Pernot's recent reconsideration of Aristides' *Roman Oration* as an example of epideictic rhetoric whose praise cannot be taken at face value. Pernot proposes, and I concur, that the discourse is "figured": that is, a coded discourse, one seeming to praise Rome, both city and empire, but actually offering an undercurrent of critique. The Greek rhetor under empire speaks from a curious position—compromised, unsafe, assimilated, complicit—at once both inside and outside Roman intellectual and political life. Scholars of the second sophistic bring the colonial relations shaping Greek rhetorical practice in the period to the forefront of analysis through a variety of approaches. Some trace cultural conflict and mark the assertion of a Greek identity (Goldhill, "Introduction"). Others concentrate on genres that allow for direct commentary on governance and advice to rulers, such as Dio's kingship discourses (Whitmarsh, *Greek Literature* and "Reading Power"). As outlined in chapter 1, my methodology draws on the stylistic analysis of Frederick Ahl, who finds in figured discourse (*eschēmatismenos logos*) subtle commentary on the conditions of empire through allusions to classical literature. Drawing on Demetrius, Ahl's method makes possible readings of the artistically wrought and strongly typified structures of second sophistic rhetoric that uncover a shadow set of power relationships embedded within intertextual references.

For Ahl, figuration often involves revisualization. Oblique references, very often to the Homeric epics, evoke through a line, or at times even a single word, narrative scenarios, often accompanied by strong visual markers, which are then reimagined by listeners within the current speech situation. All beneficiaries of the *paideia*—that is, all educated people in the Greco-Roman world—knew the epics well, and any sophist could be counted on to lace an oration with Homeric references. But Aristides' use of epic references in his encomium of Rome suggests a purposeful strategy. This line of analysis gains from Brooke Holmes' recent reading of the *Hieroi Logoi* (*Sacred Tales*). Holmes argues that Aristides self-consciously adopts an epic framework for this signature work—a record of his "interpreting and memorializing the body's suffering" (82). In this first-person account, Aristides links himself directly to Homer's Helen as a narrator, which indicates, in Holmes' analysis, "epic aspirations" and artful design in a text that may otherwise appear to be a random collection of dreams and experiences. The encomium of Rome, of course, calls for a very different ethos, as the sophist addresses a Roman audience in the physical space of the city. Instead of narrative *mētis*, the sophist in this case draws on the resources of the epic to enhance his powers of visualization.[6]

What kinds of looking are staged in the orations of the second sophists? Aristides' *Roman Oration* presents not only a *phantasm* of the imperium but also a *technē* of viewing. Finding resonance in this network of references with the category of the sublime, I pursue this effect through a reading of several striking and improbable Homeric allusions. The path of interpretation will take us through sublimity and out the other side.

Ways of seeing

What would Aristides have found in the city in 144 CE?[7] Even by Strabo's time (63/64 BC–ca. 24 CE), the city of Rome was filled with architectural splendor; after seeing these buildings and monuments, "you would easily become oblivious to everything else outside" (*Geographia* 5.3.8; qtd. in

Edwards and Woolf 5). The memorable epigram Cassius Dio attributes to Augustus (ruling from 27 BCE to 14 CE)—no doubt apocryphal—nonetheless signals the dramatic changes to the built environment that occurred under his rule: "I found Rome built of clay and I leave it to you in marble" (*Historia* 56.30; see also Lamp). As Catherine Edwards and Greg Woolf point out, the flourishing of art and architecture in Rome was thoroughly dependent on Greeks.[8] Architects, sculptors, stonemasons, artists of every variety, as well as pedagogues and rhetors, were brought to Rome under coercion in service of its cultural revival. The building continued, as historian Andrew Wallace-Hadrill demonstrates through his reading of epigraphic, literary, and archaeological evidence, through the reign of Severus in the third century as emperors and prosperous citizens engaged in a common project of rendering orderly and knowable what had been a disorganized "tangle of streets and monuments" (275). The city Aristides entered in the mid-second century was likely marveling at the newly completed temple of Venus and Roma, begun by Hadrian in 121 CE (figure 3.1). Oliver speculates that Aristides would have performed in the Athenaeum, also built by Hadrian, a theatre for rhetorical and literary performance that may have been proximal to the magnificent temple (887). Though there is no record of the location of Aristides' performance, we can speculate on the physical setting for the oration's delivery, imagining not only the grandeur of the urban architecture and sculpture but also the impressions of the young sophist, who himself participates in the complex and conflicted imbrications of Greek labor and expertise in the construction of the Roman city and empire. Even assuming space to be discursively constructed, as demanded by the genre of the city encomium, some sense of place provided by more purportedly neutral and descriptive sources throws into sharp relief the choices Aristides made in crafting a phantasm of the city of Rome.

As Pernot observes, Aristides' *Roman Oration* is notable for what it does *not* say about Rome: "he completely neglects its monuments, architecture, art, literature and language" ("Aelius Aristides" 188). This is a lot to ignore. Pernot interprets these omissions as "eloquent silence," another tactic of figured speech. We saw this tactic in use by the later sophist Libanius in his encomium of Antioch in chapter 1. Through his concentration on Rome as an imperial power, Aristides does not signal contempt for Rome's history and culture but rather, Pernot argues, calls attention implicitly to the circumstances he cannot address directly: namely, Rome's conquest of Greece. His audience may have been attuned to such a strategy, given what Helen

Figure 3.1. Temple of Venus and Roma, ancient Rome, reconstruction (ca. 145 CE). COURTESY OF FALKENSTEINFOTO/ALAMY STOCK PHOTO.

Morales terms a Roman passion for the visual: it was a "supremely spectacular society . . . a visually voracious and violent world, in which there was a heightened . . . awareness of the pleasures and dangers of spectatorial relations" (10). Even though Aristides strategically denies his auditors (and, later, readers) the ekphrastic pleasures of Rome's city sights, the oration is permeated with visuality. We can account for these effects by turning to the Greek rhetorical practices with which Aristides was trained: concepts embedded in their own political contexts.

Tracking the continuity of epideictic rhetorical practice from the democratic rhetoric of the classical era to Greek rhetoric under empire, scholars such as Pernot, Walker, and others theorize the ideological function of visuality in ceremonial rhetoric. In his work with Aristotle's *Physics*, Ned O'Gorman has usefully concentrated attention on the term *phantasia*, drawing on its capacity to act as a hinge between rhetorical production and ideology critique.[9] Remarking on the significance of spatial logic in epideictic speeches, and on the role of vision and *phantasia* in Aristotle's discussion of the *pathē* (25), O'Gorman reminds us of Nicole Loraux's treatment of Athenian democracy as imagined, operating not only via a set of political policies (citizenship, assembly, courts) and speaking procedures (*homonoia*, *isēgoria*) but also on a social-psychic level as an envisioned or imagined state of freedom and participation. O'Gorman claims forcefully that "*the primal function of public discourse is the phantasmatic*" (34; emphasis in original). To give an example from the classical period of this phantasmagoric rhetoric, we may look to the funeral oration Thucydides attributes to Pericles. There the general exhorts his listeners to look at the city: "I could tell you a long story and you know it as well as I do about what is to be gained by beating the enemy back. What I would prefer is that you should fix your eyes every day on the greatness of Athens as she really is, and should fall in love with her" (*History* 145; trans. Warner). While visualization as an ideological maneuver can operate in any genre, the funeral oration emerging from Athens in the classical era served as a prime opportunity to deliver the "psyche-sight" of a city. Aristides' admiration for Thucydides among the Greek historians he studied and his allusions to Pericles' funeral oration in the *Panathenaic Oration* suggest more than a passing relevance for this intertext (see Oudot, "Regarder Rome"). In the Roman imperial era, the city encomium provides a parallel genre to the *epitaphios logos*, but the shift in power relations changes the heuristic. We are no longer discovering how the citizen-rhetor brings Athens before the eyes of his countrymen but are led to ask now, What visions does the Greek rhetor bring before an imperial audience? To reframe the question of *enargeia* (bringing before the eyes) as an ideological act under colonial relations, we may ask, Can the power of the Greek rhetor to bring an image vividly before the eyes of a mixed audience be understood as a response or even a challenge to Roman imperium?

Aristides' *Roman Oration* is a discourse rich with scopic vocabulary and overflowing with figures. As Estelle Oudot observes ("Regarder Rome"), the city encomium cannot dispense with bringing the city into view in a gaze, and the genre demands praise, specifically in terms of magnitude and grandeur, and yet the force or style, the atmospherics of this description—one might say, the phantasm—in any particular case is not a given. Weighed against Aristides' extensive historical evaluation of the accomplishments of Rome the empire, a network of uncanny visual references strung throughout the speech unbalances its straightforward encomiastic force.

Visuality enters as a negated activity with the introductory modesty trope, which here becomes an especially forceful and convincing assertion of impossibility: Not only can I say nothing in the face of the greatness of the city of Rome, Aristides says, but the city, which becomes an empire, cannot be seen (¶6). Referring throughout to the city and her inhabitants in the third person, Aristides writes,

> For it is she who first proved that oratory cannot reach every goal. About her not only is it impossible to speak properly, but it is impossible even to see her properly. In truth it requires some all-seeing Argos—rather, the all-seeing god who dwells in the city. For beholding so many hills occupied by buildings, or on plains so many meadows completely urbanized, or so much land brought under the name of one city, who could survey her accurately? And from what point of observation? (¶6, trans. Oliver)

The passage constitutes a veritable catalogue of Greek terms for seeing: *idein*, *panoptou*, *horōn*, *katatheasaito* (to look down upon, watch from above), *skopias*. And yet with all these visual practices, the city cannot be seen by the Greek rhetor. The question of perspective caps the series. In Oudot's view, the point of perspective throughout in Aristides' account of the city-become-empire is superhuman. It is a Homeric epic frame of reference for viewing "from the summit of a mountain or another high place": a perspective of a god or of the stars, not a human perspective ("Regarder Rome" 182–83).

Where does the rhetor stand in this scenario? The superhuman or godlike perspective would certainly be within the repertoire of the second sophist, consistent with the rhetorical power described in Longinus' *Peri Hypsous* (*On the Sublime*):

> The effect of elevated language upon an audience is not persuasion but transport. . . . Our persuasions we can usually control, but the influences of the sublime bring power and irresistible might to bear, and reign supreme over every hearer. . . . [S]ublimity flashing forth at the right moment scatters everything before it like a thunderbolt, and at once displays the power of the orator in all its plenitude. (1.4.1–10; trans. Roberts)

Vision and the sublime

Vision in the *Roman Oration* seems to generate a sublime sense of the city: terrifying greatness, unfathomable size, and magnitude. In producing this vision of the city, Aristides could be seen as exercising the kind of oratorical power termed *sublimity* by Longinus, whose text may have been written before or contemporaneous with Aristides' era.[10] A treatise on the composition of prose and poetry, Longinus' fragmentary work instructs writers in achieving sublime, or elevated, effects with reference to a number of different subjects and contexts. Homer's narratives, Sappho's erotic scenes, and Demosthenes' political orations are all offered as examples of successful sublimity. But at points throughout, Longinus acknowledges the inseparability of the object of discourse and its treatment. In Homer, for example, Longinus finds the *Iliad* in general more representative of sublime composition because of the intensity of the struggle, whereas the *Odyssey* for the most part consists of "narrative . . . characteristic of old age. . . . [I]n the *Odyssey* Homer may be likened to a sinking sun, whose grandeur remains without its intensity" (9.13). For a Greek rhetor to accept the challenge of praising the city of Rome at a high point in the empire's fortunes could be seen as an attempt on Aristides' part to provide himself with a sublime subject and thus the opportunity to achieve the level of oratorical success Longinus describes.

Is there a particular affinity between empire and the sublime? James I. Porter in "Ideals and Ruins" discusses the sublime "sensibility" of Pausanius and Longinus with reference to the second sophistic. He suggests that "the sublime and its freedoms exist only in the context of threatened or real loss" (81), in this case the loss of political freedom. Loss could be experienced as a response to any political formation, depending on the positionality of the speaker. That Longinus ends his work of aesthetic/rhetorical analysis with a discussion of losses of rhetorical possibility attendant on the end of democracy (44.1–12) suggests at a minimum that speculation about the politics of sublimity in a study of postclassical Greek rhetoric is not entirely misplaced.

Some second sophistic rhetors had grandiose ambitions, seeking to dominate competitors, attain access to emperors, and gain the power of influence through their rhetorical expertise. One might say that they sought a rhetorical domination parallel with the political power of empire.[11] To see these professional behaviors as direct compensation for loss of political autonomy would be perhaps too simple (or simplistic) a reading, one that Aristides himself denies at ¶108 (though, of course, in mentioning the trope at all, he lodges it in the minds of the auditors—one of several instances of *praeteritio* in the oration). But striving, failure, and loss operate at multiple registers. At key moments in the *Roman Oration*, Aristides incorporates Homeric allusions with effects that, on first glance, seem to suggest the orator is striving for sublimity in the treatment of a subject worthy of this level of artistry and elevation. But examined more closely, and especially with reference to the epic situations from which they are drawn, the figures color or taint the sublimity they suggest. Through these odd allusions, Aristides ultimately generates something like an anti-sublime: a cynical inversion or hollowed-out shell of what the grandeur of an empire could or should be. The result is the exposure of a failure—not the failure Longinus identifies as the mark of a successful sublimity, namely, the failure of a talented writer to capture perfectly the subject of his discourse (33.2)—but rather the failure of the political entity to rise to its own vision of its grandeur. On my reading, the figured vision shadowing Aristides' *Roman Oration*, in fact, turns Longinus' sublimity inside out; it is the negative of the photograph, the absence carved out by empire where a polis would have stood. Rather than rhetorical over-mastering, Aristides achieves something even more miraculous: an obliteration. For "what one does not see neither did nor does exist" (¶13, trans. Oliver). Let us pursue this negative.

Homeric figures: A phantasmatic subtext

Other scholars have laid out the structure of Aristides' clearly organized oration (Oliver; Pernot, *La rhétorique de l'éloge* and "Aelius Aristides"). Here we will limn a set of figurative touch points: too sketchy to constitute an alternative framework but tactically placed so as to throw the regular order off balance. We can conveniently summarize the figures through their vehicles: snow, bats, walls. Would it be going too far to call this array a fantasy or dream structure underlying the orderly (but incomplete, as Pernot points out) encomium? The figures arise in a somewhat ghostly or dreamlike fashion at beginning, middle, and end, and we might productively take up Pernot's language of encryption and keys, interpreting the figures as openings onto "the secret that everybody knows" about the violence, force, and coercion of the Roman empire ("Aelius Aristides" 188–90). Immediately following the question about viewing and perspective posed in ¶6, Aristides turns to an epic figure—not to describe the city/empire but to imagine its scope: "What Homer said of snow . . . such this city also does." The sophist cites book 12 of the *Iliad*, in which Homer imagines volleys of stones, thrown over Troy's walls by both Achaeans and Trojans, as an all-covering snow:

> [As] when Zeus of the counsels, showing
> before men what shafts he possesses, brings on a snowstorm
> and stills the winds asleep in the solid drift, enshrouding

the peaks that tower among the mountains and the shoulders
out-jutting,
and the low lands with their grasses, and the prospering work of
men's hands,
and the drift falls along the grey sea, the harbours and beaches
and the surf that breaks against it is stilled, and all things elsewhere
it shrouds from above . . . (12.279–86; trans. Lattimore)

We note initially that the scene is a battle, though neither the epic poet nor the sophist takes sides. Rather, the violence of battle is distanced and subdued through the figure. Like this snow, Aristides says, Rome covers all—mountain peaks, land intervening between towns and down to the sea, indeed all of Italy. Instead of calming or pacifying the battle, it becomes a figure for a deathly, or at least stifling and cold, homogeneity and envelopment. There is an eerie stillness to the Homeric passage: the snow stills winds "asleep" in drifts, enshrouds all natural features of the landscape along with human work, quiets and shrouds the surf and "all things elsewhere." The oddity of the figure—surely snow is a rarity in Rome—generates an alien atmospherics from which the orator then announces, "Wherever in the city one is, nothing prevents him from being in its center all the same" (¶7).[12]

Movement like vision is negated within this dreamlike, labyrinthine city-state, where every place is the same place and the same time: the time of the oration gives over to timeless space.[13] Even though one is in the middle, *en mesōi*, a synonym for the Greek agora, or space of civic encounter, the scene Aristides sketches is the antithesis of civic engagement: indeed there are no people here—neither citizens nor even combatants. Under the seeming praise of a great and expansive city lurks the violence of empire that erases inhabitants and covers over the city space with the unnatural quiet, order, and harmony of the *pax Romana*. It is the antithesis or inversion of the sublimity described by Longinus, flashing forward and scattering everything before it like a thunderbolt (1.4). It is rather a production worthy of the orator who, according to Longinus, in book 15, moves away from reality and truth and into a mode of speech "poetical and fabulous . . . [breaking] into every kind of impossibility, [and thus creating] digressions [with] a strange and alien air" (15.8, 11, 12–16). Perhaps the figure qualifies as the "hyperbole upon hyperbole" identified by Pernot in his discussion of style in Greek epideictic, which, he writes, achieves "*un ton spécialement outré*," an especially bizarre tone (*La rhétorique de l'éloge* 405).

From physical geography to political organization: a major section of the oration contrasts Rome with former hegemonies—Athenian and Lacedaimonian, with reference to Persian and Egyptian—all to the advantage of the Romans (¶15–71). Ultimately, Rome dominates, but Rome's success is always cast ambiguously: "For you are the only ones ever to rule over free men" (¶36). After praising common citizenship and the actual colonization of cities, and noting that identity is now understood not in ethnic terms but rather as Roman over against non-Roman, Aristides proposes, somewhat circuitously, that "to be ruled by you has been shown to be the first course" (¶68) and denies that a city or people would think of seceding "any more than those at sea" would secede from the helmsman. This could be a safe example of the ship-of-state metaphor, as old as Alcaeus (e.g., Fragment 6), and yet the idea enters as another *praeteritio*: Who was thinking of seceding? It's also possible that Aristides sought to create a resonance with the Scylla and Charybdis episode of the *Odyssey* (12.426). In this analogy, subjects of empire are placed precariously on a ship, which risks crashing into destructive rocks, and the only escape is a plunge into the chaotic vortex. Odysseus survives by clinging to a fig tree, hanging like a bat, until his ship is spewed back out of the sea.

The next sentence echoes the disturbing figure, as the ship of state morphs into a cave, creating another eerie instance of the *outré* or anti-sublime with reference to Roman colonists: "Just as bats in caves cling closely to one another and to the rocks, so all men depend on you and are fearfully concerned that someone may fall from this chain, and it is more the case that they are afraid of being abandoned by you than that they would abandon you themselves" (¶68). The only other mention of bats in the epic is found at *Odyssey* 24.6–8, where the ghosts of the dead suitors are roused—clinging, whining, and squealing as they are led into the underworld by Hermes. As with the earlier reference, more debased figures for colonial subjects and cities are difficult to imagine. As the passage proceeds, we see that warring with—and within—the empire is replaced by "pleasant calm" (*hēdista hēsuchadzousin*), accompanied by a loss of memory. The aura of the ghostly persists, as cities lying on their funeral pyres after battles with each other are resurrected into the calm of imperial control at which they marvel: "how they reach this state, they cannot say" (¶69). The sophist as Odysseus is the bearer of memory and heroic survivor, an association Aristides also cultivates in the *Sacred Tales*, Holmes observes. The fate of both lies ultimately in the hands of arbitrary and vast powers, and both experience life as a perilous journey. All this moves quickly by, but as Aristides' allusions to the epics are not formulaic, neither are they purely impressionistic. The images or phantasms evoked draw on educated listeners' memories of the narrative to achieve their force, as we see in the final cluster of references.

The whole or hole of Rome: Sublimity, power, and failure

In the final sections of the oration, Aristides turns to Rome's "fighting force and military affairs" (¶72), outlining the practice of conscripting soldiers from colonies far and wide and offering citizenship after a term of service. Again the sophist offers seeming praise of an innovation in security while simultaneously bringing to light the harsh reality of conscription for colonial subjects. For conscription, Aristides uses the term to designate a liturgy or public service in the classical Athenian era (*leitourgia*). The soldiers, he says, henceforth, "were ashamed to declare their former origins" (¶75). Turning from conscription to walls in ¶79, Aristides presents another case of seeing what is not there in the city but what becomes another phantasm of the empire. The actual city had no substantial walls at the time Aristides was speaking, and the sophist makes clear that he is referring to walls at the outer reaches of the empire, such as those built by Trajan and later Hadrian.[14] Again through a Homeric figure, the observation becomes a trope with discomfiting effects. Citing a section of the *Iliad*, book 16 (ll. 212–17.), Aristides draws on another battle scene, in this case a moment when Patroclus is leading the Greeks, and all the tribes (Myrmidons) join together to support him, holding out their shields together like a wall, which Homer says is like house walls so carefully and closely fitted that they need no mortar.[15] The force of the figure is to bring to mind battle and conflict in the same moment as the encomiast is purportedly praising the stability and security of the empire. The language of harmony and encircling wholeness evokes images from the beginning of the oration, as does the reference to spears falling like rain evoke the earlier snowfall (¶84). In the next section, Aristides shifts the language from walling to "netting" (*sagēneuō*), a term more pointedly suggesting hunting and capture, and yet by this means "the whole inhabited world" is kept safe by "those who are partners in it" and foreigners (¶85).[16]

In further allusions scattered through the final paragraphs, Rome is compared to the realm of the Olympian Zeus (¶89), and Homer is cited in service of "the earth common to all," a realm wherein all peoples are made safe by virtue of being Roman or, Aristides corrects himself, at least being "one of those under you" (¶100). The sublime makes the many whole, Longinus writes (10.1). And so one might see Aristides' vision of Rome as a sublime vision: like an engulfing sea, hiding all rivers that flow into it; like a hunter dragging a net over the world; like a weaver, spinning all citizens, nations, and armies into a single thread. Or one might say that Aristides' style is only that—evidence of a second sophistic tendency toward excess and exaggeration, the habit of reaching for the improbable and novel through figurative language.

The analysis offered here reads the logic of figuration, and especially the Homeric references, against the grain as a phantasm of the city/empire. This shadowy network of images produces a vision of the failure of political fantasy. One cannot love (in the Thucydidean/Periclean sense) what one cannot see. But Aristides' oration teaches us that it is not the task of the Greek encomiast of the Roman empire to produce love of the empire. The postclassical sophist, like the classical eulogist, brings forth a vision, and it is our interpretive task to reconstruct that phantasm of the imperial city. On Oudot's reading, it is a perspective that constrains the visitor to being a witness of the city's power ("Regarder Rome" 192). This is certainly one of the perspectives made possible by the oration. I would suggest that the listener/viewer is not rendered abject by the oration but rather placed in a kind of suspended and uneasy space—between Rome and Athens, between sophistic oratory and epic memory, between violence and security. Aristides' power lies in his ability to lay out the historical achievements of the empire and simultaneously to flatten and deaden them, to give them the voice of the *aulos*, which "after a thorough cleaning, plays a single note": the harmony of a single keynote "taken by all, everywhere, in the same way" (¶29–30, trans. Oliver). Rather than staging his erudition through references to Homer, Aristides seems to be adopting Homer's habit of mixing registers and realms through his extended figures. Scholars have explored the disjunctions created when Homer introduces a natural, pastoral analogy into a scene of bloody battle. Aristides is doing the reverse, calling up scenes of war and peril in the subtly figured descriptions of a presumably peaceful and stable city-as-empire. Porter characterizes the sublime as an aesthetics not of wholes but of ruptured wholes; in my view, Aristides' anti-sublime produces wholes that are holes or absences: the snow, the walls enclosing walls, the single note of the *aulos*.

By introducing not only the *phantasia* of empire but by exposing the techniques of envisioning, the Greek rhetor does not exactly claim power but exposes the vacancy and emptiness behind visible marks of power, opening at key moments a door onto the uncanny and repeatedly evoking through figures the violence of imperium that brings citizens and colonials together in the city. This power is not the counter-revolutionary power of a colonized subject but the critical, creative, and rhetorical power of the second sophist to reveal the political failure of a city that calls itself an empire.

Face to face

Swain asserts that the young Aristides delivered his encomium of Rome in the presence of the imperial family (*Hellenism* 275), although the evidence for this claim is not apparent. In any case, the oration, as we've seen, makes no reference to specific emperors and goes to great lengths to establish distance between the Greek sophist and the Roman empire. Twenty years later, in 177, Aristides' beloved city of Smyrna was destroyed by an earthquake, an event giving rise to two compositions that stand in sharp contrast to the Rome encomium. In a passionate monody, composed on the occasion (which was unusual for Aristides) and not intended for circulation, we find Aristides drawing deeply on a discourse of the sublime that he had so cleverly turned inside out in the earlier occasion. Oration 18, *Monody for Smyrna*, is brief, powerful, and filled with rhetorical questions and exclamations. We can get the flavor of the work from the opening, an apostrophe to Zeus:

> O Zeus, what am I to do? Am I to be silent when Smyrna has fallen? Have I such an adamantine nature or such self-control? . . . For if all the voices of the Greeks and the barbarians, those still upon the earth and those of every age, I say if all came together, they would be too little for this calamity, even to undertake the task, not to mention maintaining its true proportion. (¶1)

Everything is out of proportion in this discourse: the magnitude of Smyrna's beauty and the disaster of the city's destruction. What could compare to this loss? Aristides asks: "The fall of Asia! The remaining cities! All the earth, and all the sea within and without Gadira! The orb of the stars! Sun who beholds all things!" (¶7). Neither the fall of Troy, nor Athens' fall to Sicily, nor any other historic or legendary loss can compare to the destruction of

Smyrna. The depths of emotion, the sense of immediacy, and the extremity of the analogies here all reinforce by contrast the distant and strained quality of the mock grandeur or anti-sublime in the encomium of Rome.

His status at this late stage and his previous contacts put Aristides in a position to appeal directly to the emperor Marcus Aurelius and his son Commodus for aid in the face of this disaster. Oration 19, *A Letter to the Emperors concerning Smyrna*, provides an opportunity to look for a difference in approach when the conditions allowed for a direct encounter. How does the Greek sophist construct the relationship to Roman power under these circumstances? Aristides makes some predictable rhetorical moves in this appeal. He begins by reminding the emperors of previous rhetorical "gifts" he provided—"pieces from oratorical contests, lectures, and such things" (¶1) and continues with several paragraphs recounting the beauties of the city they had enjoyed on a previous visit. A central appeal—one very familiar in the present day—proposes that the donor will gain in stature through the gift: by contributing and making the city new again, "what kings will you not cast in the shade? What bounds of magnanimity will you not surpass?" (¶4). Just as the bereft Smyrnian appealed to the gods for aid, he now appeals to the emperors, and in so doing seems to put them on the same footing: "Then there is no reproach in writing to you in the same fashion in which we address the gods. Indeed, for these things we pray to the gods, but you we beseech as most divine rulers" (¶5). Aristides continues with a narrative of his experience and proceeds with reminders of the generosity of the city toward the empire in previous times (¶10–13). He ends by praising the emperors' "virtue, nature, and readiness for good deeds" (¶14).

Through all these stages, the discourse proceeds in a predictable fashion. The rhetor speaks directly to the emperors but in a most respectful way, acknowledging their power in the manner of a dutiful subordinate. How better to achieve the goal of financial aid? But approaching the end of this short discourse, Aristides takes an unexpected turn, offering a somewhat contorted assurance of imperial power in a move reminiscent of the rhetorical footwork in the encomium of Rome:

> Indeed, whenever I think to myself that one of the old emperors, not of your house—heaven forfend!—nor would it be done by any of you—but that one of those former emperors in the middle of playing draughts, as it is told, said in passing that he did not wish the Nasamones to exist, and so the Nasamones perished,

> then I believe that I should reasonably expect in your case that if you wish Smyrna to exist, quickly you will show all of us what we desire. (¶9)

The "old emperor" in question is Domitian, one of the most violent and tyrannical. The effect of this contrast cum comparison has, again, the effect of a *praeteritio*: not that you would ever be like the old tyrannical emperor, but then, after all, emperors can do what they please. This sidelong reference to unfettered power takes on a more pointed effect when we learn that at this time Marcus Aurelius was traveling in the east in the aftermath of a usurpation of power led by a successful general from Syria, Avidius Cassius. Although the upstart emperor, who had a base of power in Egypt as well as Syria and other parts of the East, had been murdered and his rebellion quashed by the time of Aristides' appeal, Marcus Aurelius used his trip to "[demonstrate] that he was well and truly alive and could count on Commodus . . . to succeed him" (Gasco 475). And despite the fact that Marcus Aurelius used clemency in dealing with the followers of Avidius Cassius, the emperor embarked on a systematic destruction of all documentation related to the revolt (Cassius Dio 71.3). Thus Aristides' seemingly unmotivated reference to the tyrannical Domitian creates an uneasy resonance with Aurelius' current project of erasing resistance to his rule.

Here we experience a "moment of dissonance" (Pernot, "Aelius Aristides" 199) in the most unlikely context from the second-century Greek sophist—charismatic, wildly successful, devotee of Asclepius—with the least to gain from such a rhetorical maneuver. The impulse to rattle the chain of gold, and simultaneously the imperial cage, is powerful—produced by and rivaling the power to which it persistently calls attention.

CHAPTER 4

Julia Domna's Dilemma: Sophistic Improvisation in the Eastern Empire

In chapter 1 we encountered Philostratus' *Lives of the Sophists*, a work in which a second- to third-century sophist foregrounded the biographies and practices of others. Here we turn to another of his works, one that offers a glimpse of his own direct contact with Roman imperial power around the turn of the third century (some years before *Lives*).[1] The massive and intriguing *Life of Apollonius of Tyana* is described by Ewen Bowie as a "hybrid of which biography is the dominant parent" ("Philostratus" 28). In an extraordinary report of intellectual sponsorship, Philostratus attests that the project was initiated by Julia Domna, wife of Septimius Severus and empress of Rome from 193 to 211. Domna survived her husband and became co-ruler with her son Caracalla until his death in 217, the year of her own death as well.[2] This provocative reference linking the Syrian empress with the Greek second sophist raises fascinating questions about the dissemination of second sophistic rhetoric, about literary sponsorship and ethnic identity, and about the entanglements of imperial power. If Philostratus' text was indeed launched under the aegis of Julia Domna, do traces of that context appear in the text? Heretofore we have understood figured discourse as an oppositional strategy in response to imperial power. What changes or inflections might we see in a text produced under conditions that involve an empress in the very intellectual process of rhetorical production?

Pursuing these questions requires several stages of inquiry. First we need to ask what we can know about Julia Domna—her life as it led to her rhetorical investments. In the process we attempt to account for the significance of her various ascriptions: gender, imperial power, intellectual formation, and Syrian ethnicity. Related to this inquiry is the question of her intellectual "circle": Was there such a thing? If so, how should it be characterized? Finally we turn to Philostratus' *Life of Apollonius of Tyana* to determine how we might find traces of this relationship between empress and sophist coded in the text.

A Syrian empress

Much of what we know about Domna's life comes from historian Cassius Dio (163/64–229), a native of Nicaea in the province of Bythinia (modern Turkey) and thus a provincial elite: one with a rhetorical education and strong Greek identification who was, at the same time, the son of a Roman senator and later a Roman senator himself appointed under Commodus. He rose to the position of consul (ca. 205 and again later) and also served as governor of Smyrna. In this dual position in the empire (insider and outsider), he was a personal observer of many of the events he narrates in an eighty-book history composed in Attic Greek that encompasses the years of Julia Domna's public life.

Unfortunately, nothing in Cassius Dio's history or elsewhere is recorded about Domna's education, but her birth into the household of the chief priest in Emesa (a city founded by Arabs but also associated with the Phoenician cities of the Syrian coast) and the fact that she attracted the interest of another colonial subject with intellectual aspirations, Septimius Severus, a native of northern Africa, suggest that she did receive some significant educational experience. Anthony Birley speculates that she and her husband may have communicated in Greek, as well as in a combination of their native languages: Punic and Aramaic. This background may account for the linguistic competence and diplomatic skill Cassius Dio later reports. After her marriage in 187, she soon bore two sons and became empress when Severus declared himself emperor in the field in 193. Age twenty-three in that year, Domna accompanied her husband on many campaigns, was designated "Mater Castrorum" (mother of the camp), and upon the family's return to Rome around the turn of the third century, she reportedly began keeping company with sophists, philosophers, medical scholars, religious sages, and astrologers. When Severus went on campaign again in Africa and Britain, Domna was left as advisor to her sons to whom the emperor dictated co-rule on his death.

When Severus died in 211, joint rule, predictably, didn't go smoothly, and only a year later the older son, who came to be called Caracalla, murdered his younger brother, Geta, wounding Domna in the process as she held the younger boy in her arms. To make matters worse, Dio writes,

> she was not permitted to mourn or weep for her son, though he had met so miserable an end before his time (he was only twenty-two years and nine months old), but, on the contrary, she was compelled to rejoice and laugh as though at some great good fortune; so closely were all her words, gestures, and changes of colour observed. Thus she alone, the Augusta, wife of the emperor and mother of the emperors, was not permitted to shed tears even in private over so great a sorrow. (78.2.5–6)

At this point in a narrative that I've been recounting rather neutrally, we may recognize that Dio is offering a certain *topos* or construction of Domna: a deep pathos surrounds the figure of the grieving mother who is not even allowed her grief. In her learned and thorough biography of Domna, Barbara Levick highlights the process of constructing narrative frames for Domna, finding in her story "three dependent plots": a family romance, a story of dynastic women, and an account of the orientalizing of the Roman empire (1).[3] Evaluating these narratives or topoi based on what we've learned so far, we might envision a continuum, placing on one end the Eastern child-bride whose numerous representations in sculpture and painting show her to have a childlike, simple beauty of face and figure (figure 4.1). The child-bride becomes the devoted mother of the camp and then suffering widow, counselor of emperor-sons, and ultimately the grieving victim of her elder son's violence and oppressive control. At the other end of this continuum we might place the Julia Domna who conspires with her powerful Emesene family to join forces with the future emperor, relishes her position of power over Caracalla, and shares this role with her sister and niece, who find themselves in similar circumstances over the subsequent decades. Also near this end of the continuum would fall the impression of Domna as worshiper of an exotic Eastern religion, an impression that would have grown in light of the career of a later Severan emperor, Elagabalus (218–222), one of the most bizarre and outlandish Roman emperors in his religious and sexual practices.

These stories or narrative frames—at both ends of this imaginary continuum—have powerful emotional charges conventionally associated with the feminine in many cultural times and places: excessive vulnerability and innocence, on the one hand, and the grasping power of the orientalized woman/empress on the other. A process of clearing out and holding at bay these powerfully charged impressions will allow us to bring forward the topos that links Domna with sophistic rhetoric. The historian Cassius Dio again

Figure 4.1 Julia Domna and her son Geta, Arch of Septimius Severus, Lepcis Magna, Tripoli (ca. 203 CE). COURTESY OF THE TRIPOLI, NATIONAL MUSEUM. COPYRIGHT © LIVIUSORG | JONA LENDERING.

comes to our assistance, describing Domna's intellectual and leadership abilities in service to the emperor Caracalla even after his fratricide. At that time,

> [Caracalla] was staining himself with blood, doing lawless deeds, and squandering money. Neither in these matters nor in any others did he heed his mother, who gave him much excellent advice. And yet he had appointed her to receive petitions and to have charge of his correspondence in both languages, except in very important cases, and used to include her name, in terms

> of high praise, together with his own and that of the legions, in his letters to the senate, stating that she was well. Need I add that she held public receptions for all the most prominent men, precisely as did the emperor? But, while she devoted herself more and more to the study of philosophy with these men, he kept declaring that he needed nothing beyond the necessaries of life and plumed himself over his pretended ability to live on the cheapest kind of fare; yet there was nothing on land or sea or in the air that we did not regularly supply to him both by private gifts and by public grants. (78.118.1–3)

Here we see Domna as a woman of strength, intelligence, will, discretion, and tenacity. She is a diplomat and translator: an intellectual with an interest in the movements of language, cultural practices, and power. As such, she seems to be a strong candidate for the role Philostratus assigns her as sponsor of his biography. But the sophistic text serves as more than another piece of evidence.

In what follows, I use the text of the sophist, as well as sophistic rhetorical tactics as interpretive levers, to gain new angles of vision on this allusive ancient woman rhetor. First we examine the historical claim made by author Philostratus in the introductory frame for his biography as a way of adjudicating the question of Julia Domna's circle. We then turn to a method of reading the biography—copious, novelistic, episodic, full of movement and ideas—as a figured discourse, exploring Philostratus' strategies for coding within a complex sophistic text his own and his sponsor's precarious circumstances as subjects of empire. Of the many directions such a reading of this massive work could take, we follow two, each suggested by the situation of Julia Domna: the topos of law and lawlessness and the issue of an Eastern/Syrian identity. There is to be no unveiling of the real and true sophistic empress at the end, and a single chapter cannot pretend to offer a comprehensive reading of the *Life of Apollonius of Tyana*. These readings are more like inroads into a labyrinth—partial mappings of the crossing of the empress and the sophist—than a decisive clearing away of all mysteries.

Julia Domna's *kuklos*

Philostratus' *Life of Apollonius of Tyana* is the story of a holy man (*theios anēr*) with miraculous powers who travels the world, compares customs (much like Herodotus), matches his philosophical wisdom with that of others, and also acts as an advisor to kings. The reference to Domna, contributing to her picture as an intellectual woman bringing together prominent men for study, comes early on, as the author is providing the rationale for his work. About Pythagoras, Philostratus writes, there are many stories preserved, but the practices of Apollonius, a historical figure from the first century of the Common Era, though much like the earlier philosopher, are not well known, despite his living much later. The itinerant Pythagorean philosopher traveled to India, Ethiopia, and elsewhere in the East; stayed in temples, taught, and advised cities; and counseled some highly placed Romans, perhaps even the emperors Vespasian and Titus.

The sophist lists his sources: shrines, reports, and Apollonius' own letters. And it is here we find the empress:

> But my more detailed information I have gathered as follows. There was a certain Damis, not devoid of wisdom, who once lived in Old Ninos. This man became a disciple of Apollonius and wrote up not only his journeys, on which he claims to have been his companion, but also his sayings, speeches, and predictions. The notebooks containing the memoirs of Damis were unknown until a member of his family brought them to the attention of the empress Julia.

Philostratus continues:

> Since I was a member of her circle [*kuklou*] (for she admired and encouraged all rhetorical discourse), she set me to transcribe these works of Damis and to take care over their narration [*tēs apangelias*], since the reporting of the man from Ninos [Damis] was clear but rather unskillful. (1.3; trans. adapted from C. P. Jones)

We see here a woman, associated with an emperor, who draws together a group engaged in the discussion, preservation, and circulation of important texts. Some adjustments to Jones' translation bring out the term *circle* (replacing his choice of *salon* and thus helping us to avoid the anachronistic leap to eighteenth-century French aristocracy). We also see a concern for style, but the lexicon's assistance with the Greek *apangelia*—as a noun, "report, as of an ambassador" and, as a verb, "to bring tidings, to carry a report home, to narrate" (*LSJ*)—would suggest an interest not in style generally but particularly in the kind of narration or storytelling necessary for crossing borders, a skill (shrewdness or cleverness) that this character Damis, another Syrian, apparently lacks.

Classical scholars are of several minds on the question of Domna's *kuklos*. William Cave Wright, 1921 translator of *Lives of the Sophists*, takes it as fact that, sometime after 202 through the influence of Aelius Antipater, teacher of both Severus and Philostratus, "[the latter] entered the circle of the philosophic Syrian Empress, Julia Domna" and traveled with her and the emperor to Britain in 208, Gaul in 212, Pergamon, Nicomedia, and Antioch (x). Later scholars are more circumspect. In her review of the question, Levick finds extreme views of Domna's circle: "at first romantic and exalted . . . and more recently severely reductionist" (107). But she takes the sponsorship of Philostratus' work seriously, speculating that the commission to a sophist to write a biography of a wise man suggests "a woman who was attracted to guides to life, especially guides for rulers. She had come to power suddenly from the outer reaches of imperial society and needed guidance" (123).

On the "reductionist" or skeptical side, Tim Whitmarsh catalogues Philostratus' various uses of the term *kuklos*, finding that the sophist uses it more often as an evaluative measure than as an indicator of a physical space or actual social gathering: the *kuklos* "invokes the metaphorical idea of a boundary between insiders and outsiders" ("Prose Literature" 33). Both Levick and Whitmarsh call attention to the nature of the text, emphasizing the generic similarity of Philostratus' *Life* to the Greek novels of the era: complexly layered, highly crafted narratives that blend historical account with supernatural events. Given this parallel, and the fact that the purported source of the material, Damis, is attested nowhere else in the existing records, we might be inclined to treat a literal reading of this commission skeptically.

By reading the sophist's text rhetorically rather than historically, however, it is possible to construe something more in "the case of the woman and the sophist" than presence or absence. We would undertake such a rhetorical reading by considering the circumstances of the Greek rhetor in the imperial setting with an attunement to the possibility of finding figured discourse in this novelistic text: a "lurking meaning" shielded by the writer for the dual purposes of showing off his cleverness and keeping himself safe (Ahl). In what follows, a first pass at interpretation suggests that the potential for violence in relations with the emperor are coded within discussions of law and lawlessness; a second reading, focusing on the character of Damis, a Syrian, speculates that he may figure as a stand-in for Domna, enabling reflections on tutelage and ethnic identity.

Figuring law and lawlessness

If indeed his biography was sponsored directly by Domna, Philostratus would have been attuned to the "lawlessness" of her older son, whose assassination of Geta was only one occasion on which he "stained himself with blood." According to Bowie ("Philostratus"), Philostratus may have been connected with the imperial family from around 203 until 215, accompanying them from Rome to Gaul, Britain, Tyana, and Antioch. The sponsorship, and the work itself then, took shape during a particularly violent period in the history of the empire. Septimius Severus came to power through conspiracy and military conquest over his competitors, not in the relatively peaceful, sophist-friendly world of Hadrian or Marcus Aurelius. In the course of establishing his dominance, Severus marched into Rome with an army, entered the Senate under armed guard, ultimately put a number of senators to death, and eventually proclaimed his son Caracalla emperor-designate. Having accompanied his father on the path to rule by brutal force, Caracalla seems to have learned his lessons well. After Severus' death and the eventual return of Philostratus to Athens, imperial power through the subsequent decades kept to this pattern. The scandalous Elagabalus (218–222), grandson of Domna's sister, Julia Maesa, and Alexander Severus (222–235) were both assassinated.

Why this story, a biography of a first-century Pythagorean philosopher, for this time? Why would a sophist have spent so much effort writing about a philosopher, when the two social types—philosopher and sophist—competed for cultural capital, students, and influence in his world? If we see the sophist as interested primarily in performative competition, we could observe that, in selecting Apollonius, Philostratus gave himself the pleasurable task of appropriating his competitors' discourse and manners, outdoing the philosopher at his own game, so to speak. In Philostratus' treatment, Apollonius certainly exhibits the features of a *theios anēr* in his adoption of modest dress and an abstemious lifestyle; in his life of teaching, wandering, and poverty; and in his devotion to virtue and the pursuit of truth. But rather than practicing within a single temple, Philostratus' Apollonius becomes a sophistic Socrates, carrying his questions about virtuous behavior and wisdom to India, Egypt, Ethiopia, and, at two points, to Rome for encounters with two emperors. As C. P. Jones notes, "Apollonius is made to act very much like the public speakers whom Philostratus was later to describe in his *Lives of the Sophists* . . . travel[ing] far and wide, curing cities of their tendency to faction . . . and counseling emperors" ("Apollonius" 9). This would be an answer focused on professional identity.

In another take on Philostratus' choice of subject, we could look to the preoccupations of the two imperial figures under whom Philostratus worked at the time the composition was begun. On one hand, we have the virtuous, intellectual empress, admirer of religious and philosophical teachings, who was also in an extremely precarious position vis-à-vis her violent and unpredictable son. Apollonius as a type stands in for those brought together by Domna in her circle to provide intellectual stimulation, balance, and good judgment in a dangerous time. On the other hand, we have in Caracalla, not only a lawless and violent tyrant, but also one, so Cassius Dio reports in the same passage, with enthusiasm for companions and amusements of a lower order—magicians and sorcerers—so much so that he had a shrine erected to the historical Apollonius, reinterpreted as a master of the dark arts and the spirit world.

In choosing Apollonius as his subject, Philostratus could "speak"—indirectly—to both imperial figures. Not only did both Domna and Caracalla have a direct interest in him, though in very different qualities, but they, and other readers, would also have recognized the strong parallels between historical periods—their own and Apollonius' of 150 years earlier. With the series of conspiracies and struggle for power following Commodus' murder, Colin Wells remarks, it was the year 69 all over again. The first phase of the empire had a crisis in that year with the reign of Nero, whose ineptitude, violence, and insanity led to civil war—the chaotic year of four emperors. The crisis was overcome when the Flavian Vespasian took over and was succeeded by his sons Titus and then Domitian. While Vespasian famously founded the first chair in rhetoric, he also had a vexed relationship with philosophers. Domitian was much worse, exiling philosophers, including Dio Chrysostom, and generally restricting freedom of expression, especially criticism of himself. His death was much celebrated. Roman historian Tacitus, for example, in his biography of Agricola and his *Dialogues on Rhetoric* celebrates the release of restrictions on thought and speech following on Domitian's death.

The crisis of the late second century followed a similar pattern. Decades of enlightened and relatively peaceful rule under the Antonines (or so-called adoptive emperors) from 96 through Marcus Aurelius' death in 180 granted sophists and philosophers alike more freedom and relative safety. When Aurelius broke the pattern of adoption and turned the empire over to his incompetent son Commodus, things began to fall apart again. The parallel between the two periods enabled Philostratus to comment indirectly on contemporary affairs under the protection of historical distance and the documentary pretense of the genre of biography. Evoking through his narrative an earlier time of imperial violence and crisis, Philostratus follows the life of the philosopher through the reigns of Nero, the four emperors, and Vespasian, bringing the narrative to a dramatic climax through Apollonius' (most probably fictional) encounter with Domitian, enemy of philosophers, free speech, and virtue. By Philostratus' era a century later, the "good" emperors were finished. No longer could a sophist imagine the rich intellectual climate and potential for influence enjoyed under a Hadrian or a Marcus Aurelius. With Christians still at risk of persecution, a repetition of Domitian's exile of philosophers would not have seemed totally improbable, a net in which a sophist could have easily been caught, as was Dio Chrysostom in the first century. The recourse of the sophist was indirection, and the choice of Apollonius provided a wealth of opportunities for figuring discourse—embedding risky truths by calling into play the abundant resources of sophistic creativity: historical analogy, references to the classical repertoire, a revoicing of the holy man / philosopher, and a fictional embedding of the structures of Greek forensic rhetoric.

What was "law" for Philostratus? Although Greek sophists could have practiced law in the period in question, and Bowie ("Philostratus") suggests that Philostratus may have done so, Philostratus, like most of the prominent sophists, was more interested in law as a regulatory or normative discourse than as lowly practice.[4] Though the emperor, according to second-century jurist Ulpian, is above the law, Caracalla, like all but the most ruthless or crazed emperors, sought to legitimate his rule, cultivating *auctoritas* by periodically declaring his intention to respect, and at times actually living in accordance with, the laws (C. Wells 263). In matters of life and death, the emperors acted without check but not without being judged. To adapt the language of Giorgio Agamben, we could say that the genres of sophistic rhetoric create "constitutive fictions," bridging the distance between the arbitrary and unpredictable power of a tyrant and a vision of social order imagined through systems of law (*State* 91). For just this reason, Roman law and imperial lawlessness are topoi directly and indirectly addressed within second sophistic Greek rhetoric through a number of rhetorical subgenres: advice to kings, narratives of crime and punishment, and trial scenes.

Wedged between Caracalla and Julia Domna, and gifted with rhetorical ability, Philostratus found himself in a position to fill in that space between imperial lawlessness and the normative expectations and hopes for human survival to which law gives rise in any state. I propose that the scenes of confrontation between Apollonius and two emperors (Nero and Domitian), but particularly the apologia at the culmination of the philosopher's trial before Domitian at the end of the *Life*, offer a figured recognition of Domna's dilemma: an address to imperial violence and lawlessness and—at the same time, in a typical sophistic fashion—a self-conscious comment on the necessity for figuring discourse in dangerous times.

At the end of the narrative, Apollonius finds himself in Rome at his peril. The emperor Domitian has trusted the accusation of an informant from Arcadia who claims that Apollonius is a sorcerer guilty of human sacrifice. The Socratic character of Apollonius is fully realized in the fifty-paragraph speech of defense that Philostratus' narrator Damis relates in book 8. As a preface, readers are provided with a caveat about the style, a passage in which the sophist's source disavows the "vulgar" style of the rhetor but at the same time endorses the "concealed craftiness" of the wise man who, despite his "craft," is nonetheless to be differentiated from those "those trained in law":

> I am aware that admirers of a vulgar [*bōmolochous*] style will criticize it as lacking the finish which they consider necessary and as overdone in its vocabulary and ideas. . . . I do not think a wise man would truthfully represent his own character by cultivating balanced phrases or antitheses, and making his tongue clack like a rattle, for these things are characteristic of practiced speakers [*rhētorikois*]. . . . [F]or obvious craftiness [*deinotēs*] in court will give a bad impression, as if the speaker were plotting against the jurors, while concealed [*aphanēs*] craftiness will emerge the victor, since not letting your judges see that you are crafty is a craft [*deinotēs/deinos*] of the truer kind. (8.6.1–2; trans. C. P. Jones)

The choice of a vivid descriptor, "vulgar" style, cleverly implies a critique of the version of Apollonius that Caracalla found entertaining; *bōmolochos* is a word referring to a low jester or buffoon, one who lurks about the altars for scraps, a half-starved beggar (*LSJ*). We see next the familiar topos of division: a wise man (*sophos*) does not need artifice, thus contrasting the philosopher to the rhetor/sophist. But the sophist emerges victorious in his advocacy of "concealed craftiness" as a practitioner of a craft of a truer kind.[5] The narrator, whom Philostratus claims to quote, goes on to contrast the desirable style of a *sophos* with that of the lawyer: "When a wise man defends himself, . . . he needs a manner different from those of men trained in law—a style that is practiced [*kateskeuasmenou*] without appearing to be" (8.6.1–2). Here Philostratus uses the term for the "confirmation" phase of argument in the advanced stages of the *progymnasmata*, again drawing a distinction between his philosophic sophistic and the rhetoric of the schools.

Apollonius introduces the terms of what Foucault calls the *parrhēsiastic* game or pact (*Fearless Speech* 17 and *Government* 62–66) at the outset of the speech:

> You and I, Majesty, are playing for high stakes. You are running a risk that no emperor ever did before, that of appearing an enemy of philosophy with no justification. I am running one that not even Socrates did at Athens, since those who indicted him thought him a spiritual innovator, but neither called nor thought him a spirit. Since both of us are exposed to so great a risk, I will not hesitate to give you advice in a matter about which I am certain. They presumed that you were going to let your anger determine how you listened to me, and that you might kill me in your anger.
>
> . . . Hearing this, I was not led to be prejudiced against you, or to condemn your judgment as other than upright. I submitted to the laws, and am standing trial. This is also what I want to advise you. (8.7.1–2)

Killing in anger is, in fact, what Caracalla did when he killed Geta. Apollonius says he will not prejudge the emperor (Domitian in the story) but will submit himself to the laws and advises the emperor to do likewise. With strong echoes of Plato's *Apology*, the "defendant" goes on the offensive against the emperor at the outset, calling him to account for his prejudice against philosophers and the bad judgment of listening to an informant. Philostratus calls on his character Apollonius to contain and regulate the behavior of the emperor, perhaps especially in the interest of protecting his sponsor, the empress.

The speech itself ends with simple eloquence. Apollonius has completed his own defense: he could not, would not, and did not take a life. Nor should the emperor imperil the lives of his subjects. To the emperor he remarks, "'Human prosperity is cyclical, and pomp, Majesty, has only a brief span. . . . [T]hink of that, my Majesty, put an end to exile and an end to bloodshed, treat philosophy as you please . . . but wipe away the tears of humankind'" (8.7.49). We don't know whether Caracalla or any of his successors read or heard Philostratus' work, although the general practices of public performance in court and the circulation of written texts thereafter could have made such contact possible (Bowie, "Philostratus" 20–21). It was completed long after Domna's death. Could the text of the sophist have tempered the anger and violence of an emperor? We may only speculate that Philostratus constructed the narrative with such a scenario in mind.[6]

Julia Domna, the Syrian: Reading the East in a text of the West

Rereading with attention to character and geography, we can see the threads Philostratus pulls from this historical knot of unfettered imperial power, family, gender, and cultural difference and reweaves into a tapestry in which the emphasis is placed on religious/philosophical wisdom in a multicultural empire. In Apollonius, Philostratus has created a character somewhat like Julia Domna: virtuous, pious, philosophical. Despite his neo-Pythagoreanism, Apollonius respects the religion of the sun and its expression in the diverse cultures he visits (in Babylonia, India, Egypt, Ethiopia).[7] But notably he does not visit Syria, the homeland of Domna, where her father was a priest. In a kind of indirection that shields both the sophist and the reputation of the late empress from the orientalizing demonization of "the Syrian," ever more rampant under Elagabalus, Philostratus novelistically splits Domna into two through a kind of dream logic, in which the dreamer plays all the parts, through the creation of Damis, the Syrian amanuensis—an interlocutor very much like those interlocutors of Socrates in Platonic dialogues. A bit like a Dr. Watson in relation to Sherlock Holmes, Damis constantly asks questions that set up the wisdom of the sage.

Why would Philostratus insert a Syrian character into this project, a character decidedly subordinated to the Greek philosopher, Apollonius? One answer is that the two characters allow for debate about prudent conduct. In book 7, for example, Apollonius is brought up on charges by Domitian (the paradigmatic bad emperor) for speaking in private and in public against him. In a conversation among one Demetrius,[8] Apollonius, and Damis about what to do in the case of death penalty, Damis is loyal to the person of Apollonius but disinclined to die for philosophy. Apollonius takes the Socratic position that it is noble to die for principle, saying of Damis, "We must be forgiving of [him] for speaking timidly about our situation, for he is an Assyrian and has lived on the borders of Media, where they kowtow to tyrants, and he has no lofty ideas of freedom" (7.14.237–38). Here the character of Damis, the transcriber or translator, the cautious Syrian who wishes to live, could be read as a coded recognition of Julia Domna in her situation as Eastern empress of Rome, at risk of death and, at the same time, devotee of philosophy in its various forms (astrology, mathematics, medicine) and of religion. Apollonius gives parodic voice to the arrogance of the Greek with his ethnic slurs for Syrians from the pompous and protected position of a detached philosopher who can magically escape the leg-irons of the tyrant (which he does later in the chapter), but a reader may see in Damis, the Syrian, an admirable wish to live, to record history and philosophy, to be loyal to the philosopher, to follow him around the world, and to learn from him. This relationship marks the difference in life possibilities for the empress and the sophist. Philostratus can escape to Athens. Domna is trapped. Remembering Dio's chilling account of Caracalla's murder of Geta and Domna's situation thereafter, we may not find it very difficult to imagine a life of such fear and surveillance, one in which "all her words, gestures, and changes of colour" were observed (Cassius Dio 78.2). What enabled Domna's survival—not only survival but her exercise of political diplomacy at the highest level and the fostering of intellectual life—under such conditions? I would suggest that the resources of sophistic rhetoric could have come to her aid: the ability to strategize, to shape-shift, to create the persona necessary for the occasion.

A final glimpse into the biography will give another angle on rhetoric as a survival strategy in the age of empire. The night before Apollonius' interrogation by Domitian, Damis advises Apollonius not to sleep but to stay awake and prepare. The philosopher asks how he can prepare before he knows what he will be asked, and Damis queries, "'Will you improvise, then, [*autoschediaseis*] . . . when your life is at stake?' Apollonius replies, 'Yes indeed, Damis, . . . for my life is an improvisation [*autoschediōi*]'" (7.30). Repeating forms of a verb meaning "to act or speak off-hand, to devise off-hand, extemporize" (*LSJ*), Philostratus links through language the imperiled philosopher, sophist, empress, and imperial subject. This subject cannot count on a stable or safe future, so improvisation is essential. Preparation in the form of sophistic education—one informed by the tactics of figured speech, the control of word, gesture, and even body—can be lifesaving.

Conclusion

As we move through these readings, Julia Domna shifts in and out of focus; the figure of the empress dims as the concerns, texts, and figure of the second sophist come out more strongly. The relationship faintly sketched through these texts brings to life the subtle power of sophistic rhetoric as an intellectual acquisition but more importantly as a stance and resource that served both empress and sophist in a violent and precarious world. Sophist and empress are both bound, textually and materially, by the same chain of gold—complicity and artistry, an artistry forged within and against their complicity in the Roman imperial regime.

CHAPTER 5

Curated Visions of Manhood in Philostratus' *Imagines*

Philostratus needs no apology. There is now widespread agreement on the outstanding nature of the Philostratean corpus, as both exemplary literary masterpieces in a range of genres, in their own right, and as throwing fundamental light on a series of key historical and cultural themes in the imperial experience of Greeks in the Roman world.

—Ewen Bowie and Jaś Elsner, preface, *Philostratus*

In this epigraph, Bowie and Elsner, editors of a volume of essays published by Cambridge in 2009, boldly announce the significance of the central figure—one whose presence and influence hover over *Chain of Gold*. Neither their collection, *Philostratus*, nor the author himself, nor his corpus requires apology. Concerning the identity of this Philostratus, a name borne by several authors between the first and third centuries CE, scholarly opinion has shifted in recent years so that a single figure is now considered to have produced a large and "protean" body of work, as Elsner describes it ("Protean Corpus" 3–18). Tim Whitmarsh is even more straightforward about the rising stock of this second sophist; he announces in the same collection that "Lucius Flavius Philostratus is in danger of becoming fashionable, for the first time in 1,500 years" ("Performing Heroics" 205). I follow Alain Billault, the scholars contributing to Bowie and Elsner, and others in accepting Flavius Philostratus (referred to variously as the Athenian, the Lemnian, or the Elder) as the author of all three works by Philostratus treated in this book.[1] We began in chapter 1 by using *Lives of the Sophists* as a point of historical reference for the second sophists and continued in chapter 4 with a treatment of the long philosophical biography *Life of Apollonius of Tyana*.

This chapter focuses on a collection of descriptions, or ekphraseis, of paintings: a work commonly referred to as *Imagines* (in Greek, *Eikones*).[2] As is explained below, the mode or genre of ekphrasis has attracted critical attention from its inception. But this interest in the critical term has rarely translated into a consideration of Philostratus himself, the work as a whole, or its relation to the rest of the corpus. As Bowie and Elsner note, there have been only two monographs on Philostratus (Anderson, *Philostratus*; Billault), neither of which has much to say about *Imagines*. The detachment of ekphrasis as a topic from the work of Philostratus, notes Ruth Webb, is concretized in the choice of the Loeb Classical Library to publish *Imagines* not with other works of Flavius Philostratus but with later, similar collections of ekphraseis (*Ekphrasis* 32n55). Thus the perspective offered by the epigraph and the recent work on Philostratus, newly consolidated into a single author, is important for a rereading of *Imagines*. What changes in our understanding of this curious collection when we consider it to be the work of a second sophist who played a significant role in the imperial culture of his times? The aim of this chapter is to approach this fascinating work through a reading that brings to light the ways in which rhetorical and pedagogical practices of a second sophist both reflect and seek to shape relations between the Greek intellectual and his Roman patrons. It is necessary to begin, however, by acknowledging the important strands of scholarship that have interpreted ekphrasis.

Ekphrasis in the history of rhetoric

The term entered rhetorical theory in its technical phase as one of the *progymnasmata*, a set of brief topical exercises in writing and speaking assigned to students in earlier stages of instruction before they composed extended declamations.[3] In the course of pre-rhetorical study, taught by a "grammarian," ekphrasis usually appeared late in the list of twelve or fourteen activities constituting the preliminary curriculum (see, e.g., Crowley and Hawhee; Pernot, *Rhetoric* 219–20; Webb, *Ekphrasis* 49–50), indicating that writing a description was considered more difficult than, for example, relating a fable. Kennedy, drawing on a late source for his treatment (Aphthonius of Antioch, second half of the fourth century CE), defines ekphrasis as a description of "persons, actions, times, places, animals, and growing things" (*New History* 206). Ruth Webb's recent work puts a strong emphasis on the roots of ekphrasis in the rhetorical handbooks and focuses on the performative aspect of the definition (84–86 passim).[4] The most significant function of ekphrasis, in Webb's view, is its capacity to effect *enargeia*, "bringing before the eyes" (*Ekphrasis* 87–106), a rhetorical phenomenon of considerable interest from rhetoric's inception in the classical period before the term *ekphrasis* came into use.[5] Gorgias, for example, in the *Encomium of Helen*, has much to say about the power of the visual sense to "trouble the soul" as well as to produce delight and longing, as painters and sculptors accomplish with their creations (¶16, 18; trans. Donovan). Almost a century later, Aristotle remarks on "bringing before the eyes" (*pro ommatōn poiein*) as an important stylistic element productive of *energeia*, vividness or actualization (*Rhetoric* 1411b24–25; see also Newman 109–30; Westin).[6] Turning to other work of Aristotle (e.g., *On the Soul* and *Movement of Animals*), rhetoric scholars have more recently explored the power of visualization, *phantasia*, as a crucial factor for rhetoric—for understanding, stirring emotions, and deliberation (Hawhee, "Looking"; O'Gorman; see also Webb, *Ekphrasis* 107–30).

Thus with *Imagines* we have an ancient text that could be viewed in a minimal way as a set of rhetorical exercises intended as models for students (Fairbanks xxii); in a different light, though, we can see it as a work that taps into a longer and deeper stream of theory, practice, and speculation stretching back as far as Homer's description of Achilles' shield in the *Iliad* (18.483ff.). The sixty-eight brief discourses—"prose miniatures" as Diana Shaffer terms them—set within a narrative frame open out onto a range of topics of considerable complexity and depth.[7] Far more than merely decorative, description, in Janet Atwill's words, is "one of the most powerful normalizing strategies" (*Rhetoric* 207). "Description," she continues, "may even be more powerful than prescription in eliciting compliance to limits of behavior and desire" (208). This power comes through the impact on the reader or listener who simultaneously is invited to become a viewer, through imagination, of the subject, "whether an action, a person, a season or place, visible to the mind's eye of the audience"; thus the discourse becomes "part of an intimate communication between speaker and addressee" with imaginative and emotional consequences (Webb, *Ekphrasis* 85). The process inevitably raises the questions of mimesis and representation more generally: Can language re-present objects in the material world? How accurately and with what effects? Of course these issues were central to Plato's critique of poetry, drama, and writing, indicating a philosophical underpinning to any consideration of ekphrasis.

But the charm and challenge of ekphrasis lie in the fact that the descriptions inevitably move beyond mimesis, as the verbal representation exceeds the "real" limits of the visual image or object. That excess brings us to one of the most significant features of ekphrasis for second sophistic discourse: the famous agon between visual and verbal expression, especially when the object being described is a work of art. Whose creative achievement is the most impressive—the painter/sculptor's or the poet/rhetor's?[8] With reference to the earliest example, the description of Achilles' shield, readers both ancient and contemporary have noted that the description through Homer's poetic artistry becomes a world of its own, including far more scenes, objects, and landscapes than could possibly be engraved on any shield, even one created by Hephaestus. A few centuries later, the poet Simonides presented a more equable relationship, proposing that painting is silent poetry while poetry is painting that talks (Plutarch, *Moralia* 346).[9] That this fragment was captured by first-century CE Greek scholar Plutarch suggests the particular interest of the "inter-arts" relationship for the postclassical era. Plutarch's Latin contemporary Horace coined the famous dictum *ut pictura poeisis*—as is painting, so is poetry (*The Art of Poetry* 1.361)—reiterating a similarity between the two arts but one more often tested than accepted in future centuries. In Philostratus' *Imagines*, the narrator/sophist delivers descriptions of paintings in a luxurious gallery for a young Roman student and his comrades, thus heightening the agon through the (fictionalized) drama of sophistic performance. Elsner comments that Philostratus' project becomes "a commentary on whether the *phantasia*—or vivid visualization—evoked by the sophist can replace or even outdo in the hearer's or reader's mind the actual impression of a real gallery, a real painting, a real landscape seen directly" (Elsner, "Protean Corpus" 10–11). Taken from another angle, ekphrasis is often considered not only "one of the more difficult and elaborate exercises" (Webb, *Ekphrasis* 49–50) but part of a larger whole—positioned within an oration, a literary work such as an epic, or the emergent genre of the ancient Greek novel. As such, the mode seems to offer an acute angle of vision, as it were, into the generic capacities (and limits) of larger discourse genres.

As this brief introduction may suggest, ekphrasis has spawned a multitude of scholarly inquiries and been called into service on one side or another of passionate debates, particularly about the relationship between visual and verbal arts. One could track its appearance through Renaissance treatments of the *paragone* (comparison) of arts (Plett), on to post-Enlightenment theories of the hierarchy of aesthetic value (Lessing), and into the twentieth-century revival of rhetorical figures in the work of Gérard Genette, in whose schema description is the depiction of objects or people in stasis, a "mere auxiliary of narrative" (*Figures* 136, 134; qtd. in Heffernan 5). Appropriated by American literary theorist Murray Krieger as a "general principle of poetics," ekphrasis, Krieger argues, freezes time in space, as in exceptional poems such as Keats' "Ode to a Grecian Urn." James A. W. Heffernan has dealt with these subjects masterfully in *Museum of Words: The Poetics of Ekphrasis from Homer to Ashbery*, wherein he resuscitates ekphrasis as a "dynamic and obstetric" force in the verbal arts (5).[10] Given the reawakened interest in visual matters in the field of rhetoric studies at present, it would be a missed opportunity not to note the critical energy generated by this nugget from the ancient rhetorical curriculum. Any work of visual rhetoric incorporates ekphrastic elements, after all, and is thus subject to the many currents it has set in motion.

Philostratus' *Imagines* as a cultural text: A world of things

If the movement of ekphrasis into literary theory extracted it from its rhetorical and historical context, other strands of scholarship have pulled in a different direction. Descriptions, no matter how entrancing and imaginative, begin as descriptions of things. Several critics have drawn attention to the critical questions raised by the objects of description. In an early work, Page duBois defines ekphrasis through Walter Benjamin as a "model of the course of the world" (*History* 3). In this comparative project beginning with Homer, duBois reads epics as historical texts, and ekphraseis within them serve to "[clarify] the relation between individual and community history" (145). Writing a decade later, D. P. Fowler remarks, in an important essay on ekphrasis in the Roman context, "It is striking how often set-piece description in narrative is of things that participate particularly obviously in social systems of meaning: clothing or armour, furniture, architecture, the cultivated landscape" (27). A third example comes in an essay by Froma I. Zeitlin addressing vision in classical theatre. Here she notes that various visual and verbal idioms related to vision, including ekphrasis, come into play in the "shaping and cultivation of cultural memory (and also inevitably of political ideology) . . . as an active engagement . . . that refashions the past in the present and the present in the past" ("Artful Eye" 144–45). In each case, ekphrasis offers access—highly mediated though it may be through layers of intertextual, artistic, and interpretive complexity—to the postclassical Greco-Roman world. Even Graham Anderson, who places so much emphasis on the Greekness of the second sophists, concludes that ekphrasis is for them an "extension of cultural experience and a way of seeing the world" (*Second Sophists* 154).[11]

Perhaps the best way to enter, for the third time, into the world simultaneously imagined and inhabited by Philostratus is to lay out the narrative frame for the work. An unnamed narrator is lodging in a suburb of Naples, living in a very fine four- or five-level apartment (*insula*) facing on the Tyrrhenian Sea.[12] The narrator has traveled, he reports, to Naples, a city "settled by men of the Greek race" and "people of culture" (*astikoi*, "citified") and "therefore Greek in their enthusiasm for discussion" (1.4). Additionally, he notes that he arrived at the time of Naples' public games (also a Greek legacy). The house, we learn, "was particularly splendid by reason of the panel-paintings set in the walls, paintings which I thought had been collected with real judgment" (1.4). The narrator reports that he had already thought about speaking in praise of the paintings (*epainein tas graphas*), when the son of the host, a ten-year-old boy "already an ardent listener and eager to learn," asked the guest to interpret them for him. Without identifying the narrator as a sophist, Philostratus gives every indication to the reader of this Greek text that we are following the movement of a second sophist—calling attention to cultural Greekness within a Roman city, with a narrator ensconced in the home of a Roman patron and preparing to offer discourse. As Zahra Newby puts it, "To any reader of *Lives of the Sophists* the situation is a familiar one—a man is attended by a group of youths, eager to hear him speak, a man who can give *epideixeis* and *meletai*—he must be a sophist!" ("Absorption" 323).

Like other second sophists, Philostratus ignores or minimizes the Roman presence. Referring to "the son of my host," the narrator obscures a Roman patron / Greek subordinate relationship and his probable employment as tutor to the Roman boy and his comrades. This strategy of silence has been recognized by Laurent Pernot as one of the techniques of "figuring" discourse ("Greek 'Figured Speech'").[13] What other tactics of figured discourse might be at play in a second sophistic collection of ekphraseis? That question informs the analysis to follow, and it was, interestingly, adumbrated some two centuries ago by Goethe, in an 1818 essay titled "The Pictures of Philostratus." The great German Romantic poet had a lifelong interest in the visual arts and wrote this essay during a period of collaboration with "the friends of art in Weimar" who expressed interest in Philostratus' project (Goethe 140).[14] On his way toward a discussion of the arrangement of the paintings (about which more to follow below), Goethe makes an observation about the constraints on Greek orators under Roman rule that resonates with current readings of the second sophists: "They had long been forbidden to exercise their art upon historical and political subjects; moral problems had been used and exhausted again and again; the jurisdiction of art alone remained, and to this they fled with their scholars, to exhibit and develop their dexterity upon these harmless subjects" (141).

We can better assess "these harmless subjects" and the social context in which they come to light when we engage with the scholarship on Roman painting of this period. Eleanor Leach's definitive study on the subject, *The Social Life of Painting in Ancient Rome and on the Bay of Naples*, provides illuminating contextual detail. While contemporary readers might imagine a gallery of paintings as something like a museum, in the second- to third-century CE in Naples, painted wall decorations in a house were continuous with the world outside. Leach remarks on historical differences in visual fields: "The inhabitants of ancient cities were accustomed to seeing painted surfaces all around them occupying a far more conspicuous place in the urban landscape than is generally the case today" (3). And the house, with its visual treasures, would have been open to a parade of the patron's clients on a daily basis, as well as to aliens like the sophist, visiting students, slaves, and *liberares* (freed slaves). How did this prosperous Roman citizen come to acquire a set of paintings that the narrator views as "collected with real judgment, for they exhibited the skill of very many painters"? Leach discusses the circumstances of the Roman acquisition of Greek art: namely, theft perpetrated by Roman conquerors and governors on Greek colonies (132–33). Art collection as an imperial act can be taken as a backdrop for the scenario with which readers are presented in *Imagines*. While it's unlikely that the wall paintings the narrator describes were stolen, the artists themselves may have been Greek immigrants, some of whom, as we learned in chapter 1, were forcibly removed to Rome. Viewed in this historical context, the whole enterprise sits under a cloud of colonial appropriation (see also Lamp; Miles).

Further, Leach notes that artistic display served as a vehicle for personal and political statement in this period (5). She draws primarily on evidence from Pompeii and cities in Campania (including Naples) in the first century, but her analyses of the political uses of domestic space in the Roman house extend to the period of Philostratus' work (281–86). Acknowledging the performative nature of a second sophistic project, Leach judges that "Philostratus' [second-century] gallery [is] no less representative of a society than the material installations we have been considering [i.e., from the first century]" (281). While wall painting provided a backdrop for everyday life, stories and figures drawn from Greek mythology and literature, although conventional, might "thematically express the [Roman homeowner's] policies or interests" (5). Given that the Roman house served as a "showcase for public life," the artwork inside it should not be considered private in the post-Enlightenment sense but rather should be understood as "a parade of images, whose adoption can be seen in relationship to the social climate and conditions of the times" (17).

Greek sophist, Roman student: A colonial, pedagogical relationship

With this historical and cultural context in mind, we may now delve into the text. The project is described, in the author's preamble to the first book of *Imagines*, as a set of discourses (*logoi*) proposing to "describe examples of paintings in the form of addresses which we have composed for the young" (1.0.5). The sophist explains that he decided not to compose the descriptions, or exercises (*tas meletas*), "in public." The phrase used is *en tōi phanerōi*, which can be glossed as "open to sight" or "conspicuous." Perhaps the author makes an ironic reference here to the sophists' well-known taste for display. The lecturer, on the contrary, lodges himself in the house of a host, to which young men come "to importune him." The situation and setting are both reminiscent of the Socratic dialogues, set in the house of an aristocrat with several younger men in attendance. The Socrates-like sophist/teacher is contemplating praising the exquisite panel-paintings set in the walls of the house when he comes upon the young son of the host—designated *komidōi neos*, a well-favored boy. We might be tempted to think of the *Phaedrus* here, but instead of the one-on-one relationship of older mentor to beautiful boy, the sophist introduces a third group—other young men who have come to hear the sophist speak. He sets up the project in a self-consciously pedagogical way: "Let me put the boy in front and address to him my effort at interpretation; but do you follow, not only agreeing but also asking questions if anything I say is not clear" (1.0.35–40).

What is it that the sophist teaches via his ekphrastic lectures? The ability to appreciate fine art and discuss its technical features, as well as its intertextual relations to the Greek myth, history, and legend from which the subjects are drawn, must have been an important cultural acquisition for a Roman boy with aspirations of social and political success in the competitive imperial world. At the same time, the boy and his mates are hearing sophisticated, dramatic, and complex discourses performed spontaneously (it appears) and with imaginative force, and thus are getting a demonstration of the highest achievement of rhetorical expertise (Newby, "Absorption" 323–24). These lessons in viewing, though, concern not only what is seen but also the appropriate mental and emotional dispositions to cultivate in response to the painting and the description as well as to the scenes and figures represented. Some scholars comment on the sophistic narrator's ability to entrance the listener, spinning dazzling word webs that bind and draw the viewer/listener away, emotionally and even concretely, from the painting itself. Simon Goldhill, for example, describes ekphrastic visualization as a "rhetorical weapon to get around the censor of the intellect" ("What" 6). *Enargeia*, he asserts, is "the effect of *phantasia* . . . a way of provoking emotion, of bypassing the intellectual and critical faculties" (7). But such a characterization misses the numerous moments in *Imagines* when the sophist interrupts the viewing experience precisely to break an entrancement that would inhibit critical reflection.

The significance of this move is enforced by its occurrence at the beginning of the very first ekphrasis. "Scamander," a scene in Homer's *Iliad* (21.211ff.) in which Hephaestus comes to Achilles' aid by setting on fire a Trojan plain and the river Scamander, is filled with the bloody bodies of Achilles' victims. The subject as recounted in *Imagines* is dramatic: "fire rolls mightily like a flood over the plain . . . the river is suffering and in person begs Hephaestus for mercy" (1.1.2). But the sophist emphasizes the relation between painting and epic source:

> Have you noticed, my boy, that the painting here is based on Homer, or have you failed to do so because you are lost in wonder [*thauma*] as to how in the world the fire could live in the midst of the water? Well then, let us try to get at the meaning of it. Turn your eyes away from the painting itself so as to look only at the events on which it is based. (1.1.1)

The sophist seems here, pace Goldhill, precisely to demand that the student engage his critical faculties in assessing to what extent the painting captures or departs from its epic source. Of course there are other moments throughout the work when the ekphrasis carries the listeners and readers away—transports them through vivid language and carries them out of the frame of the picture. But each time the sophist addresses the boy, he breaks the flow of ekphrastic discourse by calling on the student—and the reader—to think, remember, and reflect on his feelings or responses, or otherwise to step outside his immersion in the viewing experience. There are eleven such occasions, by my count, interspersed at regular intervals throughout the text.[15] Newby effectively characterizes this oscillation as a movement between absorption and erudition ("Absorption"). The interruptions, however, don't always involve instruction on the part of the sophist.

The nature and occasion of exchanges beyond the first one provide insight into the relationship evolving between student and sophist. The next occurrence, in fact, presents a telling interaction. It comes in book 1 at the start of description 1.12, "Bosphoros." One of the longer descriptions, "Bosphoros" is set at the straits between Europe and Asia (just as in modern-day Istanbul) where young men are engaged in a game involving horses on the European side; women on the bank are shouting and urging them on. But the painting becomes a narrative as a boat carries the men across the straits to the Asian side, and they are received into a "charming house" (*oikia mala hēdeia*), which actually seems to be more like a stone castle with battlements built on a "lofty promontory" (*aktē hupsēlē*). In the wonderful way of ekphrastic storytelling, this location suggests a tale (*muthou*) involving a boy and girl, "both beautiful and under the tutelage of the same teacher" (1.12.3). Readers of the time would have recognized features of the Greek novel: a young, beautiful, heterosexual couple; a romantic scenario; dangerous adventures ensuing, in this case involving a possible plunge into the sea; and a woman secretly inhabiting an adjacent house, with lovers, crowned with garlands, sailing in her direction and playing music. In one of the occasional moments of mirroring, or embedding, that come along with ekphrastic discourse, we now see the woman gazing at the scene below the house, from a vantage point that parallels the beholder's stance of sophist and student. There is even more to relate, and at this point I find myself duplicating the activity of the sophist by redescribing the scene for readers at yet another remove.

Skipping to the end of 1.12 brings us to a (Greek) temple with columns that serves as a lighthouse.

It is at this point, the start of 1.13, that the boy intercedes by asking, "Why do you not go on to another painting? This one of the Bosphorus has been studied enough for me" (1.13.6). What are we to make of this interruption? One way to read it is as a sign of a young person's impatience with an extended discourse. Or, the student's confidence (or insouciance) to break into his teacher's lecture could be a sign of the power relations between hired Greek teacher and privileged Roman student. But I would like to propose yet another interpretation. As a ten-year-old, the boy perhaps is uninterested, or even made uncomfortable, by tales of romance, especially between a girl and boy close to his age. Through the interruption, Philostratus gives us an opportunity to see how the instruction works, not only in terms of a process of viewing, listening, and reflecting, but also in terms of presenting the contents of the images and stories included in the gallery. Among all the possible subjects from Greek mythology, literature, and legend, he has selected sixty-eight and arranged them in an order. He has curated them, I propose, in a way that leads us to understand some things about the cultural expectations for Roman boys, especially concerning gender and sexuality. What interests on the part of the Greek sophist might be served by seeking to influence his young Roman auditors in the realm of gender and sexuality? Is the topic of this exchange unique in the collection, or are there patterns to be discovered over the course of the ekphrastic experience? The only way to answer such questions, it seems to me, is to try to get an overview of the whole. Among all the possible mythic and legendary subjects, which ones were selected and how were they ordered?

Curation

Selecting and ordering, particularly of artworks for a museum exhibition, are acts of curation. One way to read *Imagines* is to assume that the work describes paintings in a real gallery presumably selected and positioned by the Roman aristocrat. In that case, Philostratus comes along after the fact, and the content and order of the images are not significant. The "authenticity question," as Norman Bryson terms it, has been important in responses to *Imagines* from the perspective of art history. Bryson's essay "Philostratus and the Imaginary Museum" serves as an indispensable meditation on this question and those who have pursued it. Calling the *Imagines* "one of the great ruins of antiquity," Bryson observes that Philostratus' text, even after the excavations at Pompeii and Herculaneum, "remains our most extensive account of what a Roman picture gallery, a Roman catalogue of pictures, and the Roman viewing of pictures may have been like" (255). Ultimately, Bryson's own interest lies not in authenticity but in the relations of image and text, about which he develops a thesis of considerable force and sophistication through his own reading of selected ekphraseis (267–74). But he launches the inquiry through an analysis of a very curious authenticating project by a mid-twentieth-century German émigré to the US, Karl Lehmann, who published an essay in *Art Bulletin* in 1941 titled "The *Imagines* of the Elder Philostratus." In this essay Lehmann tries to prove the possibility that Philostratus was describing an actual gallery (*pinacotheca*) and rationalizes the order of the ekphraseis using architectural principles (Bryson 257).

In this wonderfully improbable enterprise, Lehmann makes sense of Philostratus' selections and order by visualizing the paintings mounted in rooms of a hypothetical Roman house. Illustrated by several architectural drawings, Lehman's essay resolves any apparent disunity through the unity of the building: "the text's openings, interruptions, and incompleteness will be transformed, through a specific ecphrastic operation, into the wholeness of an image, an edifice, a museum" (Bryson 260). The architectural impulse, Bryson suggests, serves for the "containment and pacification" of a text that seemingly cannot be contained and overflows the boundaries of the visual image and even the constraints of realism at every turn. Bryson's reading of Lehmann reveals what is at stake in the process of curation and its interpretations. In Lehmann's "vigorous and ingenious" reading, art history emerges as "the custodian of culture working against a background of crisis and collapse" (276). The crisis, in Lehmann's view, concerns the degraded state of art in later antiquity. But Bryson observes the resonance of crisis within Lehmann's own situation as a German Jew in Istanbul contemplating the disastrous state and fate of Europe. The imposition of an architectural order on Philostratus' work contains and manages both these crises.

So the question of authenticity actually masks more fundamental investments. As Bryson notes, the authenticity debate, largely a German preoccupation, was winding down in the mid-twentieth century, and current scholarship, as I indicated above, has moved on, shifting attention to the effect of ekphrasis. I suggest, however, that we may be losing some potential for understanding if we consign questions about the whole of the work to charming but superseded methods. If, as most readers now assume,

Philostratus was not describing an existing collection but rather his own imaginary museum, then he himself selected the topics and treatments, putting them in an order that creates the narrative of the *Imagines* and offers a (highly mediated) window onto his world.

To consider Philostratus a curator puts him in a position of some interest vis-à-vis the contemporary art world—a time after the "curatorial turn" (O'Neill). In fact, curation as a practice can be found anywhere and everywhere these days. Deejays curate song lists; restaurateurs curate wine selections; travel companies curate tourist experiences. The role of the curator in the twenty-first century is to be grasped and envied, it seems; the curator moves about in a world of excess, filled with many beautiful and desirable things, and uses his or her capacity for discernment to sort, select, evaluate, and order that world for the willing consumer. From master curator Hans Ulrich Obrist, we learn that curation involves not only displaying or arranging but also caring (from the Latin, *curare*)—care for both the art and for those who view it. The curator helps viewers "simplify events in the world in order to understand them" ("Hans-Ulrich Obrist"). The current interest in curation gives weight to this aspect of Philostratus' text, a feature not taken up by those who have focused on ekphraseis in isolation. To envision Philostratus as a curator acknowledges the power and significance of his choices and leads the reader to ask, What, in fact, are the "key historical and cultural themes," in Bowie and Elsner's words, that are addressed in *Imagines*?

As Goethe, Lehmann, and others have pointed out, the order of the descriptions does not provide an obvious answer to that question. Nor have scholars since Lehmann sought to grapple with the whole collection. A typical approach to interpreting ekphrasis is to examine a few selected pieces in depth as exemplary of a technique or subject (e.g., Dubel on color; Newby on responses to *thauma*; Bann on "Narcissus"), or in Bryson's case, he examines closely two of the eight ekphraseis Lehmann omitted from his architectural order so as to establish what is repressed: to "come to see the principles of exclusion by which [Lehmann's] interpretation is structured" (265). Reading "Looms," 2.28, in relation to the preceding picture, "The Birth of Athena," 2.27, Bryson finds an effect of negativity created by the "topos of Arachne," who is absent but implied by the two scenes (265–72). This Derridean approach sees the text as "hollowed out by its own rhetorical self-awareness" and Philostratus as "belated" and "secondary": old compared with the younger student, a "Greek wandering in Italy," a critic of painting rather than a painter (274).

To approach the work as revelatory of a cultural world, on the other hand, would require an inventional process like the one Goethe conducted two hundred years ago. What are the topoi collected in the work, and can we read into their order and evaluation any kind of figured message about Philostratus' stance toward teaching and performing as a Greek sophist under imperial conditions in the third century? To answer this question, I conducted a sort of reverse curation or reordering of the sixty-eight ekphraseis, an exercise that proved to be illuminating—and really fun. Of course, the categories I've derived will say as much about my own era and investments as Lehmann's did about his. What I learned from this exercise I discuss in the next section; for my full alternative curation, organized by categories, see the appendix following chapter 8.

Recurating Philostratus' imaginary gallery

Because of my interest in imperial relations, I began by cataloguing references to geography and ethnicity. This cluster of descriptions is of considerable interest; its points of reference are reminiscent of those in the Greek novel, as we will see more vividly in the next chapter. Because the two most telling descriptions in this cluster come late in the work, I defer this topic to the end of the chapter. A new beginning, then, groups interactions between the sophist and the boy, but the other categories seemed to present themselves unbidden as cases accumulated.

Youth

For example, I found the number of descriptions involving babies, children, youths (and other small creatures such as dwarves and cupids) to be truly striking.[16] Early on, we are treated to a memorable description of a painting of dwarves swarming over the statue of the Nile river (1.5), and in the very next description, cupids (*Erōtes*) frolic in a pastoral scene, gathering apples and gems and playing ball (1.6). Anyone who has had the pleasure of viewing wall paintings in Pompeii or at a Roman museum will think of the omnipresent cupids cavorting through the scenes. We, or the boy, might consider them a neutral decorative element of painting from the period. But Philostratus takes the opportunity in 1.6 to complicate such an assumption by designating a special group of *Erōtes* "the most beautiful of all," a small group who withdraw from the rest to toss apples and engage in archery. What is the painter's meaning, the narrator asks? "This is friendship (*philia*), my boy, and yearning for one another (*himeros*)" (1.6.3). An openly approving stance toward male-male sex between free Romans in this period would be unconventional.[17] Is Philostratus grooming these Roman boys to become participants in Greek homosocial/sexual practices? Based on a reading of the group of fifteen descriptions falling into this category, I think something more subtle is going on. Some of these images—of a beautiful flute player, Olympus (1.20, 21); of the young Pelops, loved by Poseidon (1.30); of Hippolytus, a beautiful youth wronged by his stepmother (2.4)—cultivate an appreciation of the beauty of the young male body, but they do so more often in the context of aesthetic appreciation than of erotic desire.[18] Some of the beautiful boys and young men in this group perform heroic acts: Menoeceus, Creon's son, sacrifices himself at a dragon's hole (1.4); Antilochus, a young soldier in the epic, dies with a joyous and smiling face because he saved his father's life (2.7). Add to these images, then, three paintings of the well-known Greek figures of Hermes, Achilles, and Pindar—god, legendary hero, and famous poet—all represented as babies and then children (1.26, 2.2, 2.12). In each scene, the baby/child is charming and adored, even Hermes after he steals Apollo's cattle: the older god's wrath is melted by the delightful boy. Though we got a brief glimpse of the ferocious warrior Achilles in 1.1, we see him in 2.2 nurtured as a boy by his loving caretaker, the centaur Cheiron.

This cluster of images certainly confirms the view that the sophist creates and promotes a Greek world, but there is more going on. Addressing boys, the sophist offers images of loving and beloved children becoming beautiful, beloved, heroic young men. The gentle eroticism of some of these images doesn't insist on a telos of same-sex contact but does perhaps temper the harsh and militant cast of Roman masculinity. Especially for boys who may grow up to become soldiers and governors in colonial contexts, these impressions may work a kind of mollifying effect. As a group, they offer a sense that young creatures are valued and delightful, a positive pedagogical disposition.

Transformations

But nothing remains stable or fixed in this imaginary museum, nor will the bodies and lives of the Roman students taking it in. Paintings in another cluster offer visions of transformation: some involve temporarily altered states, as we see creatures (human, animal, divine) getting outside themselves through cross-dressing, drunkenness, sleeping, and dreaming. Others show more dramatic metamorphoses as girls change into trees (1.11), humans into serpents (1.18), and pirates into dolphins (1.19). Metamorphosis is a predominant theme of Greek myth, given new life by Roman poet Ovid's epic first-century treatment. It's not possible to know whether the imagined audience for Philostratus' performance might have read Ovid, especially given the sexual content of Ovid's work and the age of the boys.[19] But the world of Greek myth would have been transmitted through a number of sources and at one level would have served as a cache of entertaining tales. At another level, however, contemplating such altered states destabilizes the self and the natural and social structures within which it finds meaning. From their earliest encounters, Romans found Greek culture frightening, or at least suspicious, because of its capacities for imagining and performing otherness (see Connolly, *Vile Eloquence*). The art of persuasion, like theatre, was one of the vehicles enabling such practices. Froma I. Zeitlin has made a compelling argument that classical Greek theatre through a series of "feminine" traits (including the practice of male actors playing female roles) has the capacity for "initiating actor and spectator into new and unsettling modes of feeling, seeing, and knowing" ("Playing" 79). By placing ekphraseis of gender transformation strategically at the beginning and end of the collection, Philostratus may be drawing on the same capacity within the realm of the visual arts.

Just after they have taken in the Homeric battle scene, the student viewers encounter their second painting: in an interior scene, Comus, the spirit of revelry, leans on the door of the bedroom of newlyweds, "flushed with wine" and asleep. Another beautiful boy, the figure is not full-grown—not yet an *ephēbos*, a male eighteen to twenty years old and ready to begin military training. The figure probably has one of those faces in the bloom of youth without which, the narrator says, paintings are dull and meaningless (1.2.3), but the viewers can't see it because Comus' head is bent over in sleep, and his mind "passes over into forgetfulness of its thoughts." Lest the young students find an invitation to dissolute behavior in this image of the drunken youth, the sophist offers a mild sanction: "The moral, I think, is that persons of his age should not go revelling [the verb is *kōmadzein*, to act like or "do" Komas/Comus] except with their heads veiled" (1.2.3). Here again we find an introduction to a grown-up world with its pleasures but one delivered with a helpful caution. As the description continues, the viewers see even more dramatic transformations during reveling: "women masquerade as men, and men 'put on women's garb' and ape the walk of women" (1.2.5).

Here, at the outset of the sophist's experience with his Roman charges, the picture enables the viewer to imagine a liminal space for gender transgression and performativity.

While the social mores of the second- to third-century empire had left behind the control and rigor of Augustus' age, cross-dressing and transgender behavior would not have been within the norms for a Roman provincial aristocrat.[20] But the demand to perform one's cultural (including gendered) position through speech, thought, and movement—via *habitus*, in other words—was well accepted in Roman culture across the centuries. As Maud W. Gleason writes, with reference to her study of the masculinity of two second sophists, young men in the imperial era had need of guidance in "social and political dealing outside the circle of their fathers' friends" as "provincial aristocrats who suddenly found themselves faced with a wide world" (*Making Men* xxv). Perhaps the sophist is using images of gender mobility, alongside very positive images of young boys, to cultivate an attitude of receptivity in his students. A compelling image near the end of the collection reinforces this impression. "Palaestra" is the antepenultimate (third to last) description. In it, the narrator describes a painting of the daughter of Hermes who has discovered the art of wrestling. Her birth is fortuitous: when she comes to womanhood, "the earth seems to rejoice at the discovery, since iron as an instrument of war will be laid aside by men during the truce, and the stadium will seem to them more delightful than armed camps" (2.32.1). She is strong, "manly" (*andreias*, 2.32.2), and gender indeterminate: her figure, "if it be compared with a boy, will be that of a girl; but if it be taken for a girl, it will seem to be a boy" (2.32.3). This goddess disdains both lovers and wrestlers because she can resist the former and defeat the latter. That her figure is reddish shows that she "cares for nothing feminine" (2.32.4, or else she would be painted white). The description is offered with a neutral tone, admiring of the painter's skill and of the becoming stance of the figure, seated with an olive branch. The symbol of peace reinforces the observation quoted above: her arrival suggests that war will be set aside in favor of athletic contests.

The selection and placement of these images—Philostratus' curation—operates as a kind of figured discourse, creating a supportive surround for the Roman boys where bodies of all kinds are present and admired. Simultaneously, another kind of figuration is at work: an argument through silence. Philostratus includes none of the famously priapic images still preserved on the walls of sites like Pompeii and Herculaneum. In addition, the often-brutal sexual activity and violence against women running through Greek mythology is, for the most part, absent from Philostratus' gallery. Consider, for example, the myth of Dirce: a story not well known to many readers today but one that was often captured in wall paintings of the era. In the myth, Dirce was a naiad, a river nymph, who married a Theban king. In a plot too complex to summarize easily, this couple imprisons and mistreats a woman named Antiope, who had been raped and impregnated by Zeus. Antiope's sons discover these misdeeds, kill the king, and tie Dirce to a bull that drags, dismembers, and ultimately kills her. This dreadful scene is depicted often in the surviving wall paintings (figure 5.1) but is not included in Philostratus' gallery, an absence that fits with the curatorial choices informing the group of paintings of women.

Figure 5.1. Dirce dragged by bull, House of the Vettii, Pompeii (ca. 70 CE). AUTHOR PHOTOGRAPH.

Women

Women—mortal, legendary, and divine—are present throughout the collection, and the young viewers are offered representations of some of the famous figures from Greek myth and literature: Ariadne, Cassandra, Penelope, and Antigone, for example, make appearances. But other less-familiar characters also come into view, one of whom, a Persian warrior, I discuss at length below. What is striking about the treatment of women comes in points of emphasis and de-emphasis—moments of commentary on their narratives and suggestions for ways of looking, and looking away—that communicate respect and sympathy.[21] The treatment of women in classical Greek culture generally, and in myth specifically, has been scrutinized by feminist classicists in many important works over the past three decades, and as we all know, the report is not good.[22] Rape and other forms of violence, desertion, and disregard—such are the fates common for women, both free and enslaved, real and imagined, in stories from the ancient Mediterranean world. Philostratus' curation and descriptions, however, offer a somewhat softened angle of vision. Consider an early example: in 1.8 we see a painting of Amymone, daughter of Danaus, pursued by Poseidon. The god, however, instead of looking angry as in Homer's account, is here painted with a "radiant" and "joyous" look, "stirred by love." The sophist diminishes the violence of the god's pursuit and heightens the emotional pull. The maiden is frightened and trembling, dropping her pitcher and thus showing her distress, so the rape scenario is not denied. But the sophist invites the boy to turn away at this point: "Let us withdraw, my boy, and leave the maiden; for already a wave is arching over the nuptials" (*ton gamon*). The teacher declines to revel in the violence. In contrast, we might think of the many examples of female figures ill-treated within the progymnasmata and declamation models, their violent mistreatment offered without any qualifying comment.

In another painting, we see Ariadne, loved and left by Theseus on an island after she saved him from the Minotaur (1.15). The description confronts the ethics of the situation straightaway: "That Theseus treated Ariadne unjustly . . . when he abandoned her while asleep on the island of Dia, you must have heard from your nurse; for those women are skilled in telling such tales and they weep over them whenever they will" (1.15.1). Although the sophist sounds a bit condescending here, his treatment of Theseus in the rest of the segment passes judgment on the Greek prince's choice to follow his desire for power ("indeed he is in love, but with the smoke rising from Athens") and his neglect of the beautiful woman who aided him: "he no longer knows Ariadne, and never knew her, and I am sure that he has even forgotten the labyrinth" (1.15.3). The value in the painting lies in the depiction of Ariadne and Dionysus: "How fair a sight, Dionysus, and how sweet her breath! Whether its fragrance is of apples or of grapes, you can tell after you have kissed her!" (1.15.3).

Philostratus includes some of the many flawed women in the Greek panoply, but he downplays their missteps. A description of Pasiphaë, made to fall in love with a bull, follows that of Ariadne, but the act is not depicted, only the skill of Daedalus in crafting the cow framework to be used for the union. The Bacchantes who tear Pentheus apart in Euripides' tragedy are excused: "they do not see what they are doing" (1.18.1); "[p]itiful also we must consider the state of the women" (1.18.3). Phaedra's attempted seduction of her stepson, Hippolytus, and her subsequent betrayal of him is mentioned but not emphasized (2.4). Antigone, defiant resister of Creon's rule, is praised for her strength in lifting the body of her brother and controlling her fear (2.29). The emphasis in the painting is on the maiden in the moonlight as she buries her brother, controlling her desire to cry out in lamentation and gazing at his body (2.30).

A possible exception to this tendency to present women in a favorable light, on the reading of Bryson, could come in 2.28, "Looms." The ekphrasis begins with a beautifully constructed sentence referring to the boy and his discovery of a painting of Penelope's loom. We come to understand the detailed description of the loom—its warp, threads, and shuttle, with Penelope shedding tears and unraveling her work—as the boy's own ekphrastic composition. Here is a fine pedagogical moment. The sophist then draws attention to a nearby painting of a spider weaving webs in an abandoned house (2.28.2). Bryson reads the spider as an evocation of the mortal Arachne punished by Minerva for pitting her own skill as a weaver against the goddess's. Ovid's version of the metamorphosis of mortal woman into spider, writes Bryson, is an opportunity for the Roman poet to draw attention to his own craft, positioning it somewhere between Arachne's loom and the tapestries woven by the divine Minerva. In Bryson's intricate analysis, Philostratus' repetition becomes a "comic transformation of Ovid's contest, down-scaled, with Penelope in the place of Minerva and spiders in the place of Arachne" (272). According to Bryson, Philostratus places his own project, the *Imagines*, "somewhere between the higher artists (Homer, Hesiod, Ovid, etc.) and the beasts" (273). This reading aligns with Bryson's vision of the sophist's project as "self-mocking and self-defeating" (273), "haunted by an inescapably secondary or belated relation to pictures" (274).

As artful as it is, Bryson's reading doesn't accord with my sense of Philostratus' persona in this work; with the energy, vitality, and buoyancy of his oeuvre more generally; or with the tone of this ekphrasis in particular. To interpret the description of the spider's "repulsive fuzzy surface and its savage nature" as a fall into nature, signaling the ruination of human effort, like the ruined courtyard, Bryson must overlook Philostratus' praise of the painter who successfully "wrought the spider itself in so painstaking a fashion [marking] its spots with fidelity to nature" as a good craftsman, one skilled at depicting the truth (2.28.3).[23] This passage immediately precedes the "For look!" moment in the ekphrasis: the epiphanic or ecstatic moment when the image carries the viewer away, in this case via the wonder of a delicate web with its tight lines and concentric circles. Indeed, there are numerous points in the volume where the narrator moves from the representation of nature into an explanation and appreciation of nature itself (e.g., 1.9, a description of wetlands; 1.13, tuna fishing on the Euxine Sea; 2.17, an extensive description of islands; 2.34, Horae, the harvest). If we reevaluate the "beast," then Philostratus' position seems less hollowed out and more fully present, not only to the art of representation but also to the life surrounding him: nature and its variously designed creatures.

The most striking ekphrasis of a woman in the volume moves us away from nature and back into the world of human history, drawing on a source close in time and concerns to Philostratus' world. And with this description, the categories of "women" and "geographies and ethnicities" overlap. The subject is Rhodogoune, daughter of the Parthian king Mithradates I, who lived 171–38 BCE and built his eastern kingdom (geographically proximate to Iran) into a thriving empire. The line of Mithradatic kings led to Mithradates VI (134–63 BCE), a dynamic leader who presented the Romans of his era with the most dangerous challenge to their imperium ever launched (see Mayor). This history would necessarily be in the minds of listeners and readers in Philostratus' day. Elsewhere, Rhodogoune appears as a vivid figure in a work by second-century CE Macedonian author and rhetor Polyaenus, whose *Stratagems of War* was dedicated to Marcus Aurelius (ruled 161–180) while he was engaged in war against the Parthians.[24] Rhodogoune also appears in an anonymous first-century BCE work, *Tractatus De Mulieribus*, translated as *Warrior Women* by Gera. A more vivid character, one better suited for ekphrasis, is difficult to imagine. Having led the Persians to victory over the Armenians, who had broken a treaty, she is captured by the artist in battle gear, including shield and spear, pouring out a libation in honor of the victory. Her hair is disarranged because, as the story goes, the attack began while she was washing her hair, so she is pictured rushing into battle with an incomplete coiffure (*Imagines*; trans. Fairbanks 145n1). After describing Rhodogoune's fine horse with precious stones on the bridle, the sophist moves to the woman warrior's clothing: scarlet girdle, robe, trousers, and chiton fastened with brooches. The narrator notes that, unlike the Amazonian off-shoulder look, this warrior's shoulder is covered. At this point, the sophist interrupts with an address to the boy: "It seems, my boy, that you have a feeling for the beauty in this figure and desire to hear something on this point also, so listen" (2.5.4). What follows is an analysis of the queen's indisposition toward love based on her face and posture in the act of pouring a libation to the gods and on her victory over men. The lengthy description divides her features into pairs, with one half suggesting conventional feminine beauty and the other qualifying it in some way that is attributed to her status as a ruler. Of the woman's eyes, he writes, "the joy they show is due to the occasion, their beauty is a gift of nature, while their haughtiness arises from her authority as a ruler" (2.5.5). When the sophist describes her mouth as "delicately formed" and "most sweet to kiss," the description reaches its most explicitly erotic detail. But even that element is qualified when the boy is reminded that she is uttering a prayer of victory. The ekphrasis ends with a playful move outside the frame of the painting: "if we care to listen attentively, perhaps [her mouth] will speak in Greek" (2.5.5).

With this extraordinary entry, Philostratus' representations of women move from sympathetic to admiring. The Roman students, having been reassured in their status as young men, are thus introduced to women not as sexual objects, abject sufferers, or passive placeholders in the family but as three-dimensional characters acting in the most fulfilling of life's dramas. At the same time, the particular and quite unusual choice of Rhodogoune allows the sophist to figure a response to Roman empire in a number of ways. Mithradates VI, charismatic and powerful ruler of Parthia, was historically, and remained in reference, the archetype of colonial resistance: "Rome's deadliest enemy" in the subtitle of Mayor's biography of him. Envisioning Persian forces in a successful battle refigures the most famous surviving floor mosaic of this period and region: a magnificent battle scene in which

Alexander triumphs over the Persians (figure 5.2). Here we have another example of figured discourse through silence—or in this case, invisibility. Recreating Alexander's victory is safe given the thoroughly successful conquest of Greek cities by the Romans. But given that potentially rebellious cultures continue to threaten on the eastern borders of the empire, Philostratus' vivid and sexualized evocation of Rhodogoune reminds viewers of the always-tentative status of colonial military control.

Geographies and ethnicities

Anderson and others make the point forcefully that a central aim of second sophistic practice is the glorification of Greek culture, history, and identity (e.g., Anderson, *Second Sophistic*; Goldhill, "Introduction"), but, as I argued in chapter 1, I think the aims of second sophists are more complex and multilayered. All the paintings in Philostratus' collection are drawn from Greek mythology and literature, so they obviously immerse the reader and putative viewer in a classical Greek world. But geographical and cultural references scattered throughout suggest an imperial perspective. The touch points are similar to those deployed in the Greek novel, as we will see more vividly in the next chapter. The geographic/cultural loci of Asia and Europe are referenced (1.1, 1.12 and 13, 2.28), and we see a strong presence of Africa

Figure 5.2. Alexander mosaic, House of the Faun, Pompeii (ca. 70 CE). COURTESY OF THE NATIONAL ARCHAEOLOGICAL MUSEUM, NAPLES. PHOTOGRAPH BY DEA/G. NIMATALLAH. CREATIVE COMMONS.

through the figure of Memnon, the Ethiopian general (1.7, 2.7), Perseus and Andromeda (a white Ethiopian, 1.29), and the Nile dwarves (1.5). But what world is this? References to barbarians (1.28, 1.30) and the overt "othering" of Memnon as a black Ethiopian create an ethnocentric stance. In 2.7, a scene from the epic, Memnon kills Antilochus in front of his father and is "terrible [*deinos*] to look upon because of his black skin color, lion skin attire, and sneering expression" (2.7.4). The more positive view of Ethiopians in 1.29, with Perseus and Andromeda, is equally alienating by describing "charming Ethiopians with their strange colouring and their grim smiles" (1.29.3). Such descriptions are reminiscent of Herodotus' ethnographic adventures, which kept Hellenic culture at the center.

But two significant ekphraseis trouble a conventional Hellenocentric geographic and cultural perspective precisely through their reference to ancient historical encounters between Greeks and the East. Rhodogoune is one, and the other is the penultimate description in the collection. This ekphrasis makes an explicit comment about Greek history through the figure of Themistocles, a Greek general who played a heroic role in the Persian War (early fifth century BCE), leading to a decisive naval victory, the Battle of Salamis. But his loyalty and behavior later became suspect: Themistocles was ostracized in 472 BCE and ended his life in service to the Persians. Instead of focusing on the general's treachery, Philostratus' sophist reads him as a Greek among barbarians: "a true man among those who are not men, inasmuch as they are ruined and dissolute, surely an Athenian to judge by his coarse cloak, he addresses some wise discourse to them, I think, trying to change their ways and make them give up their luxury" (2.31.1). To Greeks among Greeks, Themistocles was a cautionary figure, but to Greeks among Roman colonizers, he becomes the rugged and pure Athenian among the oriental excesses of the barbarians—advising them of the wisdom (*agoreuei sophon*) of giving up their fancy ways. Notice what the guide praises in the extended description that follows:

> The painter does not ask to be praised for his fine representation of tiara and tasselled cloak or sleeved jacket or of the monstrous shapes of animals with which barbarian garments are embroidered; but he should be praised for the gold which he has painted as threads skillfully interwoven in the cloth and preserving the design to which it has been constrained, and by Zeus, for the faces of the eunuchs. (2.31.1)

Could we interpret "preserving a design to which it has been constrained" in terms of the options open to colonial subjects—subjects metaphorically emasculated by the imperial powers? The Greek root of the word translated as "constrained" is *anankē*, the fate that wields irresistible power throughout early Greek myth and literature. Perhaps this is an example of the indirectness or subterfuge through which figured discourse operates: a description disguises a comment about Roman power as a comment on taste in costuming.

Philostratus goes on to describe Themistocles speaking to the Medes (Persians, or "Orientals") not in Greek but "using the Median tongue, which he took the pains to acquire there" (2.31.2). He is bold, not perturbed, but there is "hesitance in the thoughtful expression of the eyes, due to his speaking a new language recently learned" (2.31.2). This linguistic transcultural moment speaks back to the Romans, who made few efforts to interact with, or allow themselves to be influenced by, the peoples they conquered.

Conclusion

I've sought in this chapter to argue that Philostratus' curation of scenes from Greek culture not only teaches a critical approach to visual arts and demonstrates sophistic practice but also recommends to the Roman boys he tutors desirable and useful dispositions: ways of seeing themselves and other actors in the late empire that will enable them to thrive and treat their colonial subjects with care. Bryson, in his treatment of the pedagogical scenario in the text, argues that the staging of interpretation by the sophist/critic shows the student how to internalize aesthetic effects in a technology or discipline of the self. The teacher models this internalization for the student, and the student copies, in a parallel exercise, a scenario supportive of Foucault's vision of the ascetic in *The Care of the Self.* But in my view, the behavior modeled here extends beyond the narrow discipline of the ruler and his advisor, a relationship Michael Warner critiques as an "englobing duo" ("Queer Theory"). There is a larger world imagined within these many, diverse scenes. Different both from the architectonic space of the museum and the individualized technology of a self, space in these ekphrastic moments is constructed dialogically as pedagogical, cross-cultural, positively sexualized, and colonial. Philostratus uses ekphrastic technique to construct a space that enables the Roman boys to imagine not only the pleasures held out by their privileged futures but the consequences and responsibilities of acting in a power-laden multicultural, imperial context.

CHAPTER 6

No Animals Were Harmed: Sophistic Rhetoric in Heliodorus' *Aithiopika*

Ancient Greek novels are intricately crafted prose fictions (*plasmata*) that have been widely recognized as a form of sophistic practice. Authored by culturally Greek writers from colonial outposts, these long, adventure-filled romantic narratives are packed with all manner of rhetorical performances—mock legalistic defenses, laments, ekphraseis, and other progymnasmatic embeddings. Regarding Heliodorus' *Aithiopika* (*Ethiopian Story*), my object of analysis here, one critic finds that, within it, the author "exhausted the arsenal of rhetorical 'pyrotechnics'" (Futre Pinheiro 80). We encounter one pyrotechnical performance in what follows, but my aim is not to catalog such moments. I instead take up a larger concern for the novel—one that has perhaps not yet been given the depth of attention it warrants—that of religion and, specifically, the traditional/pagan practice of sacrifice staged dramatically in the final book.[1]

Numerous critics describe Heliodorus' novel as religious or as permeated by religion. Froma I. Zeitlin, for example, coins the term "mysteriosophic" to describe it ("Religion" 104); translator J. R. Morgan calls it "religiose" (350). Ken Dowden's study of divine power in the novel captures the pervasive presence of gods and addresses to them throughout the work. Gods are everywhere and nowhere, Dowden finds. They are rarely distinguished by name but rather constitute a collective captured by the expression *kreittōnes*, the better ones, a word that crosscuts pagan and Christian texts and appears in the writing of a number of fourth-century authors (including Julian and Libanius). Dowden in fact creates a tabulation of such uses to make the case for a fourth-century date for the work, a date endorsed (for various reasons) by numerous other critics. I find these arguments persuasive and would like to explore the possibility of locating the work more precisely in or after the reign of Julian, the last pagan emperor.[2] As a starting point, we may put the author's "signature" (*sphragis*) coming at the very end of the novel in conjunction with Julian's *Hymn to King Helios* (362?).

In the final sentence, Heliodorus writes, "Thus ends the Ethiopian story of Theagenes and Charikleia: the work of a Phoenician of Emesa, of the clan of the descendants of the Sun, Heliodorus, son of Theodosios" (10.41.4). Here the author marks a colonial location (Emesa in Syria) and perhaps a priestly vocation: clan of the sun, "sun-loving" and "god-loving" in the names of son and father. Julian's *Hymn to King Helios*, a passionate encomium of the god Helios, "common father of all mankind" (131C), places him solidly within this discourse. In this oration, Julian expounds the doctrines of the Syrian Neoplatonist Iamblichus in far more detail than we find in the fictional world of Ethiopian sun worship as it appears in Heliodorus. But Julian's frequent efforts to link Helios with the ancient Greek gods resonate strongly with the Greek/Ethiopian alliance in the novel. We find Julian proposing that "Zeus is in no wise different from Helios" (149B); likewise Athena, Apollo, and Aphrodite assist Helios and are very near to Helios (149–50). Further, Julian mentions Emesa as "a place from time immemorial sacred to Helios" (150D; see also Hilton). Syncretism is a crucial feature of fourth-century religion across the empire and within the world of the novel. But a close look at the final book takes us beyond this general impulse toward religious pluralism and into an engagement with the principal controversy of the fourth century: the struggle between pagans and Christians. Though sun worship plays a role in the final chapter, I suggest, following Hunter, that the novel does not advance a particular religion but rather creates a multivalent commentary on imperial religious crises, and particularly on the emperors' involvement in them. I hope to show how Heliodorus crafts a figured intervention into this controversy toward the staging of a specifically rhetorical response to it. The question Heliodorus poses and responds to in a figured way is, How should an emperor negotiate religious controversy? Figured discourse, as we have seen in previous chapters, can appear in a variety of genres. Approaching the technique in Heliodorus requires some preliminary engagement with the fascinating phenomenon of the ancient novel and the critical questions surrounding it.

The ancient novel as sophistic practice

Earlier chapters established that second sophists were members of a culturally Greek intelligentsia active during the Roman imperial era. As such, they combined practices of oratorical performance and pedagogy with certain political functions possible for colonized subjects (some of whom were also Roman citizens). The texts we've examined so far exemplify generic diversity and inventiveness—Dio's hybrid narrative/exhortation, *Euboean Discourse*; Aristides' grand encomium of Rome; Philostratus' religious biography, *Life of Apollonius of Tyana*, and the collected descriptions in *Imagines*. In each, as I've argued, the sophist offers a more or less "figured" response to the political circumstances of colonial life under empire. We've noted narrative and fictive elements in Dio's castaway fable (chapter 2) and Philostratus' biography (chapter 4), but with the novel we move into a familiar and thoroughly literary mode. Barbara Cassin enables us to see a continuity across these genres by drawing connections among historical topics of declamation, the character development aspect of epideictic rhetoric, and the novel as sophistic practices (*L'effet* 457–97). Following Philostratus' emphasis on history as a defining feature of the second sophistic (*Lives* ¶481), Cassin exploits the multiple meanings of the Greek *historia*—also available in the French *histoire*—as inquiry, narrative, and story to make a case for the second sophistic as a "historicizing rhetoric" (*rhetorique historisante*, *L'effet* 459). Reading such texts requires literary hermeneutics, rhetorical analysis, and an attunement to cultural and political history.

For those texts interpreted in the previous chapters, speculating about figured meanings was aided by our knowledge of the particular situation of the sophist in question, his relation to imperial power, and identifiable moments of historical reference, despite the coding or obscuring that operated in each case. But for the novel as a genre, and for Heliodorus in particular, we are in a somewhat different terrain. We know nothing of the author other than the dubious information in the final sentence of the novel. And as a genre, the ancient Greek novels (like second sophistic discourse in general) studiously avoid direct reference to contemporary Roman reality. They are all set in classical times and seem to enclose their characters in fictional worlds organized along a predictable narrative trajectory: a heterosexual couple—beautiful, virtuous, in love—are separated and endure long, perilous journeys but ultimately are reunited and joined happily in marriage. The ancient Greek novel is considered to be "an imperial genre" (Reardon 8), but how and to what end historical and political contexts are mediated by these fictions is an interpretive question to which critics have offered various responses. All the major novels seem to have been authored by writers from colonial outposts, in the case of Heliodorus, as we have seen, the city of Emesa in present-day Syria.[3] By narrating geographic expansiveness in a picaresque and touristic mode, Greek novelists can be said to convert imperial space into a delightful literary landscape. Some critics emphasize the novels' sensationalism, taking it as a sign of an "appetite for entertainment" among Greek elites (Reardon 11). On this view, the novels signal a retreat to the world of the private in the face of empire. In the words of Niklas Holzberg, the novel served the Greek subject of empire by creating "a literary world of fantasy which reflected the reality of his own life and reconciled him to it" (32–33). Some critics find support for this view in the novels because of their focus on romantic love, a private concern removed from larger political considerations (e.g., Konstan, *Sexual Symmetry*). Assuming that novels were read silently, consumed for popular entertainment, such critics emphasize the stabilizing social effect of the heterosexual union and thus the distance between public and private spheres. Reardon has suggested that, as the empire became larger, the individual became smaller and more absorbed in himself. On this view, literature is superstructural and inconsequential for public life, and rhetoric finds a new home there because it has been cast out of the realm of public deliberation in the era of empire.

A different approach is offered by scholars who find that Greek novels, and the second sophistic more generally, "speak to empire" by securing Greek cultural identity as a persistent value (Goldhill, "Introduction"; Whitmarsh, *Second Sophistic*). The analysis offered in this chapter is related to this approach in the sense that I argue, ultimately, that the novel offers a utopian vision of pagan religious ritual, but the "cultural" in my reading is construed as a material engagement with imperial economies, human/animal relations, and civic survival. This approach is influenced by a position on "rhetoric" and "literature" developed by scholars such as Jeffrey Walker (*Rhetoric and Poetics*, with reference to the Hellenistic era and the early empire) and Peter Brown (regarding late antiquity): that rhetoric did not decline after the fall of democracy into a trivial, secondary literariness but rather flourished in a wide range of forms. Taken together, these forms demonstrate that Greek intellectuals continued to produce rhetoric, not as something to do while they weren't ruling, but rather as creative responses to their changed political and geographic situation.

The scholar hopes that any critical method brought to bear somehow measures up to the magnitude or challenge of the work itself. In the case of Heliodorus' novel, that is a tall order. Morgan remarks that it is "a work on an altogether grander scale than any other extant Greek novel, a work whose structure and execution express an ambition to be considered at the highest level" (349). In his introduction to a collection of essays on the work, Richard Hunter writes of *Aithiopika*'s "irritant power": "the remarkable romance gets under your skin (quite literally, of course)" (Preface). *Aithiopika* is a textual performance in which every marker of social, political, and geographical stability is happily undermined: human "nature" (including the human/animal distinction as well as skin color as a fixed marker), parentage, gender, cultural and ethnic identity, native/foreigner status, juridical and political procedure, ritual, and true speech. But in putting all these signs in play, the novelist does not resort to what we might see as a free-floating, postmodern detachment from the imperial condition (although Whitmarsh's readings often move in that direction, and he has suggested "postmodern" as an appropriate description for the second sophists). Rather, these displacements always demand or give rise to newly asserted "anchorage for belief" (610) as Jonathan Crewe puts it in an essay on *Aithiopika* as "critical romance."

To begin with the geographical, *Aithiopika* is strictly speaking a *nostos*, a return, as Charikleia, the ingénue/protagonist, is born in Ethiopia and returns there in the end. But other trajectories are arguable. Whitmarsh, for example, sees in the novel a movement outward: from Greece through Egypt to Ethiopia with no return. He writes, "the end of *Aithiopika* is also the limit of the known world" ("Birth" 98), but this is not an alien or foreign territory or people. Even given the ethnic stereotype operative since Herodotus—of Ethiopians as a virtuous people—the ruler Hydaspes is especially distinguished as a model of judicious military and political action. So we are not so much taken to an exotic outpost as brought to a new world, a political sphere run by a benevolent leader, and also one capable of change. Change comes when the return of Charikleia provokes a shift in ritual practices: as a Greek and alien, she is proposed as a human sacrifice; but when it is revealed that she is actually Ethiopian and cannot be sacrificed, the way is opened for Sisimithres, the gymnosophist, to object to living sacrifice in general—human or animal. And this change is adopted. The "Greek" protagonist returns "home" to a home she never knew, one transformed through her intercession. It is a home that becomes so not through nature—even though she was born there—but must be won through sophistic practice, in this case a legal action.

The potential for transformation runs through the narrative at every level: when the young couple we thought to be Greek and "white" marry in

Ethiopia, they fulfill a Delphic oracle, finally remembered by Charikleia, that foretold they would travel to the black land of the sun and receive a crown of white on blackening brows (*melainomenōn*, 10.41.2), not black but blackening. Heliodorus' sophistic practice keeps everything in motion continually—not only cultural identity and political institutions but also nature itself. The story of *Aithiopika* begins, in fact, with the most natural of acts.[4] Readers are invited into the bedroom of the Ethiopian royal couple, both black-skinned, who conceive a child while Persinna, the queen, is looking at a painting of Andromeda (the mythic white Ethiopian rescued by Perseus). As a result of "maternal impression," the child from this union, Charikleia, is born white, leading Persinna, in fear of being suspected of adultery, to expose her. Subsequently, Charikleia falls under the loving care of three substitute fathers: Sisimithres, an Ethiopian gymnosophist ("naked" philosopher); Charikles, a merchant from Delphi; and Kalasiris, an Egyptian priest. Growing up in Delphi, the princess, ignorant of her origins, becomes the epitome of Greek beauty and learning, committed to the worship of Artemis. But on the occasion of a festival, she falls in love with a Thessalian champion, Theagenes, who returns her affection. Kalasiris steps in to reveal the truth of Charikleia's birth, which she accepts enthusiastically as does Theagenes, and the three begin their journey back to Ethiopia. They suffer many trials involving merchants, pirates, and brigands. After their capture by bandits on an island in the Nile delta, they meet another Greek, the Athenian Knemon, who serves as their translator for a time in Egypt. His own story of sexual pursuit and betrayal by a predatory stepmother is embedded as a novella within the major story. Traveling up the Nile, the lovers are captured, and Theagenes is tortured by Arsake, a lustful Persian queen, but they ultimately make it back to Meroe, the capital city of Ethiopia, where, through a series of trials, Charikleia is revealed to be the true daughter of Hydaspes and Persinna. Theagenes is accepted as her husband, and the two are married and proclaimed priests.

Although some parts of this adventure take the lovers to Egypt, especially the Nile delta, I will focus here on the Greek/Ethiopia axis, a cultural geography organized not by contrast but rather by linkage via Charikleia's heritage and through the homologous scenes of ritual pagan sacrifice in book 3 in Delphi, where Charikleia meets Theagenes, and repeated with a difference in book 10 in the celebration of the Ethiopian king's military victory. On his way back to Meroe from battle, Hydaspes is eager to prepare for sacrifices to express gratitude to the gods for his success, but upon arrival he is taken aback by the people clamoring for him to perform a human sacrifice—an old and infrequently performed ritual allowed on the occasion of a military victory. Charikleia and Theagenes, captured as ancillary trophies in the battle, are the best candidates. The sacrificial victim cannot be a native, but Charikleia is not recognized as Ethiopian. Her white skin, dress, and (for the Greek speakers) rhetorical proficiency all identify her as Greek. Both members of the Ethiopian royal couple respond intuitively to Charikleia, feeling an odd familiarity with her and resisting the impulse to sacrifice her. In addition to these intuitive hesitations, Hydaspes receives direct advice from Sisimithres, a gymnosophist, to sacrifice neither humans nor animals (10.9.6–7). Finally, Charikleia brings a legal case against Hydaspes, exercising her impressive rhetorical skills (enhanced by certain inartistic proofs such as tokens left with her as a baby by her mother and a birthmark) to persuade him against sacrifice. These forces combine to convince him to free her and Theagenes from peril. The story ends with Charikleia and Theagenes embraced by their Ethiopian parents/in-laws and taking on roles as priestess and priest of the religion of the sun.

Figuring sacrifice

If Heliodorus is engaged in a figured discourse here, what is his object? Is it possible to read Hydaspes as a "mask" for Julian, the last pagan emperor?[5] The Ethiopian king, like Julian, is a benevolent autocrat with recent military success. Although Julian's popularity with the people during his short term as emperor ebbed and flowed, scholarly sources emphasize his early scholarly training and preoccupation with religion and ethics, his unexpected military success and favor with his soldiers, and his highly principled approach to polis life. Both Ammianus Marcellinus and Libanius (*Funeral Oration*) attest to Julian's virtue and his efforts to put the welfare of the cities at the forefront of his policy decisions. So far as his fictional mask, Hydaspes, is concerned, we hear from the narrator in book 10 that the predicament of the city is resolved through "the righteousness of one man" (*eunomian andros*) (10.1.1) and, a bit later, that Hydaspes' righteousness, combined with his civility and graciousness toward his subjects, had instilled "an almost filial devotion in his people's hearts" (10.3.3).[6]

For Julian, traditional sacrifice is the central practice associated with the return of civic responsibility to the city. In his essay *Misopogon* (beard-hater), addressed to the people of Antioch, where he moved the court and enacted his religious reforms, he stages the scene of sacrifice over against the lapses of the city as he found it:

> In the tenth month, according to your reckoning, . . . there is a festival founded by your forefathers in honour of this god, and it was your duty to be zealous in visiting Daphne [a suburb of Antioch]. Accordingly, I hastened thither from the temple of Zeus Kasios, thinking that at Daphne, if anywhere, I should enjoy the sight of your wealth and public spirit. And I imagined in my own mind the sort of procession it would be, like a man seeing visions in a dream, beasts for sacrifice, libations, choruses in honour of the god, incense, and the youths of your city there surrounding the shrine. . . . But when I entered the shrine I found there no incense, not so much as a cake, not a single beast for sacrifice. (361D–62A)

Julian's disappointment was noted by the sophist Libanius, who provides a rich account of Julian's career in his *Funeral Oration*, Oration 18. Libanius narrates Julian's return to the city of Antioch after he was made emperor:

> It was this that shook him to the core, as he saw their temples in ruins, their ritual banned, their altars overturned, their sacrifices suppressed, their priests sent packing and their property divided up between a crew of rascals. If one of the gods promised him a cure for these ills at another's doing, I am sure that he would have insisted on refusing the throne. His anxiety, therefore, was not for power but for the well-being of the cities. (23)

Like his historical counterpart, Hydaspes is focused intently from the outset of book 10 on carrying out traditional sacrifice. He sends instructions to Persinna ahead of his arrival, requesting that "herds of oxen, horses, and sheep, of zebras, and griffins and other creatures of every variety, [be] taken across the river to the sacred glade to await the ceremony . . . a hecatomb of each and every species to be offered in sacrifice [*thusian*]" (10.4.1). Figure 6.1, a view of the magnificent ruins of Lepcis Magna, built by the emperor Severus early in the third century, shows oxen at a sacrificial altar.

Figure 6.1. Animal sacrifice, Arch of Septimius Severus, Lepcis Magna, Tripoli (ca. 203 CE). COPYRIGHT © LIVIUSORG | JONA LENDERING.

But why human sacrifice? Although the Carthaginians were said to have sacrificed human children within historical memory,[7] Ethiopians, on the contrary, were known for their virtuous religious practices. Three passages from Homer mention gods visiting Ethiopia to participate in grand and festive sacrifices (*Iliad* 1.423–4, 23.205–07; *Odyssey* 1.21–25). Addressing this question requires a broader engagement with the topic of sacrifice in the Greek tradition—a deep and complex inquiry. As Marcel Detienne observes, sacrifice is a system that "eludes clear and explicit analysis" (5). I draw here on the foundational work of Walter Burkert and on Detienne. In his 1985 work on Greek religion, Burkert reviews a range of approaches to sacrifice. Those methodologies that seem most relevant for a reading of Heliodorus understand religious ritual as an action with a semiotic character. Such acts have a function in "the creation of solidarity, or the negotiation of understanding among the members of a species" (54). This reading of cult practices places them solidly within a communal public sphere (55). Where animal sacrifice is concerned, Burkert advances an interpretation that understands sacrifice as straightforward and far from miraculous (55). The ritualized slaughter of the animal is followed by a "meat meal," a sustaining distribution of food to the people. This aspect of sacrifice is vividly and repeatedly enacted in the epic texts, thus establishing its material/economic function.

We may turn to Detienne for illumination regarding the semiotic and sacred dimensions of sacrifice. With reference to Hubert and Mauss' *Essai sur la nature et la fonction du sacrifice*, Detienne describes a "double process" of communication by means of a victim called on to play a mediating role between humans and gods (14). On one reading, the victim serves as an intermediary between human and divine (see Bradbury, "Julian's Pagan Revival," on Iamblichus), allowing for communication across radical difference. Exemplifying this theory, Heliodorus' novel thematizes problems of communication. For example, the queen Persinna, upon recognizing Charikleia as her daughter, "burst[s] into tears, and unable to control herself for joy, set[s] up a kind of animal howling [*mukēthmos*], (for a surfeit of pleasure often gives rise to a mournful wailing)" (10.16.1), and readers are reminded of the sounds of the sacrificial animal. Communication with the divine comes through the prayers of the priest and the setting aside of a portion of the animal for the gods.

From another perspective, we might be led to interpret the proposal of human sacrifice to stand in for Christian abhorrence of pagan animal, or "blood," sacrifice. This practice was a site of intense struggle across the third and fourth centuries, with Romans persecuting Christians on the grounds of their unwillingness to sacrifice animals as a verification of their faith. As Christianity became more acceptable and was ultimately embraced by the emperor Constantine (and all but one other fourth-century emperor), pagans were put on the defensive and animal sacrifice deemed objectionable even when it was not outlawed (Cameron 74). So we could see the possibility of human sacrifice in the novel as an imaginary intensification of the issue of blood/animal sacrifice. This intensification could work as a veiled criticism of the excessiveness of Julian's practice. Ammianus Marcellinus—generally positive in his presentation of Julian—finds fault with the pagan emperor on this account:

> He offered repeated victims on the altars of the gods; sometimes sacrificing one hundred bulls, and countless flocks of animals of all kinds, and white birds, which he sought for everywhere by land, and sea; so that every day individual soldiers who had

> stuffed themselves like boors [*incultius*] with too much meat... were placed on the shoulders of passers-by, and carried to their homes through the streets from the public temples where they had indulged in feasts which deserved punishment rather than indulgence. (*Roman History* 22.12.6)

In Heliodorus' novel, it is the people who demand the human sacrifice. Perhaps Heliodorus is suggesting the excess and indulgence of people who get carried away with a sacrificial practice gone too far. Another interpretive possibility arises through the role of the gymnosophist who gives voice to a key principle of neo-Pythagoreanism: the sanctity of all life. This is a very old line of Greek religious thinking running from Pythagoras through Plato, in the classical period, to Plotinus and Porphyry in the postclassical period, and it was given vivid treatment in Philostratus' biography of Apollonius of Tyana, as we saw in chapter 4.

In my view, what is at stake in this issue of human sacrifice at the close of the novel is not the advocacy of a specific religious practice but rather broad cultural identification. For many Greek and Roman peoples across the empire (both elite and common), the ritual of animal sacrifice provided a vehicle for identification through a practice signifying the values of civic pride and duty in provincial cities. As Christianity grew more popular, blood sacrifice stood for the public expression of civic ties and responsibility over against the more narrowly communal and private nature of the new religion (Stroumsa). The emperor Julian and sophist Libanius of Antioch make this point forcefully in the texts quoted above, as Julian looked forward to "the sight of your wealth and public spirit" in the sacrifices he had hoped to find at Daphne, and Libanius points out that the reconstitution of pagan religion for Julian was a matter not of power but of the "well-being of the cities." Blood sacrifice (human or animal) was confrontational toward Christians, and in practicing it so vigorously, Julian politicized religious issues, creating divisions that could lead to reprisals with a regime change (Bradbury, "Julian's Pagan Revival" 347). Thus the working out of the plot in book 10 has the effect of moderating extremes of both Christian and Julianic dicta.

Sophistic solutions

Given the crucial role of sophistic rhetorical practice in the resolution of the crisis, the emphasis here is more political than doctrinal. Let's turn then to the sophistic/rhetorical elements in the scene and in the narrative resolution of the conflict. In the face of the threat, Theagenes is at first sanguine when he assumes that Charikleia will reveal her identity to her natural parents and their suffering will be over. Charikleia, however, delays. In all the Greek novels, but especially in *Aithiopika*, a strong, culturally Greek female character dominates the narrative. This characteristic leads some to see the novel as a feminized genre because of its investment in the private realm, and it has even prompted speculation about a female readership (Hägg). Feminist critics (e.g., Haynes) note that the heroines manage their own protection against sexual, social, and economic threats in the wider, more dangerous world of the empire. To carry the analysis further, we might propose that, if one of the standard operations of colonization is disempowerment through feminization, a heroine such as Charikleia—as strong rhetor—provides a subversive counterstatement: she is the mistress of wily tactics necessary for perseverance in a world where people move from place to place across lawless territories and in and out of shifting systems of signification—linguistic, economic, and cultural—within which women themselves are tokens of exchange.

Heliodorus repeatedly calls attention to systems of signification. He often stages scenes of failed communication: of language difference and the inability to translate, and of misunderstanding, forcing readers to attend to the polyglot realities of language in empire and to more profound limits to human communication. On occasion characters resort to animal-like sounds and gestures, sometimes miming their messages. But alongside this motif runs a commentary on how best to speak to the powerful. Charikleia, perhaps the best example of the active heroine that characterizes the genre, is also the most rhetorically adept character in this or any of the Greek novels. When her Greek "father," Charikles, tells the story of her upbringing in that country from the age of seven (2.33), he reports that "she makes great play with that subtlety *(hēn poikilēn edidaxamēn pros kataskeuēn)* in argument whose various forms I taught her as a basis for choosing the best way of life" (2.33.5). This Isocratean view of the value of rhetorical teaching, set alongside her consistently virtuous behavior, prepares the reader to give moral weight to her rhetorical performances throughout the novel.

But Charikleia uses deceit over and over to save herself and Theagenes from death and to preserve her chastity and independence from multiple seduction plots and proposals of marriage. Her handsome boyfriend is often confused and upset by her strategies, but they carry the day. Not only Charikleia but also her Egyptian guardian Kalasiris and, finally, her Ethiopian birth father, Hydaspes, the model of a good ruler, tell lies to persuade others to do what is good. Charikleia's lies, like her skin color, are deeply situational: we might even say, they are only skin deep. At one point, she frames her strategy in the form of a *sententia*: "Sometimes a lie (*pseudos*) can be good, if it helps those who speak it without harming those to whom it is spoken" (1.26.6). These faculties—subtlety of argument, attunement to the situation, a flexible relationship to "truth"—qualify Charikleia as a sophist.[8]

This rhetorical élan is on display in book 10 when her life is on the line, and she casts her defense as a legal case against the emperor. Against "those who hold sovereign power" (10.10), she demands rights. Hydaspes is amused, finding it an "outrageous insolence" to be confronted as a king with a case at law by an alien/captive woman. The scene allows Sisimithres the gymnosophist to voice strong egalitarian/democratic sentiments: "Justice does not stand in awe of station"; "at law there is but one king: he who has the stronger case"; and "a person's character is as important as the color of his face in reaching a judgment." But Hydaspes is certain that Charikleia will say nothing worth listening to: "She will just give us a string of fictions (*plasmata*) to buy herself time, typical of people whose lives are in danger": a perhaps overly dramatic but apt description of the function of Greek rhetoric under Rome more generally.

Hydaspes is convinced through Charikleia's rhetoric, and he then finds *himself* in need of a sophistic practice to somehow mollify the people who are agitating for the traditional human sacrifice. His solution is to lie (to speak *a contrario*), a rhetorical practice Charikleia used strategically earlier in the novel to defend Theagenes. Hydaspes delivers an impassioned concession to his people's will: "I am resolved to sacrifice her to the gods for your sake" (10.16). But as he leads Charikleia to the altar, he prays "that his oration, whose rhetoric he had contrived to ensure its ineffectiveness, would fail to carry his point." He does not miss his guess, as the people refuse to let him sacrifice Charikleia; and in a reversal of the myth, Heliodorus contrives that Hydaspes correct the horrible error of Agamemnon in slaughtering Iphigenia, who, as we recall, is likened to a virgin heifer in Euripides' *Iphigenia at Aulis* (11.1079–84).[9]

At the end, Hydaspes does finally stand before the altar, but the whole spectacle surrounding the ritual is carried out in a jubilant and comic way, transforming other violent elements of traditional Roman practices such as the slaughter of human and nonhuman animals at gladiatorial contests. As a spectacle occasioned by a military victory, it has the features of a triumph—a parade of people and goods from distant places along with games. But the visiting dignitaries present their gifts/tribute willingly, and in fact receive gifts in return, altering the imperial economy. No one is enslaved, and no humans or animals are harmed in the contests. These fictional modifications to traditional Roman practices could also be considered a figured commentary: an implicit critique of colonial exploitation and violence. That Heliodorus is vague about the precise nature of Hydaspes' sacrifice is significant. The participants (and readers) are allowed to accept it as a bloodless (and wordless) ritual that serves all: it is a collective practice that requires no common language, pantheon, ethnicity, skin color, gender, nor even a shared species. Picturing the ruler, Hydaspes, officiating at a sacrifice suggests the "benefaction" that constitutes a significant socioeconomic dimension of the ritual (Bradbury, "Julian's Pagan Revival" 349) and perhaps gestures toward Julian's frustrated attempts to get the city leaders in Antioch to fulfill their duties to the people.

The whole episode can be seen as dramatically endorsing a centuries-old characteristically Greco-Roman style of civic life. In so doing, it operates somewhat differently from the other figured discourses analyzed in preceding chapters. In the other cases, Greek rhetors obscured their critiques of Roman power. Here the object of critique may more pointedly be the pagan emperor himself. If the novel was in fact written after Julian's reign, during the Christian backlash, presenting such a full and positive account of the pagan rites would itself have constituted a figured discourse—a risky proposition in a Christian context. According to Bradbury, "Julian, Libanius, and Eunapius all make clear that to sacrifice in the public eye under Christian emperors was to exercise 'boldness' and 'daring'" ("Julian's Pagan Revival" 343). But setting aside blood sacrifice in favor of a bloodless celebration pointedly nullifies the aspect of pagan religious practice most objectionable to Christians while preserving the collective rite. Seen in this way, the narrative makes an accommodation to Christianity—and to Christian emperors—without endorsing the religion or capitulating to it; instead, it keeps in play religious alternatives such as the sun worship practiced by the Ethiopian characters and, by association, the whole panoply of "oriental" religions popular in that era. Charikleia takes up her new role as priestess of the moon in a seamless transition from her original status as a virgin priestess of Artemis in Delphi.

One could read the final passages as refuting my claim that the significant forces are rhetorical and political. Divinity seems to be given priority by the narrator as he speculates about how the people were persuaded:

> The populace cheered and danced for joy where they stood, and there was no discordant voice as young and old, rich and poor, united in jubilation, for though they had understood very little of what was said, they were able to surmise the facts of the matter from what had already transpired concerning Charikleia; or else perhaps they had been brought to a realization [*huponoias*] of the truth by the same divine force that had staged [*eskhēnographēsen*] this whole drama and that now produced a perfect harmony of diametric opposites: joy and sorrow combined; tears mingled with laughter; the most hideous horror transformed to celebration; those who wept also laughed; those who grieved also rejoiced; they found those whom they had not sought and lost those whom they thought to have found; and finally the offering of human blood, which all had expected to see, was transformed [*metaballomenōn*] into a sacrifice free of all stain [*eis euageis thusias*]. (10.38)

But consider the humorous or figured ambiguity embedded in the idea of a divine force staging the drama: it could refer to the gods, but also to Hydaspes, or to the novelist himself as the scene-writer. The people are inspired (from *theiazō*) by the "scene" itself and find in it the *huponoias*, "the real meaning which lies at the bottom of a thing, deeper sense, especially covert meaning (such as is conveyed by myths and allegories)" (*LSJ*). In fact, the passage could even be gesturing toward the novelist's practice: with *huponoias*, readers are "brought to a realization—a conjecture," the payoff for successfully interpreting figured discourse. The confirmation by Sisimithres that, in fact, the gods do not want blood sacrifice—and that Hydaspes ought to have realized this long ago—has a *parrhēsiastic*, or truth-telling, quality.[10] But its force is diminished by its post hoc position in the dramatic action. The religious philosopher's opinion enters into the mix of voices, but ultimately it is a rhetorical/sophistic solution rather than divine truth or religious doctrine that has determined the outcome.

Theagenes is accepted as Charikleia's husband, and the two are married and proclaimed priests. Via life-sustaining fiction and the true lies of sophistic rhetoric, Heliodorus projects a comic, even utopian, vision of a Greco-Roman empire in which religious practice sustains civic health, and no animals—including human animals—are harmed.

CHAPTER 7

"Tiresome" Libanius: Speaking to Empire, Addressing Emperors

What we see in these second sophistic discourses from the early centuries of the Common Era are not only self-serving performances by elite Greek intellectuals making their mark in imperial culture but also experiments in the construction of political subjectivity. And yet we cannot really speak of a single stance or subjectivity emerging from these diverse works. The second sophistic was not a systematic movement; it would do an injustice to the *poikilos* nature of these sophists' productions to culminate this study by fitting them into a single mold.[1] Rather, we might locate their rhetorical strategies on a spectrum, at one end of which would appear the centered biographical subject, speaking in his own voice. Here we can place, for example, the second half of Dio's *Euboean Discourse* and Aristides' plea for aid to the city of Smyrna. Somewhere in the middle of the spectrum would fall the city encomia of Aristides and Libanius and the *Imagines* of Philostratus, discourses in which a named author delivers the oration (or circulates the written text), but the genre allows for considerable distance and complexity, as we have seen. Then at the "literary" end of the spectrum, we find the novelistic play and multivocality of Philostratus' biography and Heliodorus' novel. Political subjectivity in these two works is not absent but, rather, is dramatically decentered. The subject constructed via these literary genres and launched into the precarious world of imperial culture is elusive and mobile, protected by layers of mediation from the risk of direct confrontation with Roman power.

We saw at the outset the consequences of such confrontation when Dio was exiled by Domitian in the first century. Written three centuries later, the extensive autobiography and oeuvre of Libanius offer another window on the dangerously shifting fortunes of the Greek sophist in relation to imperial power.[2] We met Libanius earlier in the roles of encomiast of the city of Antioch (chapter 1) and supporter of the emperor Julian (chapter 6). In the final decade of his life, near the end of the fourth century, Libanius produced a set of "political" orations within which he adopts the stance of *parrhēsiastes*. As a sort of introduction to these discourses, we have a curious piece in which Libanius speaks directly about his own political investments and stances, an analysis of which provides the core of this chapter. How are we to interpret this shift in rhetorical stance of a fourth-century sophist? Are there implications in Libanius' choices for periodizing the second sophistic?

A biographical approach

Given that we have so much material from Libanius, including an extensive autobiography and many letters, a biographical reading should certainly be taken into account, although most scholars who study this fascinating figure caution against reading his artful and sometimes self-serving self-representations at face value (e.g., Cribiore, *Libanius* ch. 1; Van Hoof, "Introduction"; Watts). A *syncrisis* (comparison/contrast) with Aristides, another second sophist with a strong personality who drew attention to himself, offers a way into the character of Libanius and brings to light some surprising similarities.[3] Both were precocious in youth, fixed on a sophistic career at an early age, sought a rhetorical education in Athens, and achieved early success. Libanius, born in 314 to a distinguished Antiochene family, was driven by a lifelong devotion to his hometown, as was Aristides to his adopted city of Smyrna. Yet Aristides avoided financial obligations to the city and rarely got involved in its affairs. Libanius, on the other hand, did all in his power to arrange for an appointment as chief sophist in Antioch and achieved his goal in 355. Although he received immunity from financial obligations to the city by virtue of his appointment, he spent the balance of his long life teaching there and spoke up in opposition to problems created by mismanagement of the city on the part of both Romans and local elites. Indeed, in the second paragraph of his monumental *Autobiography*, Libanius links his love of Antioch and oratorical prowess with what we might call today political activism: "My family was one of the greatest in a great city—in education [*paideia*], wealth, the provision of shows and games, and in the oratory [*logoi*] which opposes itself to the excesses of governors" (¶2). While Aristides distanced himself from emperors for the most part, Libanius seemed destined by family history, talents, and disposition to be closely tied to them, for better or worse.[4] His family's fortune having been stripped away arbitrarily by Diocletian a decade before his birth, Libanius began life as a victim of imperial violence. Early in his career the mandate of Constantius II forced him to serve as sophist at Constantinople against his wishes, but his admiration for Julian (361–363) created a strong if sadly short-lived bond. As we will see below, the powerful and influential emperor Theodosius (379–395) became an invoked audience in the final phase of Libanius' career. Finally, for all their differences, an intriguing similarity between the two sophists is their poor health. Libanius suffered from migraine headaches, gout, and depression—maladies, like those of Aristides, of a potentially psychological etiology.[5]

Despite his physical problems, Libanius carried out an amazingly active professional life, one in which his sophistic talents served both pedagogical and political purposes. Examples from the *Autobiography* illustrate the mix of motives, styles, and demands driving Libanius' prolific rhetorical production over some five decades. When he was allowed to return to Antioch in 354, he entered a city plagued by imperial violence:

> [T]he whole community was tempest-tossed by the murderous anger of the emperor [*caesar*, or second-rank emperor, in this case] Gallus. Some were dead already, others he had arrested for execution, and all were men of parts. Among them I saw even my old teacher Zenobius, for I went to their prison and, crossing the threshold, I fell on my knees and wept among them as they all lamented. Next day they were released, and the rumour spread that some kindly spirit had entered with me, and by its agency the storm had been stilled. On the day following, I made an address to the emperor [Gallus], and being asked to deliver another oration, unwillingly and fearfully I gave a panegyric, trying to get round him. (Oration 1 ¶96–97)

This passage shows the range of influence a sophist could exercise, from his mere presence as a mollifying force, to a speech of praise, offered "unwillingly and fearfully" on demand, but in the interests of calming Gallus' "murderous rage" directed at the influential men of the colonial city.[6] The locution of "getting round" (*perierchomenos*) the caesar seems to work figuratively the way it would in colloquial English: somehow avoiding his wrath through indirection. Libanius' various tactics worked in the event, as Gallus expressed delight and released the prisoners, including Libanius' teacher.

In better times, under the more reasonable Roman official Strategius, the sophist's talents came into play more comprehensively as Libanius "set about helping those whose help I thought I should need" (¶106). While his days were occupied with oratory, he spent the evenings helping to construct arguments on behalf of citizens under bad favor with previous administrators. But lest we lose sight of the sophist's ever-present desire for recognition, Libanius offers this account of a rhetorical exchange:

> The prefect [Strategius] was more desirous of praise than other men were of office, and he demanded of me a panegyric as repayment of the debt I owed him, since I had promised a speech in his honour once he had attained his present office. . . . I said that I would settle my debt if he left his quarters and came to listen to my oration in the city hall, for this would be something without parallel for the prefect to do, and it would form the first part of my speech that he had honoured eloquence so. (¶111–12)

Here we get a fascinating glimpse of the elaborate system of give and take between the Roman ruler, who needs local support and at the same time craves praise, working in tandem with a sophist who uses his friendship to advance the fortunes of his fellow citizens and his oratorical abilities to wrangle a bit of notice for himself and his art from his Roman patron. Here, in the moment, the chain of gold seems to yoke the colonial rhetor and Roman master comfortably together. And as we noted in the previous chapter, the few months of Julian's reign were, for both emperor and sophist, golden as they shared principles of civic virtue based in traditional religious practices.

Following the death in 363 of Julian, Libanius' ideal emperor, the sophist was in a vulnerable position in Antioch society. Backlash against Julian's anti-Christian reforms by the next three emperors (Jovian, Valentian, and Valens) made the ensuing decade a difficult one for Libanius—so risky that he virtually stopped presenting public orations for a time. The accession of Theodosius in 379, however, seemed at first to turn the tide in a more hopeful direction, but the use of the incompetent and corrupt gentry as a "private audience" impeded Libanius' attempts to reach the emperor (Norman, "Introduction to Oration 2" 6; Wiemer 205–19). Nonetheless, Libanius used this period of relative safety to produce a set of speeches notable for their deliberative aims. A subset of the "political orations" (the category also includes orations addressed to Julian; see Malosse 83–87), some eight orations (*logoi*) addressed to the emperor Theodosius between 379 and 388, speak directly to problems affecting the city. In one of the most famous, *To the Emperor Theodosius for the Temples* (386), Libanius makes a plea for an end to violence against pagan sanctuaries by "monks, fanatical bishops, and overzealous officials" (Malosse 86). As we saw in the previous chapter, for Libanius as for his revered emperor Julian, pagan ritual was strongly linked with responsible civic behavior, so the argument here is not about religious doctrine but rather about the well-being of the city. Other topics concerned the treatment of prisoners and of farmers who, on coming into town, faced the threat of being forced to work for corrupt officials. Still other orations argued for honesty and disinterest on the part of Roman governors adjudicating legal cases, or for dedication by provincial elites to the city council (a theme we saw in the encomium of Antioch discussed in chapter 1).

Hans-Ulrich Wiemer, in a recent and thorough discussion of Libanius' relationship to emperors, asserts that the sophist never met Theodosius, the great Christian emperor, face to face (197–202), but given Libanius' distinguished career and close connection with at least one emperor, it seems appropriate to read the political discourses as more deliberative than epideictic. The orations are addressed to Theodosius by name, and there is clear evidence that the emperor at times looked favorably on the sophist and made decisions that accorded with Libanius' views (Wiemer 200–01).[7] Given the timing of the emperor's decisions and the uncertain paths of delivery, it does not seem that Libanius was actually positioned to persuade the emperor to take one action or another in most cases (e.g., Wiemer 201; Quiroga Puertas). Rather the sophist played the role of interpreter of events and legitimated the good decisions of the emperor. As Jeffrey Walker frames it, for sophists under empire, "rhetoric shapes and sustains the prevailing modes of public judgment to which the sovereign power must be responsive, and itself embodies that judgment to the sovereign power" (*Rhetoric and Poetics* 133). At times, this role occasioned an audacious stance. In Oration 50, for example, in making an argument against requisitioning the forced labor of peasants during a time of food crisis in the city, Libanius calls attention to the brutal behavior of the Roman administrators: "[T]hese people act as though they were laws unto themselves . . . and the government of the Roman empire has broken down, and then they make their appeal to authority, though they know full well that not even to you, Sire, is all permitted. For it is the very essence of monarchy that its holders are not omnipotent" (¶18).

Indeed, almost twenty years after the high-water mark of his career, in this period Libanius found himself often sailing against the prevailing political winds. Changes in the higher strata of Antiochene society created a newly hostile reception for the venerable sophist. Norman writes, "*Honorati, principals*, military commanders, governors and the varied hotch-potch of imperial agents and secretaries, whose presence made Antiochene society more incoherent and unbalanced, . . . used such distinctions for their own elevation to undermine the established system of local organization" ("Introduction to Oration 2" 5–6). In the face of these local difficulties, Libanius turned to the new emperor himself, one with whom the sophist shared an ethical commitment to good governance despite their religious differences. Labeling the political discourses *prosphonetic*, as does Malosse, raises the question of the nature of Libanius' address. A *prosphonetic* speech, a category found in Menander Rhetor's list of epideictic subgenres, is one addressed to a ruler and may be understood somewhat formulaically or reductively to refer to a formal speech of welcome for a visiting dignitary, for example (see Kennedy, *Classical Rhetoric* 39; Pernot, *Epideictic Rhetoric* 16-17, 50). Libanius' political orations, on the contrary, were not composed for ceremonial occasions but rather offered forceful and hard-hitting arguments about specific civic problems; thus the impetus seems deliberative and the stance *parrhēsiastic.*[8] How should we interpret Libanius' change of direction in this period? Might we read it as an indication of a larger-scale shift in fourth-century rhetoric?

From biography to periodization: A third sophistic?

Considerable scholarly attention is being paid of late to changed circumstances for Greek rhetors and the empire itself in the fourth century. While we have encountered the second sophists featured in this book in chronological order and placed each within specific historical and geographic circumstances, the emphasis has been on the consistent elements of the relationship between Greek sophist and Roman imperial power over three centuries. The inclusion of Heliodorus' novel and of Libanius—obviously not mentioned in Philostratus' third-century catalog—raises questions about the limits of the phenomenon and about periodization. The second sophistic arose in response to the Roman empire, which persisted even after the second-century crisis dividing rule into two geographic regions. But the rise of Christianity over the course of the fourth century—its embrace by Constantine I in the early decades leading to its adoption as the state religion by Theodosius in

380—worked complex changes on the relation of the Greek/pagan sophist to the Roman/Christian emperor.

A number of scholars are exploring questions of the periodization of the second sophistic in light of the fourth-century rise of Christianity (Fowler and Quiroga Puertas; Pernot, *Rhétorique de l'éloge* 271). Decades ago, in 1993, Laurent Pernot proposed the term *third sophistic* for this period in his monumental study of the rhetoric of praise, *La Rhétorique de l'éloge*; he reiterated the claim in his 2005 *Rhetoric in Antiquity* (206). Even though Christian rhetoric in the fourth century "supplanted" pagan rhetoric, Pernot asserts, the process came about as a kind of summing up or culmination (*aboutissement*) of the Greco-Roman (second sophistic) tradition (*Rhétorique de l'éloge* 273; *Rhetoric in Antiquity* 206), which simultaneously experienced a flourishing. Pernot details features of the new Christian rhetoric, seeing especially in the New Testament "great linguistic and literary difference, compared to contemporary pagan texts" (*Rhetoric in Antiquity* 204). But he also notes Christian rhetors' appropriation or "recycling" of pagan rhetoric (205). Pernot has recently taken up the question of a third sophistic anew and presented an open and inventional approach to the topic at a meeting of the International Society for the History of Rhetoric in the summer of 2017. There he suggested that both pagan and Christian rhetors constitute a third sophistic ("Third Sophistic"). Pernot points out that Christian rhetors such as John Chrysostom and Gregory of Nazianzus studied with Greek rhetors, produced orations on sophistic models (encomia and funeral orations, for example), and placed a high premium on eloquence. Kennedy takes a similar approach, calling Gregory's encomium of Basil the Great "probably the masterpiece of sophistic Christian oratory" (*Classical Rhetoric* 140–46).

Alberto Quiroga Puertas, on the other hand, sees in a third sophistic a new direction in Greek/pagan rhetorical practice. He identifies features of this phase, including a diminishment in the uses of declamation and the imitation of classical models (35). Rhetoric becomes more pragmatic, Quiroga Puertas asserts, as rhetors turned to realistic situations. Despite the pragmatic turn, however, rhetors were not able to take up the directly deliberative genres of the classical period given the conditions for exchange under empire. Rather, they aimed "to analyze and explain the facts at the core of the transition towards a Christian order" (35). Quiroga Puertas, then, is interested in the pagan side of this shift, while Pernot and Kennedy have looked more toward the new Christian contributions. Christianity, posits

Quiroga Puertas, "speeded up the impact of rhetoric in society" and demanded that pagan rhetors redefine what it meant to be pagan (38).

The relation between Christian and pagan rhetoric in the fourth century is a topic far too capacious to be treated comprehensively in a single chapter. My purpose here has been to present several suggestive strands of analysis offered under the notion of a third sophistic, particularly as they apply to the late orations of Libanius. While the sophist may have ignored or dismissed Christianity, his concern with the moral function of rhetoric created more continuity than rift with the new religion, his focus remaining on the city at risk in the new order rather than on individual behavior. The task of (re) constructing an ethical, pagan, sophistic identity in the face of Christianity could be a way of understanding the aims of Oration 2, a curious discourse composed just prior to the era of Libanius' political orations.

The "tiresome" Libanius: Pathos, melodrama, identification

There is surprisingly little scholarly work on Oration 2, one that, according to Malosse, "merits more attention than it has hitherto received" (95). Perhaps Anglophone scholars confronting the work in the Loeb edition may have been put off by A. F. Norman's translation of the title as *To Those Who Called Him Tiresome* (*Pros tous barun auton kalesantas*). Composed in 380 CE when Libanius was 67, the oration stages an argument against "some people" who (on the report of his students) have brought this charge of "tiresomeness." These are members of the Antiochene elite upon whose support—in the form of their endorsement of his good character and judgment—Libanius had relied for the maintenance of his position as chief sophist of this important provincial center. Nonetheless, he risks in this oration the practice of *parrhēsia* in opposition to them. In Oration 2, we see the rhetor defending his use of plain speaking and, in the process, reflecting on the cultivation of political identification through empathy for others.[9]

Libanius begins by asking, Why should this particular charge of "tiresomeness" be brought now? He follows with a series of other potential accusations that could be made against him: he was offended when imperial officials did not visit him, perhaps (¶8); or he talked too much about his family (¶10); or perhaps he mentioned his labors in rhetoric, here and abroad, including accepting a chair in Antioch (¶12). With these denials we have a fine example of *occupatio* (or *praeteritio*): mentioning a thing by saying you will not speak of it. Because Libanius is guilty of none of these things but in fact embodies their virtuous opposite, we are presented with a brief apologia: he has a good reputation in the "workshops" (i.e., with the laboring class) as well as with governors; he has been offered distinctions in the past and declined to take advantage of them; he speaks well of his family; he doesn't call attention to his skill at rhetoric (except with his students); he visits the sick (¶14–25). These passages can sound, to a contemporary reader, pompous and self-serving. In fact, though, most of Libanius' claims can be verified by independent accounts. His efforts on behalf of workers, peasants, ordinary soldiers, and provincials are well attested (Norman, "Introduction to Oration 2" 5). And we have seen above an array of social problems toward which Libanius would direct his attention in the decade to come. So, when it comes to the charge of tiresomeness, meaning the burdensomeness for listeners of being reminded of unaddressed civic ills, Libanius replies: guilty as charged. The oration can be charted in terms of Hermogenes' system of *staseis* as *dikaiologia*: relating to a past action. Because Libanius ultimately admits that, indeed, he is guilty of bringing grievances against his fellow citizens, it is an *antithesis* (opposition), granting the intentionality of the actions and defending them via *antistasis*, that is, because they are beneficial (see Kennedy, *Invention*).

At the crux of the accusation, we learn, is his sin of constantly praising and yearning for the past. Libanius calls into service for political arguments the very feature of sophistic rhetoric that is said to remove it from politics. The contrast between the well-governed city of the past and the corruptions of the present leads Libanius to reframe the accusation: he is not tiresome to all but only to those for whom the bad fortune (or decline) of the many serves their own good (¶28). He then catalogues grievances against the imperial administration of Antioch and the corrupt councilors (or the upper-class Antiochenes who now decline the responsibilities of serving on the councils, or *curiae*): the burdens of taxation on workers, the excesses of administrative expense, the poor treatment of soldiers. (It's striking how familiar these grievances sound to twenty-first-century US ears.) Among these complaints are included the proscription against what Libanius famously endorses as the civilizing practices of pagan worship and the decline of Greek rhetoric in favor of "Latin and law" (¶44).

We might now think that, again, the political edge of the oration is given over to a self-serving and nostalgic fixation on rhetoric, but at this point Libanius fuses the loss of rhetorical art with the misfortunes of the less privileged and, by extension, the kind of sympathy required for any form of identification across social difference. How, he asks, does sympathy with the unfortunate become a crime? "I regard it," he says, "as perfectly proper to be upset by not just the troubles of one's own, but by those of others too" (¶47). Consider the practice of emotional identification fostered by reading ancient Greek tragedy, the sophist suggests. One is able to experience sympathy with the disadvantaged by reproducing the emotional effects of reading (or being reminded of) the sorrows and losses of literary figures such as Niobe, Hecuba, and Oedipus. Libanius offers here an education of the emotions for political efficacy.[10] This education proceeds in a stepwise fashion. The practice for these modes of identification begins with the subject experiencing grief through reading and feeling for the figures of Greek tragedy: Niobe's and Medea's children, Laius and Oedipus, Hippolytus, and the thousands harmed by the Trojan War. The exercise of *prosopopoeia* from the *progymnasmata* comes to mind here. Anyone who came up through the schools would have been required at some point to compose an oration in the voice of another, and often the subjects faced emotionally dramatic situations drawn from literature and myth.[11] Moving away from literature, Libanius then proposes that a person would certainly grieve for the death of a child of another family (not one's own), and if so, wouldn't one grieve for a wrong to one's city, or damage to another city (such as the inhabitants of Cyprus) who suffered from an earthquake? Linking onto this chain of emotional identifications, Libanius asks if it is possible to extend sympathies to those in other walks of life—even the uneducated—and, if so, to a whole province or people (*ethnos*).

A focus on grief and suffering in this oration may seem to fit into a pattern across Libanius' life: frequent references to emotional and physical maladies on the personal level as well as monodies (laments) in response to dire events such as the destruction of Nicomedia by earthquake and the death of Julian. Historian Edward Watts has offered a persuasive account of Libanius' "rhetoric of suffering" in such discourses, urging a textured reading that sees such emotional outpourings not merely as autobiographical reports but rather as part of the creation of textual personae useful for specific rhetorical goals. Rhetors and literary critics would certainly endorse such an analysis. The rhetorical phenomenon of making emotions vivid—of eliciting pathos, of moving the listener—has a long history in Greek rhetoric (in, for example, Gorgias, Aristotle, Longinus, and Hermogenes). What is striking in this case is Libanius' advocacy of using such emotional effects (in tragedy and epic) not to persuade an audience to feel for or agree with the orator himself but to enact a kind of empathy across difference that would then change the listener's perspective on the polis. Such identification would generate an emotional disposition toward actions good for the city—actions inspired by pain or grief.

In light of this argument, the key word of the title, *barus*, a word appearing frequently in ancient Greek texts, deserves more careful attention.[12] Reviewing the many uses of *barus* suggests that to translate it as "tiresome" is a trivialization, obscuring a range of significations from physiological to emotional. *Barus* is first of all heaviness, a material weight that moves to the metaphorical sense of psychological burden: oppressiveness and grief. Achilles, for example, sighs "heavily" as he speaks to his mother, in book 1 of the *Iliad* (1.364), of his sadness at losing Briseis. The word speaks of the heaviness of fate for Aeschylus' Agamemnon and Euripides' Helen. The chorus of Sophocles' *Antigone* also uses the word to refer to the weight of her grief. The stranger in Plato's *Sophist* remarks that monarchy, when bound by good written rules—that is, laws—is the best of all the six forms of government; but without law, it is most oppressive (*barutatē*) to live with (302e). The gap between this richness of reference in contrast to the disdain connoted by the word *tiresome* seems to me a symptom of the critical disposition I discussed in chapter 1: an angle of vision that obscures the "weightiness" of the imperial relationship. (Norman also refers to Libanius as "cantankerous" and attributes to him an inclination toward morbidity.)

In giving voice to grief, Libanius may be enacting what some contemporary political theorists might consider a crucial aspect of constructing a political identity. Anne Anlin Cheng, for example, in *The Melancholy of Race*, poses the question in just such terms: "How does an individual go from being a subject of grief to being a subject of grievance?"—from suffering injury to speaking out against that injury? (3).[13] In the case of Libanius, the injury is not directly against him (or only against him) but against the civic order, the city, and the whole range of its inhabitants. For the success of this project, myth and literature, and the rhetorical *paideia* within which they are introduced, have an important role to play. The *paideia*, then, becomes not merely the valuable cultural capital of the Greek intellectual but the very means of becoming the kind of colonial subject who can confront challenging political conditions.

In this unusual oration, Libanius does not "figure" his message, but neither does he employ *parrhēsia* in a conventional way. He seems to be laying out the preconditions for engaging in political discourse at all, responding to the question, Why speak? Why bother to analyze the conditions necessary for addressability? Although I've suggested that the political orations to follow in his career were addressed to the emperor in a more direct and serious way than mere formula, we learn that Libanius was not under any illusions about his access from remarks he makes in Oration 2 about the circumstances of delivery. He writes, "This then is the sum of one matter that induced me to speak [his reputation], but there is another, no less weighty. I hope that my remarks would have some effect, and would serve as a cure and corrective, transmitted from person to person until it reached the emperors' ears" (¶70). But because of the obstructionist actions of the elites he accuses of mismanaging the city, "[t]his has been a vain hope and I have not succeeded. Those who have the ear of our rulers converse with them on any matter but this, neglecting things of importance and reporting only what will win them favour" (¶70–71). The additional impediment Libanius fails to mention here is the devoted Theodosius' greater receptivity to Christian bishops as advisors on provincial matters. In an era of waning Greek/sophistic influence, Libanius sought to make a case not only for himself or for his city but also for a kind of rhetorical subject with the ethical gravitas to compete with Christians for the ear of the Christian emperor. If the fourth century did give rise to a third sophistic, then perhaps a more directly expressed concern for access or addressability is one of its distinguishing features.

CHAPTER 8

Conclusion: Refractions of Empire

It can be argued that rhetoric in our contemporary era of empire produces a dilemma for citizens something like the one Libanius faced. Teachers who see rhetoric as a crucial tool for confronting political problems cultivate in their students a form of subjectivity through which pathetic appeals generate responsiveness and rational argument makes the case for political change. This process can be termed a communications model of rhetorical action that grounds the discipline's uptake of political rhetoric from the classical period forward and provides the commonsense backdrop for so much of our current discussion about teaching writing and speaking, as well as many of our analyses of political discourse. The history of social movements in the US since the 1960s gave renewed force to the rhetorical idea that speaking truth to power—even in the performative and disruptive mode of protest—was the essential and strongest means of confronting political wrongs, including imperialism. But recently—say, since 2001—such communications seem to be seriously broken; many feel a sense of impotence where political communications are concerned. A nadir of inefficacy was reached in February of 2003 when people worldwide staged the largest public demonstrations ever recorded, in opposition to the impending US invasion of Iraq; millions demonstrated in Rome, Paris, London, and across the US. When George W. Bush was queried the next day about his response, he pronounced that "democracy is a beautiful thing" and proceeded to launch a war with Iraq in the next month ("Bush Says"). And, from a national perspective, what need did the US president have for world opinion when news polls showed national support for an invasion of Iraq? (Borger and White). There was no "tiresome" Libanius facing him in an imperial court nor a Dio standing on his chariot to alert him to the devastating consequences of his actions. There was no relation or access to the emperor.[1]

Perhaps readers may be thinking that this is a somewhat simplistic way of marking the difference between the conditions of communication in a premodern era and those in the current moment characterized by speed, distance, electronic mediation, layers of bureaucracy, and mass distribution. And, in any case, there were certainly some actual humans standing at former president Bush's shoulder as he made the fateful (and fatal for many) decisions in the early aughts, but those relations come under a special heading. Such communications are of a kind that ordinary people learn about only years later in journalistic exposés such as Bob Woodward's *Plan of Attack* (2004), a behind-the-scenes account of how Bush decided to go to war that the author based on interviews with key administration insiders, transcripts of phone calls, and even "PowerPoint presentations from military computers" (Freedland). All the brilliant, passionate, carefully reasoned free-speaking arguments against the war were not heard. There was no relation enabling their reception and thus their potential force. And there was no place for the empathetic subject described by Libanius. As many have observed, political discourse in the twenty-first century is often produced in an echo chamber of niche communication channels, consumed by those who are already convinced and rarely circulated in meaningful ways to decision-makers or to those whose views might be changed by it. And yet we (rhetoric scholars, ordinary citizens, political actors, et al.) continue to act as though such free speech has a weight or status, the potential for effect, that qualifies it as the favored style of public discourse and justifies its continued centrality in our pedagogical schemes.[2] And we feel the weight—the heaviness and frustration—felt by Libanius in 380 CE when our speech falls on deaf ears.

Farewell to modernity?

This contemporary dilemma of political rhetoric mirrors the communication conditions of the postclassical Mediterranean world: a severely truncated role for free speaking—through rational argument and direct persuasion—along with a flourishing of aesthetic modes of figuration or indirection. Indeed, we postmoderns seem to have entered a new era ripe for figured discourse. In the age of *pax Americana*, we're awash in outrageous political rhetoric and layers of neoliberal affective currents. It's an era that has seen a proliferation of genres, media, and modalities—and arguably a growing role for satire and humor in political life. The precarities of life under neoliberal empire are met by performative and unruly protests (such as Occupy Wall

Street) with a high degree of visuality and circulation but often with unclear demands and aimed at powers whose addressability is questionable.[3] At the same time, free speech as a stance, the subject through which it speaks, and its styles are still essential to political life. It is impossible to renounce the importance of free speaking and, simultaneously, impossible to deny the power of figuration in the current climate.

To illustrate this contemporary rhetorical situation, consider two news items from June 2017. Liveright Publishing announced that it would publish the prison correspondence, much of it as yet unavailable, of Nelson Mandela; the press's editor in chief, Robert Weil, observed that "Mandela's actual words . . . reflect his courage, his wisdom and the unspeakable horrors he went through" (J. Williams). In the same week, a production of Shakespeare's *Julius Caesar* in Central Park made news because the actor playing the Roman usurper was dressed to resemble the forty-fifth president. Protestors and some sponsors objected to the enacted assassination (Ehrbar), and commentary and comedy unfolded in the aftermath, as commentators debated whether this embedded figuration was an act of symbolic violence or a confirmation of democratic/republican principles. No doubt, there were many who, like me, greeted both these events with pleasure and enthusiasm; they made me think about conditions for political speech, and they stimulated my political interests. Rather than making a choice between two postures, or hierarchizing them, we are seeing them flourish in parallel tracks. But also, at times, we find a creative resituation of the one within the other.

Parody news programs are prime examples of such embedding. Starting with *Saturday Night Live*'s "Weekend Update" segments (1975–today) but really catching fire with Jon Stewart's *Daily Show* (1999–2015), their influence has been profound. During the presidential election of 2000, a Pew Research Center poll announced that almost half of US adults between the ages of eighteen and twenty-nine were turning to late-night television for election "news" (Yahr). We are seeing here a new phase of the "literaturization" Kennedy found in the postclassical period of antiquity. Another example comes from the memoir of a young political organizer. With *Dreams from My Father*, published in 1995, Barack Obama reversed the typical sequence for politicians who write books to further their political careers. Before he was elected to office, he became the literary hero of his own autobiography, a book that "leaves an impression of candidness and authenticity" (J. Scott). Stanford professor Arnold Rampersad found the book "so literary . . . so full of clever tricks—inventions for literary effect—that I was taken aback" (J.

Scott). Master of serious oratory over his eight years as president, Obama also created a comedic persona at White House Correspondents' Dinners, on late-night television, and on social media. In twenty-first-century national and international spheres, the power of parody, the blending of journalism and entertainment, and the proliferation of new-media sites for political engagement have dramatically decentered "straight," instrumental rhetorics of civil exchange and argumentative order. And now the gold-encased world of the forty-fifth president and his products are forging yet another chain. The scholar of figured discourse notes with pleasure these days the wide use of one of the signature moves of the second sophists against Roman power—the self-conscious omission of reference to it. One small gesture of defiance and disregard, one that I'm practicing here, refuses to repeat the name of the president who has trumpeted his brand high and low, far and wide. We see here yet another resonance between the old and new empires.

Not only in this small way but in other literary/rhetorical practices we can see how contemporary critics of empire artfully figure the power of *parrhēsiastic* practice within pleasurable and accessible literary genres. New versions of a twenty-first-century global Sophistopolis proliferate, and some participants are using tactics that we observed in the second sophists. In several works, we saw the sophist embed mock-deliberative or legal scenes within narrative: the trial in Dio's Oration 7, the confrontation of the philosopher and the emperor in Philostratus' *Life*, and the trial scene in Heliodorus. When the political subject is barred in real life from the benefits of democratic practices—or when those procedures seem to have lost meaning and force—the sophist brings them to life in fiction. *Bamako*, a 2006 film from Mali by director Abderrahmane Sissako, takes its name from Mali's capital city and its premise from world economics. The film stages a trial pitting the plaintiff, "African society," against the defendant, the World Bank. I learned of this film from a fine article by Bret Benjamin, who artfully blends aesthetic and rhetorical criticism. In "Making the Case: *Bamako* and the Problem of Anti-imperial Art," Benjamin writes that "the film is invested in social transformation through the aesthetic project of figuring the impossible and the rhetorical project of constituting a counterpublic in opposition to neoliberal development by making a public case against the World Bank" (199). With respect to ancient rhetorical genres, Benjamin notes that the film "actively takes up the questions of epideictic rhetoric even as it figures a moment of forensic exchange" highlighting the "challenges and stakes of rhetorical legibility" (200). What makes possible such a reading is Benjamin's construal of "empire" as a historical and analytic category rather than as "merely a pejorative descriptor of aggression, power, or territorial expansion" (203). The latter definition is likely to produce readings that focus on resistance and, in so doing, miss the complexities of a figured response and also the opportunity for reflection on the possibilities for and limitations of "rhetorical legibility" in specific contexts.

Another second sophistic tactic, projection, involves the imagining of possible worlds from within genres whose purpose seems to be more limited: something like a generic overflow or excess. We saw Dio offering a utopian vision in the *Euboean Discourse*, Aristides staging a negative anti-sublime within an encomium, Philostratus (*Imagines*) projecting forms of ideal life within school exercises, and Heliodorus imagining a religious collective without the sacrifice of life in his novel. To exemplify the tactic of projection in the twenty-first century, I turn to a 2017 novel, *Exit West*, by Pakistani author Mohsin Hamid. Set in an unnamed Middle Eastern city, the novel features a young heterosexual couple, as in the ancient Greek novels. Even as their romance blossoms, Saeed and Nadia find life becoming increasingly harder as their city falls apart during a military siege. Movement, food, and electricity become scarce. They learn of "agents" who, for a fee, provide access to doors that serve as portals to elsewhere. They take the chance, ending up first on the island of Mykonos, then in London, and later in Northern California. Movement across dangerous geographies produces an episodic structure.

Not quite fabular, not quite magical realist, the work seems to offer a kind of soft utopianism. In London, for example, migrants at first arouse hostility but eventually move to "London Halo," a suburb where they can have a new dwelling in exchange for labor (169). The work has a sophistic feel: generically hybrid, it's full of vivid ekphrastic detail, engaging multiple senses but also projecting a new sense of order. Although the ancient sophistic examples of world projection are generally sunnier than this contemporary work, both operate on the assumption that a sharp divide between free speaking and conventional literary genres is inadequate for responding rhetorically to the wrongs wrought by empires.[4]

From chain to rain

With the embeddings and projections of *parrhēsia*, we have displaced the truth teller imagined by Foucault in antiquity and lauded by the political movements of the modern period: heroic and forthright, with persuasion as the aim. In the alternative scenes highlighted here, the colonized sophist/artisan plays with and within available genres but without an easily identifiable aim and lacking a sure sense of reception. These conditions call to mind Kenneth Burke's observations about persuasion and freedom: "Persuasion involves choice, will; it is directed to [a person] only insofar as he [or she] is *free*" (*Rhetoric of Motives* 50, emphasis in original). Under various conditions of unfreedom, Burke suggests, "we could with more accuracy speak of persuasion 'to attitude,' rather than persuasion to out-and-out action." He turns at this point to Roman rhetoric with its Latin vocabulary, drawing on Cicero's offices of eloquence for a shift from *movere* (move) to *flectere*, to bend. Further, Burke posits that "the notion of persuasion to attitude would permit the application of rhetorical terms to purely poetic structures . . . when these devices are considered for their power to induce or communicate states of mind to readers, even though the kinds of assent evoked have no overt, practical outcome" (50).

We might enhance Burke's "persuasion to attitude" by turning once more to the French "school" of second sophistic analysis, which has coined a term for the dispersed effect of figured discourse: *rayonnement*. Translated in English as "influence," "effulgence," "radiancy," or "fervor," *rayonnement* impresses and shines; it names rhetorical acts with radiant energy and cultural influence (Oudot "Regarder Rome"; Pernot, *Rhétorique de l'éloge*). *Rayonnement* does not take aim in a direct way, but it influences nonetheless. As Philostratus writes of Aristides' appeal to Marcus Aurelius to rebuild the city of Smyrna after an earthquake, the emperor was less persuaded than "incited by good advice and by eloquence, [to] shine out more brightly and press on with ardour to noble deeds" (*Lives* 2.9.¶583; trans. Wright 219). *Rayonnement* is multivalent; it figuratively blends the visuality of rhetorical style with cultural/rhetorical circulation infused by energy generated both by the discourse and by the rhetor him- or herself. There is in this concept a kinship worth exploring with contemporary Anglophone theories of visuality and affect, but it stands in contrast both culturally and temporally to twentieth-century North American conceptions of rhetoric as constitutive or identificatory. Rather, we may think of this brilliant dispersion as embracing and scintillating—less a chain of gold than a rain of golden words, falling on the powerful and powerless alike.

The French scholarship I've drawn on here and throughout the volume has expanded my outlook on second sophistic rhetoric. One of the aims of the project has been to call attention to broader scholarly frames of reference in the interest of pushing our US and Anglophone field toward a more fully comparative approach. Another, more central goal has been to call attention to one of the history of rhetoric's "lost geographies," the postclassical period of ancient Greek rhetoric. I hope that this book persuades rhetoric scholars to expand their sense of the scope, variety, and potential for rhetorical scholarship in the ancient world—particularly for its political potential—setting aside a narrow understanding of classical rhetoric as an uncritical exercise in the veneration of canonized texts from Athens in the fifth and fourth centuries BCE and Rome in the first centuries BCE and CE.

That classical heritage is sometimes negatively characterized in terms of the restrictive gender and race of its major figures. Another hope I have for this study is that it has troubled any simplistic assumptions about gender and ethnicity in ancient Greek rhetoric. Through the analysis of Philostratus' *Imagines* and Heliodorus' novel, *Aithiopika*, we have discovered that masculinity and femininity, sexuality, and skin color are mobile signifiers in postclassical rhetoric. And our encounter with Julia Domna revealed that women were not completely absent from rhetorical activity in the period. So many more complexities across these sociological axes remain to be discovered in studies of ancient rhetoric. Finally, where politics is concerned, I hope that this encounter with postclassical Greek rhetoric will shine some light on rhetorical possibilities in our current imperial era.

APPENDIX

NOTES

WORKS CITED AND CONSULTED

INDEX

APPENDIX: A RECURATION OF PHILOSTRATUS' *IMAGINES*

Some entries are listed in more than one category. Numbers on the left refer to the book (1 or 2) and to the description therein, and numbers in parentheses indicate pages in the Loeb edition.

I. Interactions between the sophist and the boy

- 1.1 Scamander—look away from the painting. (7)
- 1.8 Amymone—daughter of Danaus, pursued by Poseidon; "Let us withdraw, my boy, and leave the maiden; for already a wave is arching over." (281–82)
- 1.13 Bosphoros (continued)—from the boy: "Why do you not go on to another painting? This one has been studied enough for me." Sophist: "What do you mean? I have yet to speak of the fishermen." (55)
- 1.15 Ariadne—"You must have heard from your nurse; for those women are skilled in telling such tales and they weep over them whenever they will." (61)
- 1.24 Hyacinthus—the tale is terrible and incredible, but "we are not here to criticize the myths and are not ready to refuse them credence, but are merely spectators of the painting." (95)
- 1.28 Hunters—tricked by the painting: "I shout at them as though they could hear and I imagine that I could hear a response. You [the boy] didn't help: you were just as overcome, deceived, and stupefied as I." (109)
- 2.1 Singers—"Do you wish us to pour a libation of discourse on the altar?" (129)
- 2.5 Rhodogoune—"It seems, my boy, that you have a feeling for the beauty in this figure and desire to hear something on this point also, so listen." (147)
- 2.8 Meles—as the sophist is describing the way the river water / male lover will create a chamber for the two, he says, "Why

do you seize hold of me, my boy? Why do you not let me go on and describe the rest of the painting? If you wish, let us next describe Critheïs, since you say you are pleased when my tale roams freely over such things." (161)

2.17 Islands—"Would you like, my boy, to have us discourse about those islands just as if from a ship, as though we were sailing in and out among them in the springtime . . . ? But you must be willing." Boy: "I agree, let us go sailing"; then, "let us examine the city that has been built upon the island." (209)

2.21 Antaeus—the giant from Libya; "I think you must be afraid of him, my boy." (225)

II. Geography and ethnicities

A. Imperial/world

1.1 Scamander—"forces of Asia against Europe." (9)

1.5 Niles dwarves. (19)

1.7 Memnon—the Ethiopian general, son of Eos, black skin; Nile river. (29–31)

1.11 Phaëthon—falls into the river Eridanus, in the far west near the end of the world (the Po or the Rhone, source of amber from the North Sea). (49)

1.12 Bosphoros—youths on horseback playing a game on the European side and then going across to Asia. (51)

1.17 Hippodameia—in Arcadia: her father, Oenomaüs, like a Thracian, "a barbarian and savage of aspect." (71)

1.19 Tyrrhenian pirates. (75)

1.28 Hunters—pigments brought from a great distance; "barbarian." (109)

1.29 Perseus—Ethiopians and a Greek man in Ethiopia (115); Andromeda, fair of skin though in Ethiopia, very beautiful; "charming Ethiopians with their strange colouring and their grim smiles; and they show that they are pleased and most of them look alike." (117)

1.30 Pelops—detailed description of his beautiful body until the parts that "might be mentioned" are concealed by garments favored by the Lydians and "upper barbarians." (123)

2.5 Rhodogoune—Persian military leader (related to Mithradates); alliance of Persians and Greeks. (145)

2.7 Antilochus—Memnon the Ethiopian kills the young Greek

in front of his father, Nestor (155): he strikes terror because of his black skin color (155–57). Memnon is "terrible [*deinos*] to look upon, in the army of the Ethiopians, holding a spear and wearing a lion's skin and sneering at Achilles." (157)

2.8 Meles—as the sophist is describing the beautiful girl, he mentions Athenians colonizing Ionia. (163)

2.28 Looms—a reference to the Seres, people of the country of silk somewhere in eastern Asia. (249)

2.31 Themistocles—a Greek among barbarians; he speaks Median with hesitancy. (259–61)

B. Greek sacrifice and religion

1.4 Menoeceus—Creon's son sacrificed at the dragon's hole. (15)

1.12 Bosphorus—on the Asian side, a temple with columns. (55)

1.27 Amphiaraüs—Theban who fought in the Trojan War; as he sinks beneath the earth, his look is holy and oracular. (107)

2.1 Singers—female singers led by a woman with her first wrinkle sing to Aphrodite. The altar is full of frankincense, cinnamon, and myrrh; it gives off a fragrance as of Sappho. (129)

2.5 Rhodogoune—pictured pouring a libation for her victory over Armenians; a woman praying. (147)

2.16 Palaemon—received at Corinth by Sisyphus; the meaning, garb, etc. reserved for the mysterious rites, altogether secret. (193)

2.24 Theiodamas—Heracles steals and eats an ox; there follows an explanation for a sacrifice in Lindian Rhodes. (239)

2.25 Burial of Abderus—a victim of the flesh-eating mares of Diomedes; Heracles carries the partially eaten body, erects a city with his name, and establishes games. (241)

2.27 Birth of Athena—two peoples already sacrificing to her on the acropolis, Athenians and Rhodians. (246)

2.30 Evadne—leaping onto her husband's funeral pyre, she is adorned with wreaths and gold like other sacrificial victims. (257)

2.33 Dodona—the oracle of Zeus, an oak: priests come to hang garlands, utter prayers, attend to sacrifice. (267)

III. Human conditions

A. Babies, children, youth

1.4 Menoeceus—Creon's son sacrificed at the dragon's hole. (15)

1.5 Nile dwarves—on the statue of the Nile they speak. (15)
1.6 Cupids—they (*Erōtes*) gather apples, fragrance, gems in their baskets: "This is friendship, my boy, and yearning of one for the other." (16)
1.11 Phaëthon—youth thrown from the chariot. (47)
1.20 Satyrs—gaze lovingly (and lustfully) on Olympus, a pupil of Marsyas (whose gruesome flaying by Apollo is not described in the *Imagines*). (81)
1.21 Olympus—the flute player, beautiful like Narcissus. (83)
1.26 Birth of Hermes—Hermes as a baby stealing Apollo's cattle; the god's amusement conquers his wrath. (99–101)
1.28 Hunters—who should be hunting the boar get distracted and begin hunting a beautiful youth: "Why do you touch him? . . . Why have you turned toward him?" (109); of the most beautiful, the sophist says, "I admire his spiritedness [*phronēmatos*] . . . he is conscious of the fact that he is beloved [*eratai*]." (111)
1.29 Perseus—Eros is a youth rather than a child. (117)
1.30 Pelops—loved by Poseidon; "a lad with a beard just beginning to grow." (119)
2.2 Education of Achilles—Achilles as a child "not yet conscious of valour"; nourished by milk and marrow by the centaur Cheiron. (133–35)
2.4 Hippolytus—beautiful youth wronged by his stepmother and father; his beauty lingers even after he is wounded. (143)
2.7 Antilochus—in the prime of youth; loved by Achilles; killed by Memnon the Ethiopian. He died with a joyous and smiling face because he saved his father's life. (157–59)
2.12 Pindar—as a babe; bees at work molding the child to be inspired with harmony and music; statue of Rhea by the door. (179–81)
2.16 Palaemon—a dolphin bears the sleeping child. (193)
2.17 Islands—the city built on the island is a small plaything for a royal child complete with a theatre and a racetrack for little dogs. (209)
2.22 Heracles among the Pygmies—they are trying to kill the god, but he rises up and laughs at them, sweeping them up in his lion's skin. (229–31)

2.25 Burial of Abderus—a still beautiful youth, victim of the flesh-eating mares of Diomedes; Heracles bears his body on a lion skin. (241)

B. Women mortal, legendary, divine

1.6 Cupids—gathering apples; Aphrodite is invoked but doesn't appear. (29)

1.8 Amymone—Poseidon's rape is off-scene; figured as "a wave arching over." (281–82)

1.11 Phaëthon—the daughters of Helius become trees and shed golden (amber) tears. (49)

1.12 Bosphoros—a woman pursued by lovers inhabits a secure house; she "gazes at the scene from her house . . . and laughs down at the crowd." (53)

1.15 Ariadne—sleeping on Naxos; Theseus is unjust; Dionysus is loving. (61–63)

1.16 Pasiphaë—lusts after the bull; the act is not shown; instead the workshop of Daedalus. (67)

1.17 Hippodameia—in Arcadia: a chariot race for her hand; white horses of Pelops are "comrades . . . of Persuasion" (69); beautiful couple dressed in wedding garb. (71)

1.18 Bacchantes—a forgiving attitude toward Pentheus' mother and aunts for tearing him apart: "they do not see what they are doing." (73)

2.1 Singers—female singers led by a woman with her first wrinkle; singing to a statue of modest Aphrodite; references to Sappho. (129–33)

2.4 Hippolytus—the father's injustice is worse than the stepmother's. (143)

2.5 Rhodogoune—a resplendent warrior pouring a libation; like a bacchant; her eyes show merriment but also the "haughtiness" of a ruler. (145–49)

2.9 Pantheia—in a story from Xenophon's *Cyropaedeia*, the sophist declines to describe the destruction of war, burning of houses, and ravaging of Lydian women but rather describes the beauty of the woman who has killed herself to die with her husband; her eyes show "great intelligence [*te noun theōrōmen hosos*] . . . and virtue of the soul [*tēs psychēs agathōn*]"; they "show the courage of reason rather than of rashness." (165–71)

2.10 Cassandra—a figure of pathos trying to protect the dying Agamemnon from the crazed Clytemnestra. (175–77)
2.18 Cyclops—ends with the nymph Galatea driving dolphins over the sea. (215)
2.27 Birth of Athena—emphasis on the rainbow colors of her armor; both Zeus and Hera rejoice at her birth. (245–47)
2.28 Looms—Penelope at her loom, shedding hot tears. (249)
2.29 Antigone—her strength in lifting the body of her brother and controlling her fear; she masters her cry of lamentation in keeping watch. (253–55)
2.30 Evadne—leaping onto her husband's funeral pyre: a sweet and pure fire for those who have dealt so well with love. (259)

C. Adult men and gods

1.1 Scamander—the painting ignores the battle and represents the river, plain, fire, and Hephaestus running. (7–9)
2.6 Arrichion—won the pancratium contest and died just after winning; painted as a victor, "perspiration fresh on his body." (155)
2.19 Phorbas—a barbarian boxing with Apollo: savage and swinish. (219)
2.20 Atlas—bearing the earth; Heracles wants to take over: detail of straining bodies. (221)
2.21 Antaeus—a giant from Libya wrestling Heracles, painted as strong, symmetrically developed, skilled, red-blooded with passion; Antaeus resembles a wild beast. (227)
2.22 Heracles among the Pygmies—asleep after the battle; they're trying to kill him, but he rises up and laughs at them, sweeping them up in his lion's skin. (229–31)
2.23 Madness of Heracles—the horrible act of his killing his children; graphic description of the dead infants. (233–35)
2.24 Theiodamas—a rough, aged peasant curses Heracles for eating his ox. (237)

IV. States of being and behaving

A. Altered states: drunkenness, revelry, sometimes lusting; sleeping, dreaming

1.2 Comus—spirit of revelry pictured asleep, leaning in a doorway to a bedroom. (13)

- 1.16 Pasiphaë—in her desire for the bull she has a helpless look; the bull has a proud mien, "already experienced in love," and gazes fondly at the cow. (67)
- 1.19 Tyrrhenian pirates—Palaemon rides on a dolphin's back sound asleep. (81)
- 1.22 Midas—capturing a drunken, sleeping satyr. (85–87)
- 1.25 Andrians—inhabitants of Andros are drunk on their river of wine, singing, dancing, reclining, but powerful in the assembly and good to friends. (98–99)
- 1.27 Amphiaraüs—consulting the oracle requires sleep; god of dreams in a "relaxed attitude." (107)
- 2.8 Meles—the woman in love with the river is in a dream, thinking the man to be a river. (161)
- 2.11 Pan—set upon by nymphs when he is asleep at noon. (177)
- 2.13 Gyraean rocks—Poseidon punishing Ajax's insolence: Ajax gazes out over the sea like a man emerging from a drunken sleep. (183)
- 2.16 Palaemon—dolphin bears the sleeping child, swimming noiselessly so as not to disturb his sleep. (193)

B. Transformations, metamorphoses; cross-dressing; hybrid creatures

- 1.2 Comus—reports of revelers cross-dressing and masquerading as the other sex. (13)
- 1.3 Fables—stories of animals in human roles. (15)
- 1.6 Cupids—a digression on the male hare who bares young "contrary to nature." (27)
- 1.8 Amymone—Poseidon's sea chariot drawn by "hippocamps," web-footed horses. (33)
- 1.11 Phaëthon—the daughters of Helius become trees and shed golden (amber) tears. (49)
- 1.18 Harmonia and Cadmus—turning into serpents: "in astonishment they embrace each other . . . holding on to what is left of the body." (75)
- 1.19 Tyrrhenian pirates—turned into dolphins by Dionysus. (79)
- 2.2 Education of Achilles—the painting of centaur Cheiron glosses over the juncture of man and horse. (137)
- 2.3 Female centaurs—how beautiful they are, the delicacy of their female form gains strength from the horse in union with it; baby centaurs gambol beneath their mothers. (139)

2.15 Glaucus Pontius—a man who eats an herb on shore and then dives into the sea and becomes a sea deity: part human, part fish. (191)

2.16 Palaemon—also transformed into a sea god. (193)

2.32 Palaestra—in Arcadia, Palaestra, daughter of Hermes, has discovered the art of wrestling. The maiden has a manly aspect and would not marry or bear children. Her figure is gender ambiguous: "if compared with a boy, will be that of a girl, but if it be taken for a girl, it will seem to be a boy." Her breasts are like those of a boy of tender years. She cares for nothing feminine. (263–65)

V. Nature, natural phenomena

1.9 Marsh—wetlands description; cupids riding swans; a bridge of date palms across the river; palms are male and female; the male tree falls in love and falls over the river, offering menial service to humans to cross. (41)

1.10 Amphion—receives a lyre and plays to the stones; he sings "a hymn to Earth . . . she, creator and mother of all things" (43). The stones all run together toward the singing; they listen and become a wall: "eager in rivalry, and happy, and devoted slaves of music." (45)

1.11 Phaëthon—"the Earth raises her hands in supplication, as the furious fire draws near her"; the river laments and offers its bosom to receive Phaëthon. It will catch the amber drops (tears). (49)

1.13 Bosphorus (continued)—tuna fishing on the Euxine Sea; brown and charming men catch lots of fish and let some go. (57–59)

1.31 Xenia—beautiful description of fruit in a still life (figs, chestnuts, pears, apples, cherries, grapes, honeycomb, foaming milk). (123–25)

2.14 Thessaly—Poseidon breaking through the mountains to create plains, letting a river through. (185)

2.17 Islands—very extensive natural description of islands. (195–211)

2.26 Xenia—in this one, the painting speaks of its gifts of hospitality: a hare, ducks, bread, poppy-seed bread (that brings sleep), fruit, confection. (243–45)

2.28 Looms—the painter has wrought the spider and her web in a painstaking fashion, with fidelity to nature. (251–53)

2.34 Horae—goddesses of the seasons come in their appropriate times: "the Earth in her wisdom brings forth for them all the fruits of the year" (269)

VI. The arts

A. Speech; eyes speaking, speaking painting

1.5 Dwarves—on the statue of the Nile, they "are not without the gift of speech." (19)

1.26 Birth of Hermes—Apollo seems to talk. (103)

2.4 Hippolytus—the painting itself mourns, having composed a sort of poetic lament in his honor. (143)

2.8 Meles—a story of a woman in love with a river: "She keeps up a conversation with it as though the murmur of the water were human speech." (159)

2.26 Xenia—the painting offers its gifts to the farmer: a hare, ducks, bread, poppy-seed bread (that brings sleep); fruit, confection. (245)

2.33 Dodona (penultimate entry)—the oracle of Zeus, an oak: the place is "replete with the divine voice"; a vessel resounds most of the day. (269)

B. Artistic technique

1.23 Narcissus—the realism of the painting; bee settling on the flowers; Narcissus does not see through the artifice of the pool. (89)

1.28 Hunters—after the boar is killed, everyone gazes at the lad, still in the posture of throwing his javelin, "as though he were a picture." (115)

2.29 Looms—the painter himself, like a weaver, captures nature successfully. (251)

2.34 Horae—the painter himself is caught up in the dance of the Horae, a final honor. (269–71)

C. Poetry, music

1.10 Amphion—receives a lyre and plays to the stones, which all run together toward the singing: "eager in rivalry, and happy, and devoted slaves of music." (45)

1.21 Olympus—about the flute player: "Your breast, I should say, is filled not merely with breath for the flute, but also with thoughts of music and meditation on the tunes you will play." (85)

1.25 Andrians—inhabitants of Andros are drunk on their river of wine, singing to their wives and children. (98–99)

2.2 Education of Achilles—Cheiron the centaur plays the lyre, a mark of his culture and soothing to children. (137)

2.5 Rhodogoune—"Is she not elated and proud of the victory and conscious that she will be celebrated for her exploit with lyre and flute and wherever there are Greeks?" (145)

2.12 Pindar—attending his birth, bees are not in hives but in a city: Athens! (179)

2.34 Horae—goddesses of the seasons sing and whirl in dance. (271)

NOTES

Preface

1. See Kagan et al. for one vision of US supremacy offered in 2000. The Bush-era National Security Strategy policy statement, issued in September 2002, reiterated the advocacy of a *pax Americana*. On the *pax Romana*, see Hopkins; Woolf, "Roman Peace." Woolf's nuanced treatment shows how an ideological formation is not merely an imposition from above but also gives shape to a "range of opinions in a developing debate" (182). See also Lamp on the related phenomenon of "Augustan political myth" (38–57).

2. On comparisons between the Roman and US empires, see the following: from classics, Rose, "Cicero" and "Theorizing Athenian Imperialism"; from political and cultural theory, Foster; Ignatieff; Steel; P. J. Williams; and from communications studies, Hartnett and Stengrim.

3. In terms of historiographical categories, I subscribe to Richard Rorty's view that historical and rational reconstruction "can never be that independent" but rather should be seen as "moments in a continuing movement around the hermeneutic circle" (53n1).

1. Rhetorical Possibilities under Empire: Captivity, Complicity

1. The category of second sophistic, coined by third-century rhetor Philostratus in *Lives of the Sophists*, serves as a convenient but not in each case precise label for the rhetors included in this project. Fourth-century sophist Libanius of Antioch and the novelist Heliodorus, also thought to have composed in the fourth century, obviously could not have been included in Philostratus' catalog. I use the term *second sophist* in the lowercase to designate the major subjects of this study and others, such as Lucian, who do not appear in Philostratus' *Lives* but who have strong family resemblances to the group. I return to the question of periodization in chapter 7.

2. See also Mattingly's archaeological study of sites in Britain, Jordan, and North Africa: *Imperialism, Power, and Identity.*

3. Where classicists working with second sophistic material use theory, they often turn to the cultural sociology of Pierre Bourdieu, focusing their analysis on the question of national or ethnic Greek identity. See, for example, Goldhill, *Being Greek*; Whitmarsh, "Greece."

4. See Woolf, "Becoming Roman," on Romanization.

5. See Hopkins on the "relative peace" of these centuries; this peace excepted imperial expansion in Britain and Dacia (modern Romania) and involved "internal pacification of conquered provinces" (193).

6. See Ackerman and Coogan, and N. Smith on the concept of lost geography.

7. See Conley for an economical summary of older and newer views of the second sophists (59–62). See recent studies by Goldhill (*Being Greek*, 1–28), Pernot (*Rhetoric in Antiquity*, 128–201), and Whitmarsh (*Greek Literature*, 1–38) for general discussions of this group, including the problematic nature of the "second sophistic" label and for an extensive bibliography. All subsequent dates will be in the Common Era unless specified.

8. See chapter 4 for a reading of Philostratus' extensive biography of the neo-Pythagorean sage, *Apollonius of Tyana*, and chapter 5 for a discussion of his collection of descriptions, *Imagines*. Chapter 5, note 1, offers more information on the Philostratus family names.

9. The scholarship on the second sophistic is extensive. Oxford has now compiled a *Handbook of the Second Sophistic* (Richter and Johnson, eds.). For overviews, see Anderson (*Second Sophistic*); Bowersock; Gleason (*Making Men*); chapters in Goldhill, editor (*Being Greek*); Kennedy (*New History*, ch. 11); Swain (*Hellenism*); Walker (*Rhetoric and Poetics*, ch. 4); and Whitmarsh (*Greek Literature* and *Second Sophistic*).

10. See Walker, *Genuine Teachers*, on declamation.

11. See Alcock on Greek cities after Roman conquest; Miles on the Roman plundering of Greek art.

12. The British relationship to India, especially where the cultural/literary traditions of Sanskrit texts and art are concerned, may approximate that of Greece and Rome. See Said, *Orientalism*.

13. See A. N. W. Saunders' introduction to his collection of Greek political oratory on the complexities and mediations of "political" oratory in the classical period. Jeffrey Walker makes a powerful case for epideictic as the primary and dominant rhetoric mode from Homer through the second sophistic and beyond (*Rhetoric and Poetics*). See Josiah Ober on questions of access to spaces of public speech in classical Athens.

14. See Aune on Marx's "anti-rhetoric" and J. Smith on rhetoric in Hegel.

15. See C. Miller for an illuminating and carefully documented discussion of "concealment" as a transhistorical feature of rhetorical practice. The question here concerns the choice of tactics under specific historical and material circumstances.

16. On Thersites, see Rose ("Plural Voices"); Thalmann. For a recent treatment of rebellious Antigone, see Butler.

17. The English translations of these lectures appear under the following titles: *Hermeneutics of the Subject*, *The Government of Self and Others*, and *The Courage of Truth*. *Fearless Speech* is a transcription of lectures delivered in English at the University of California, Berkeley.

18. See Rose ("Cicero" 366–67) on the use of Pierre Macherey for an analysis of Cicero's response to imperialism in the orations.

19. The rhetorical posture of the *parrhēsiastes* translated easily to republican Rome, with its legend of heroic challenge to tyranny, and became coded in a fusion of masculinity and national identity: "Rhetorical education was designed to instill in Roman boys habits that would make their masculinity literally visible to the world: along with constructing logical arguments, handling narration and interrogation, and creative ways to use words, they learned to stand up straight, look others straight in the eye, gesticulate with grace and authority" (Connolly, "Virile Tongues" 86).

20. For a clear exposition and elegant analysis of figured speech in a Byzantine-era Greek text, see Walker, "These Things I Have Not Betrayed."

21. For accounts of the reigns of the two emperors who became the epitomes of violent misrule, see Suetonius, *The Twelve Caesars*, on Nero (213–46) and on Domitian (299–314).

22. On the literal level, the comment may be taken to refer to language differences, but translator Wilmer Cave Wright, in his annotation, finds it "probable" that "Trajan understood Greek" (Philostratus, *Lives* 20–21n5). The best education was conducted in Attic Greek, but Roman public life and legal actions were conducted in Latin, which not all of the Greek intelligentsia deigned to learn. It is assumed that many vernacular languages were spoken in the empire, although very few written records remain. Among them would have been demotic Greek, Celtic, Coptic, Punic, Aramaic, Syriac, and numerous others. On this topic, see Brunt, *Roman Imperial Themes* (277–80), for an overview and bibliography.

23. See Whitmarsh (*Greek Literature* 181–246); Millar (*Emperor*).

24. Whitmarsh (*Greek Literature* 207, 246) argues for the unlikelihood that any of the kingship orations were presented to Trajan. Within Whitmarsh's theoretical paradigm, searching for extratextual contexts and effects dooms the historian-critic to an "expressive-realist" methodology (see 20–38). His emphasis on the textuality of second sophistic rhetoric is accompanied by a diminished recognition of material circumstances.

25. See Rose ("Cicero" 367) and also Poulakos (*Speaking for the Polis* 4) on the political orientation of Isocrates' rhetoric in the classical era.

26. For a reading of figured discourse in Anna Comnena's Byzantine-era history, *Alexiad*, see Quandahl and Jarratt. For readers of French, Laurent Pernot offers *L'Art du Sous-Entendu* (the art of hidden meaning): a lively exploration of the phenomenon in historical and contemporary settings. On Greek figured discourse in the Roman empire, see chapter 5 (55–146).

27. Born too late for Philostratus to include him with the second sophists, Libanius nonetheless may be considered in relation to them, for he carried on the rhetorical practices of the Greek revival in the Roman East. For background on Libanius, see his *Autobiography* (Oration 1); Norman, "General Introduction" (*Antioch* xi–xviii); and Cribiore (13–41).

28. See Norman, "General Introduction" (*Antioch* xi–xiii).

29. See Libanius, Oration 11 (31). For another translation, see Downey.

30. For Libanius' financial circumstances, see his own extensive *Autobiography* and Norman's "General Introduction" to *Antioch*. On Libanius' school, see Cribiore (111–73).

31. The noun also means "cord" or "cable." Different spellings of transliterated forms reflect inflections (case endings) in ancient Greek. The term also appears in the final battle scene in the *Odyssey*. When the sneaky goatherd, Melanthius, is caught delivering more weapons to the suitors, Odysseus, "lord of suffering," ordered that he be tied "with a knotted rope and hoisted . . . to the rafters" as a form of torture (22.180–200; trans. Wilson).

32. See also Lattimore (Homer, *Iliad* 8.18–27), who translates the phrase as "cord of gold" and "golden rope."

33. In a fascinating study, Lévêque traces the uses and signification of this analogy through ancient Greek literature, ending with a discussion of Byzantine Michael Psellos. In the epigraph to the volume, Lévêque quotes Psellos writing that he is full of fear in the face of this analogy.

34. See Libanius, Oration 11 (¶34–36).

35. But elsewhere Kennedy acknowledges that it is difficult to draw a line between artificiality and the indirectness or subterfuge necessary for making political observations in eras when the rule of law did not protect citizens from arbitrary acts of political retribution (*Classical Rhetoric* 114).

36. See Henri Lefebvre on the dialectical relation of imagined to actual space.

37. Longinus' *On the Sublime*—written, says the author, for "public men" (*andrēous politikous*)—includes a narrative of decline. Two prominent Roman texts incorporating this theme are Tacitus' *Dialogue on Oratory* and book 10 of Quintilian, *The Orator's Education.*

38. See Barbara Cassin, "Time," where she argues that "Rome governs space whereas Athens frames time" (41). See chapter 2 for Aristides' representation of Rome as everywhere and nowhere.

39. See also Hawhee, "Looking"; Plett.

40. I have not devoted chapters to two of the more colorful figures in this period: Favorinus, a first-century hermaphrodite from Gaul, and Lucian, a scathing ironist from Syria. The key work on the former is Maud W. Gleason's *Making Men*; on Lucian, see C. P. Jones, *Culture and Society in Lucian.*

2. Sophist in Exile: Dio Chrysostom's *Euboean Discourse*

1. Philostratus is ambiguous about whether Dio's exile was commanded or self-imposed. He writes that Dio left "through fear of the tyrants in the capital [Rome] at whose hands all philosophy was suffering persecution" (*Lives* ¶488). But a few lines earlier we read that "he had not been ordered to go into exile" (*Lives* ¶488). Dio himself claims that he was in fact exiled not because of his own speech but by association with an influential Roman assassinated by Domitian (Oration 13, *On His Exile*; C. P. Jones, *Roman World* 45–46).

2. The bibliography on Dio is extensive. Essential recent studies from classicists that inform this chapter include C. P. Jones (*Roman World*), Swain (*Dio*), and Whitmarsh (*Greek Literature*). Kennedy (*New Rhetoric* 233–37) and Pernot (*Rhetoric in Antiquity* 191–92) discuss Dio from the standpoint of rhetorical studies.

3. Greek texts with English translations of Dio's discourses are published in five Loeb volumes translated by J. W. Cohoon (vols. 1–3) and H. Lamar

Crosby (vols. 4–5), 1932–51. Two of the eighty (37, *The Corinthian*, and 64, *On Fortune*) are now believed to have been authored by Dio's student Favorinus (Cohoon, vol. 1, x).

4. See Whitmarsh on the problem of bringing the assumptions of "expressive realism" to second sophistic rhetoric (*Greek Literature* 30).

5. See Walker on the stock themes of Roman declamation and debates about their value as training for political life (*Rhetoric and Poetics* 96–99). In his discussion of declamation (both Greek and Roman) in the Augustan period, Kennedy characterizes the practice as "literary composition, in which dangerous subjects could be touched on implicitly, subtly, or in an apparently imaginary context" (*Classical Rhetoric* 172).

6. See Jameson, *Political Unconscious*, especially "Conclusion: The Dialectic of Utopia and Ideology" (281–99), on reading literature for both critical and utopian impulses. Jameson's use of Burke's concept of the symbolic act, wherein the cultural performance is "affirmed as a genuine *act*," is particularly useful for second sophistic rhetoric, located at the boundary of the literary and the instrumental (80–81; emphasis in original). For scholarship on ancient rhetoric employing Jameson's approach, see Rose (*Sons of Gods*) and Poulakos.

7. Kennedy (*New History* 235) calls the *Euboeic Discourse* one of Dio's finest speeches. Kennedy and others refer to the discourse as the *Euboikos*. I follow Cohoon, who terms it the *Euboean*, the adjective derived from the name of the region, Euboea. References are to the Loeb edition (1949), translated by J. W. Cohoon.

8. Berry remarks that "narrative of any kind is unusual in Dio," and he further notes that, in the *Euboean Discourse*, "the pastoral comes to life with a realism which we do not usually associate with orations of the Second Sophistic" (71).

9. Goldhill asserts, "This is the first time that an attack on prostitution as such is articulated in the ancient world" ("Rhetoric" 239).

10. Ma interprets the scene both as an imitation of deliberation in the classical polis and as a reflection of actual practice in Greco-Roman cities (especially 117–24). The situation is also reminiscent of Dio's experience in his own city of Prusa recounted in the early Oration 46 (C. P. Jones, *Roman World* 19–25).

11. A familiar Greek critique of Roman law joins here with a Stoic doctrine from Epictetus: "Let others labour at forensic causes, problems and

syllogisms: do you labour at thinking about death, chains, the rack, exile" (Discourse 2, ch. 1).

12. See Ma on this point (especially 122–23).

13. See Ma on redistributive economies of the Greco-Roman city (112 passim).

14. See Desideri for an analysis of four spatial orientations appearing throughout Dio's works: the city of Rome, an idealized countryside as the site of freedom, barbarian spaces of possibility at the margins of empire, and the homeland offering a new vision of the city.

15. In a reading finely attuned to Dio's multiple personae, Ma proposes that his account is "not about the polis, but about images of the polis, and the use of such images to talk to the polis about itself" (109).

16. Dio compares himself with Odysseus overtly in Oration 13, *In Athens*, about his banishment. We've also seen this analogy in the Philostratus anecdote about Dio's behavior after the announcement of the assassination of Domitian (*Lives* ¶488).

17. When Dio disallows "representing the sorrows of Niobe or Thyestes by song or dance" (¶120), he dissents from a more common second sophistic endorsement of classical performative traditions and emotional states (see chapter 7 on Libanius). He mentions specifically Athenian and Theban dramatic traditions, though he does admit the value of sacred choruses.

18. Scholars are cautious in their assumptions about the performance situation for these discourses. Trajan is not mentioned, and there is no external evidence that Dio delivered them (in person or writing) to the emperor. On the other hand, there is internal evidence, especially in Oration 3, that Trajan is the audience (Cahoon, vol. 1, 1, 103). Jones suggests that the imagined dialogues, Orations 2 and 4, may have been delivered before Trajan (*Roman World* 115n5, 193). Whitmarsh keeps the question open about whether or not Trajan heard the works and proposes that Dio presented them publicly to a Greek audience in a "theatre or civic assembly-space" (*Greek Literature* 187). Informing my reading is Whitmarsh's extensive discussion of the kingship orations in a section of his chapter 4 called "Staging the Dionic Man" (183–216).

19. For readings of these orations, see C. P. Jones (*Roman World* 115–23), Moles ("Kingship"), and Whitmarsh (*Greek Literature* 186–216). Davis and Vitanza have some interesting comments on Dio's fourth oration in their entry on Diogenes of Sinope in Ballif and Moran.

20. For extended treatments of Foucault's work with Greek rhetoric, see Walzer, "*Parrēsia*, Foucault, and the Classical Rhetorical Tradition," and Jarratt, "Untimely Historiography?"

3. An Imperial Anti-sublime: Aristides' *Roman Oration*

1. Marcus Aurelius ruled Rome jointly with Lucius Verus from 161 to 169, and when his son Commodus came of age, Marcus made him co-emperor (180–92).

2. Among Aristides' most important works for rhetoric as a discipline is his lengthy argument for the art of rhetoric in opposition to Plato: *Against Plato in Defense of Rhetoric*. See also Atwill and Portz for a new engagement with Aristides' Egyptian connections.

3. See Whitmarsh, *Greek Literature* (especially 29–38), on his method of reading for a "politics of imitation": "literature in this period is a fundamentally creative *act* that possesses its own materiality and ideological immediacy; it is not simply the monumentalization of the author's psychic preoccupations" (32; emphasis in the original). I find Whitmarsh's method particularly apt for Aristides. But Whitmarsh's concentration on literature and deemphasis on rhetorical context doesn't work as well for situations where a sophist addresses auditors, including Roman emperors, directly in his own voice, as in the *Letter to Smyrna* discussed in the last section of this chapter. See chapter 7 for a fuller discussion of such *parrhēsiatic* moments.

4. I rely on Oliver's 1953 edition and Behr's 1981 translation with some adjustments, except where noted.

5. With reference to Polybius' *Histories* and Dionysius of Halicarnassus' *Roman Antiquities*, Oliver asks, "how much did Aristides owe to the rhetorically educated historians of the Hellenistic Period?" (882).

6. Zeitlin remarks on the uncanny quality of visual encounters within Homeric figures and places in the second sophists' rhetoric. Her analysis highlights the theatrical or spectacular in orations of Dio Chrysostom and texts by Lucian with similar qualities ("Visions").

7. Charles Behr's biography of Aristides based on *Sacred Tales* has much to say about the disastrous voyage to Rome in 144 CE and the young orator's subsequent course of treatment in Pergamum as an incubant in the Temple of Asclepius (41–60). Behr asserts that, because of Aristides' bad health during his first stay, he could not have delivered the oration on that occasion and argues for a date of 155. Swain also accepts that date (*Hellenism* 265–66).

Pernot ("Aelius Aristides" 176) and Oliver believe that Aristides delivered the oration on his first visit to Rome (143 or 144). I accept this scenario and work from the premise that the young Aristides arrived at Rome, delivered his encomium, and then fell ill. The possible connection between the stress produced by the performance in a colonial context and Aristides' illness has been explored by P. C. Miller.

8. The scholarship on this topic is extensive. Mary Beard and John Henderson provide a spirited introduction. Miles offers a fascinating investigation of the Roman plunder of Greek art and some attendant political, cultural, and material consequences for Rome from the earliest conquest of Greek cities up to the fourth-century CE relocation of the empire's capital to Constantinople.

9. The use of the term *phantasia* in psychoanalytic theory bears some relationship to its Aristotelian source and rhetorical applications. Although the term can refer to an individual's daydreams or unconscious wishes, according to Laplanche and Pontalis, "phantasies are still scripts (scenarios) of organised scenes which are capable of dramatisation—usually in a visual form" (284).

10. Porter offers a useful summary of the debates about the identity and chronology of Longinus. He finds that "one broad consensus opinion puts the treatise in the first century A.D." (274n1).

11. Philostratus' biography of Herodes Atticus, a contemporary of Aristides, offers an example of this type of sophist (*Lives* 2.545–66).

12. Another possible resonance of this figure comes from the description of Odysseus' rhetoric in the *Iliad*, book 3. At a pause in the conflict, Helen has been summoned by Priam, aloft the ramparts of Troy overlooking the field of battle, to identify the Greek warriors. Helen begins to describe Odysseus and is then assisted by Antenor, a Trojan leader who had hosted an embassy for Helen's release (11.203–24). He proceeds to contrast the rhetorical style of Menelaus, who spoke "rapidly, in few words but [was] exceedingly lucid," with that of Odysseus, who pretended to be sullen and a fool, but when he let loose, words drifted "down like the winter snows" (trans. Lattimore).

13. On Rome as a space of power, see Cassin "Time of Deliberation." On city space as labyrinthine and dreamlike in the Greek novel, see Nimis.

14. The Servian Wall built in the fourth century BCE became irrelevant in the first centuries of the empire as the city grew beyond it. The Aurelian Wall was constructed in the third century to keep out the Germans tribes. See Fields and Dennis. Woolf ("Roman Peace") discusses the rhetorical effects of discourse about walls.

15. Here the poet anachronistically describes the hoplite battle formation, which came into use far later than the period of the legendary Trojan encounter.

16. The verb here refers to catching fish in a net and metaphorically to sweeping up humans in a dragnet (*LSJ*). The figure of the net recalls Libanius' reference to the cable or chain of gold that Zeus threatens to use against the other Olympians in the *Iliad*, book 2, to control their actions. See chapter 1.

4. Julia Domna's Dilemma: Sophistic Improvisation in the Eastern Empire

1. C. P. Jones ("Apollonius") dates the *Life of Apollonius of Tyana*, the longest biography surviving from antiquity, after Domna's death in 217 but before the publication of *Lives of the Sophists* in the 230s. Bowie puts it somewhat later ("Philostratus" 29).

2. It is thought that the Latin "Julia" was probably added after she became empress, so she is referred to as Domna in the scholarship (Levick).

3. Levick's evaluation of previous histories, both those written in Domna's era and nineteenth-century imperializing ones, calls attention to gender and ethnic biases. Her method has a kinship with that presented by Susan Romano for a similar project: trying to piece together the life of a woman from sixteenth-century New Spain from a very few textual and visual sources. Such feminist historiographical methods have recently been advanced under the term *critical imagination* by Royster and Kirsch.

4. We saw the same phenomenon in chapter 2 with Dio Chrysostom's fictionalized trial. The narrator is concerned that the rural family get justice but treats the legal process and its rhetoric with disdain.

5. Jones translates *deinos* as "craft": what Demetrius in the first century BCE identified as the forceful style. See also Ahl on *deinos* as a feature of *parrhēsia* in chapter 1.

6. A similar scene is enacted at the climax of Heliodorus' novel, *Ethiopian Story*, analyzed in chapter 6.

7. Scholars are divided on the question of Syrian religion as sun worship. The most current view is that this is a mistaken association. Philostratus may include it in the biography because of the resonances with Neoplatonic philosophy: both imagine a harmonious universe ordered by a virtuous force.

8. It's worth mentioning that the character Demetrius bears the name of the author of the Hellenistic text *On Style* that introduces *eschēmatismenos logos*: figured speech.

5. Curated Visions of Manhood in Philostratus' *Imagines*

1. In order to keep these questions of identity open, some scholars refer to the Philostrati (plural) as the "author" of various works. Those who wish to pursue the mystery of Philostratan identities may consult Bowie, "Philostratus" (19–25); Wright, introduction to *Lives* (ix–xxii); and Fairbanks, introduction to *Imagines* (xv–xvii).

2. The term ekphrasis (like logos, doxa, and polis) has become so common in English that it is rarely italicized. I follow that practice for the singular noun (ekphrasis), its plural (ekphraseis), and the adjective (ekphrastic/ecphrastic).

3. Although the term *progymnasmat*a appears in the fourth-century BCE *Rhetoric for Alexander*, a full written account of this Greek curriculum first becomes available, in the extant classical literature, through Quintilian's *Orator's Education* in the first century CE. The curriculum is treated fully in the Greek handbooks of Theon, Hermogenes, Aphthonius, and Nicolaus (first–fourth centuries CE). See Kennedy, *Progymnasmata*; Pernot, *Rhetoric* (146–51); Webb, *Ekphrasis* (49–59).

4. Webb offers a welcome reorientation toward the handbook tradition and a helpful focus on rhetorical effect, but she is not enthusiastic about modern appropriations of the term to refer almost exclusively to works of art (*Ekphrasis* 5, 45, 81–83). Thus Philostratus' *Imagines* plays a fairly minor role in her erudite and otherwise comprehensive study (187–90).

5. For an extended discussion of ancient ekphrasis with reference to its appropriation in the early modern age, see Plett (37–50).

6. Much ink has been spilled over the terms *enargeia* and *energeia*, with authors claiming vigorously that one is meant when the other is used. I find it helpful for distinguishing them to think of the roots: *argos*, shining, bright, glistening; *ergon*, work (*LSJ*). Andrew Sprague Becker offers a useful overview of Greek definitions of the terms in the rhetorical handbooks from Aelius Theon (perhaps first century CE) through Nikolaus of Myra (fifth century CE), all of whom use forms of the word *enargeia* to emphasize vividness and the effect of "bringing-before-the-eyes" (8–9). Webb's discussion of the combined influence of the two terms in the phenomenon of ekphrasis is illuminating: "There is a certain associative logic in the way in which ekphrasis is both a force acting upon a listener [*energeia*] and a means of depicting action in words [*enargeia*]" (*Ekphrasis* 86). She emphasizes

that ekphrasis "does not only have objects existing in space as its referent but has a temporal dimension" (85); thus, "there is an association between movement, and its rendering of space through time, and vividness: between *energeia* and *enargeia*" (85–86).

7. I am grateful to Diana Shaffer for research assistance in the early stages of this project. Her own fine essay on the subject has informed my reading.

8. Dio Chrysostom's *Olympic Discourse* (Oration 12) from 97 CE offers one of the best examples of this *topos*, as the orator views a monumental statue of Zeus and constructs a debate between the sculptor and poet about representing the grandeur of the god.

9. Anne Carson, in her provocative essay "Simonides Painter," refers to the fifth-century BCE poet as a "proto-sophist" because of his interest, alongside Gorgias and Protagoras, in artistic illusion, both verbal and visual. Her note 1 (61) offers a useful summary of work on the comparison between poetry and painting. See also Rosenmeyer on Gorgias and *apatē* (artistic deception).

10. W. T. J. Mitchell's chapter "Ekphrasis and the Other" from *Picture Theory* deserves mention in this context as well. Mitchell takes the ekphrastic paradigm to be that of (Hegelian) subjectivity: an object confronts a speaking/seeing subject who interpellates it as "other" and must do something with that otherness: bridge it, fear it, be indifferent to it.

11. Anderson remarks that a "tendency of Greeks to persevere in the preservation of things Greek would have provoked admiration from [Romans] in search of a complex of historical and legendary traditions longer and more illustrious than their own" (*Second Sophistic* 7). He emphasizes the second sophists' efforts to preserve a "strong sense of continuing Hellenic identity" (3), characterizing their concentration on the past as a survival strategy under the political impotence of their present time (101). I concur with these observations, but when Anderson suggests that the second sophists imaginatively collapsed past and present (83), he moves toward the historiographic positions of Kennedy and Brown refuted in chapter 1—toward nostalgia and calcification and away from the potential for critical history.

12. Billault finds the persona in *Imagines* among all those created by Philostratus to be the one most like the author himself.

13. See chapter 3 and Pernot, "Aelius Aristides," for more about second sophistic silence regarding Roman imperial presence and colonizing activities.

14. John Gage, in the introduction to his collection of Goethe's writings on art, notes that the author was less interested in developing a coherent critical position than in "approaching experience visually" (ix). For Goethe, Gage

writes, "the contemplation of art was . . . above all an imaginative activity" (xv). Given these dispositions, we can see the attraction of Philostratus' ekphrastic project for Goethe.

15. Exchanges between the sophist and the boy interrupt the flow of description at the following points: 1.1, 1.13, 1.15, 1.24, 1.28, 2.1, 2.5, 2.8, 2.17, 2.21, 2.34. I take the order of the ekphraseis as we have them today to be Philostratus' design. There are risks in such an assumption. References to "Philostratus" and works attached to that name in the tenth-century encyclopedia known as the *Suda* are confused and in any case do not include a table of contents for *Eikones*. The earliest manuscripts appeared in the thirteenth and fourteenth centuries, and the work enjoyed five editions (German and French) in the eighteenth and nineteenth centuries. As I am not a specialist in manuscript studies, I cannot pronounce definitively on the issue, but in none of the scholarship on the text that I have read does anyone question whether the order that has come down to us is indeed Philostratus' (see, e.g., Webb, "Greek Grammatical Glosses"). Questions concerning the logic of the order—whether or not it is "confused"—are another matter, about which the rest chapter 5 has something to say. I hope my interpretation presents convincing internal evidence for self-conscious ordering—a curation, so to speak—that informs the educational aims of the work.

16. My interest in youth as a category has been inspired by Jasmine Lee's dissertation: "Appraising Our Investments in Youth: Rhetorical Education in the Age of Neoliberalism" (University of California, Irvine, 2018).

17. Foucault's assertion that the love of boys in this period "was still common and still regarded as a natural thing" (*Care* 189) is contradicted by his observation that Roman law in the period, while not forbidding homosexuality, protected free adolescents from abuse and violence (190). Richlin points out the difficulty in determining whether the second sophist refers to sexual practices of his day or those of an earlier period, thus performing a kind of "retrosexuality."

18. In his extensive study of Roman sexual practices, Craig A. Williams notes that male-male sex is unremarkable between Roman men and slaves but unacceptable between free men. As in the Greek culture that the Romans ambivalently adopted, young male beauty is prized.

19. Quintilian mentions Ovid in book 10.1 in a discussion of the kinds of reading suitable for aspiring orators. He finds the work lacking in seriousness, even the epic (10.1.88). In the genre of elegy, Ovid is "more sportive" (*lascivior*) than other Roman poets (10.1.93); in tragedy, however, "Ovid

shows, in my opinion, to what heights that poet might have risen if he had been ready to curb his talents instead of indulging them" (10.1.98).

20. Michel Foucault's account of sexual practices in the postclassical era would seem to contradict this statement (*Care*). But he is working from Greek materials. It's unclear whether his findings would apply to Roman men in general. The excesses of particular emperors also stand as an exception. Elagabalus, for example, during whose reign (218–222) Philostratus lived, plumbed the depths of almost unimaginable depravity, some of them involving outlandish and violent sexual practices. He is characterized as transgendered in some accounts. See *Historia Augusta*, "The Life of Elagabalus." Again, the dissemination of such practices would seem to be limited.

21. Richlin briefly addresses Philostratus' treatment of women in *Lives*, finding the text informed by a "butch aesthetic" and by "virulent misogyny."

22. The bibliography is too extensive at this point for a quick summary, but those seeking a point of entry might consult an important early collection of essays from 1984 (Peradotto and Sullivan) that still offers crucial touch points by major scholars.

23. The Greek words translated by Fairbanks as "repulsive fuzzy surface" include *to erion*, wool, and *hupomochthēron*, an unusual word that means something like "in a wretched condition or sorry plight related to toil or labor" (*LSJ*). "Savage" is a translation of *agrios*, which can also mean simply "wild." This translation injects a tone of moral sanction not necessarily present in the original.

24. Parthians occupied the territory now known as Iran. This territory was earlier inhabited by Persians, and there was a cultural blending of Persian and Parthian dress, manners, and customs. Mithradates VI, for example, was a Parthian who self-consciously styled himself in Persian ways (Mayor).

6. No Animals Were Harmed: Sophistic Rhetoric in Heliodorus' *Aithiopika*

1. In *A Million and One Gods*, Page duBois makes a case against the use of the term *pagan* to refer to ancient polytheistic religious practices. From Latin *pagus*, meaning a territory or region, the term came to refer pejoratively to country people or rustics, and it was taken up by early Christians to designate, and denigrate, those who practiced polytheistic religions. I respect her reading of the term, but I've chosen to use it as a neutral designation

for traditional Greco-Roman religious practices because of its continued use in much of the scholarly work on ancient religion (see, e.g., Bradbury, "Constantine" and "Julian's Pagan Revival"; Kennedy, *Classical Rhetoric* 143; Pernot, *Rhetoric in Antiquity* 204; Rives).

2. Although he was raised a Christian within the Constantine dynasty, Julian (born 331/32) embraced the Greek *paideia* and studied in Athens, where he encountered Neoplatonism and the Mithraic mysteries. His religious beliefs are expounded in his Oration 4, *Hymn to King Helios* (perhaps composed in 362). Other sources for Julian's life and beliefs are Libanius' *Funeral Oration over Julian* (Oration 18) and the historical fragment of Ammianus Marcellinus, a Roman soldier from Antioch who fought with Julian in his final campaign. Julian entered public life in 355, became emperor in 361, and was killed in battle against the Persians in 363. For a detailed review of dates proposed for Heliodorus' novel, see Bowie, "Literary Milieux."

3. A short catalog of the complete novels with the authors' cities of origin includes Chariton (Aphrodisias/Turkey), *Chaereas and Callirhoe* (mid-first century?); Xenophon of Ephesus (Turkey), *An Ephesian Story* (mid-second century?); Achilles Tatius (Alexandria, Egypt?), *Leucippe and Clitophon* (late second century); Longus (Lesbos, Greece?), *Daphnis and Chloe* (200?); and Heliodorus (Emesa, Syria) *Aithiopika* (mid- to late fourth century?).

4. I use the term *story* in its technical, narratological sense to indicate the actual chronology of events as opposed to their order in the narrative (discourse). Arguably the most narratively complex of the extant novels, the narrative (or discourse) begins with Charikleia and Theagenes in Egypt in the aftermath of a slaughter by bandits. Byzantine rhetor Michael Psellos offers a vivid figure for the narrative structure of *Aithiopika*: "like a coiled snake, concealing the head inside the coil, it displays the rest of its body . . . the onset falls in the middle, elevating the centre to the beginning" (qtd. in Agapitos 133–34).

5. In "Greek 'Figured Speech' on Imperial Rome," Pernot sets out several categories of figured speech, including cases in which a character in the text serves as a stand-in, or "mask," for a historical figure. His example comes from Dio Chrysostom's second *Discourse on Kingship*, wherein Alexander, in dialogue with his father, Philip, may serve as a mask for the emperor Trajan (140–41). While Pernot points out the ambiguity of masks in Dio's sophisticated use of the technique, I'm proposing a more direct correspondence between the fictional king Hydaspes and the emperor Julian.

6. The Greek edition consulted is Héliodor, *Les Éthiopiques*, published by Budé. Translation by Morgan (Reardon, pp. 349–588.)

7. Rives attests to human sacrifice in "the Punic cities of the western Mediterranean, various German tribes, and perhaps some Celtic tribes as well" but finds evidence for human sacrifice among Greeks and Italians in the ancient period "controversial" ("Human Sacrifice" 66). See also S. Brown.

8. On Charikleia as a masterful rhetor, see Pernot, "Chariclée." See Winkler on the "mendacity" or "strategic falsehood" of Kalisiris in the novel. On lie versus fiction (*pseudos, plasma*) in second sophistic rhetoric, see Cassin, *L'effet* (473–79).

9. In Aeschylus' *Agamemnon*, Iphigenia is compared to a sacrificial sheep (11.1415–18). Cassandra, in the same drama, characterizes her own execution as a sacrifice. The chorus asks, "how can you walk to the altar so bravely,/ like some sacrificial cow driven by the gods?" (11.1297–98; trans. Meineck).

10. Lucian's viciously sarcastic oration *On Sacrifices* presents a disgustingly vivid version of the argument that the gods do not want blood sacrifices.

7. "Tiresome" Libanius: Speaking to Empire, Addressing Emperors

1. *Poikilos* is an adjective meaning multicolored, changeful, various, elaborate, variegated, intricate, riddling, ambiguous, artful, and cunning (*LSJ*).

2. Libanius was an incredibly prolific speaker and writer. We have preserved from his voluminous corpus sixty-four orations, over fifteen hundred letters, the autobiography, and a collection of *progymnasmatic* exercises (recently edited and translated by Gibson). A manageable selection of the work is usefully sorted into three Loeb volumes by Norman. *Selected Orations*, volume 2 (published in 1977), includes the oration analyzed here plus a number of political orations from the same period. Both roman and arabic numbers are used in this volume, so, for example, the "tiresome" oration is titled Oration 2 but referred to in the running head as Oration II.

3. Edward Watts discusses the "kinship" between Aristides and Libanius, referring to an extraordinary letter the latter wrote thanking a friend for sending a portrait of the second-century sophist. Libanius' behavior—he composes the letter while viewing the portrait and reading Aristides' work—suggests to Watts something like idol worship (39–40). See also Van Hoof ("Introduction") and Cribiore (*Libanius* 90).

4. Wiemer is a crucial resource on this point. Walker provides a lively overview of encounters between second sophists and emperors from Philostratus' *Lives*, including Aristides' appeal to Marcus Aurelius for aid to Smyrna (*Rhetoric and Poetics* 83–85). On this event, see also chapter 3 of this book.

5. Was simply existing as a colonial intellectual in the Roman empire hazardous to the health? Studies by Holmes on Aristides' body and by Gleason, *Making Men*, on masculinity, sexuality, and the body in the famous agon between Favorinus and Polemo suggest that the sophistic body under colonial rule is a subject ripe for further research. See Hawhee on the healthy gymnastic embodiment of sophists (*Bodily Arts* 110–13).

6. Norman's extensive and historically informed notes remind the reader that Libanius, like most autobiographers, is capable of distortion, selective memory, and other self-serving rhetorical tactics. In this case, the beloved teacher whom he represents himself as saving was also the object of his intense professional impatience. Libanius wanted his teacher to step down from the position of the city's chief sophist in favor of himself, his student. Zenobius' death by natural causes resolved the impasse.

7. Wiemer places fourteen to sixteen orations in the category of political orations during this period (201).

8. See Pernot's review of Malcolm Heath's 2004 *Menander: A Rhetor in Context* for a discussion of the intersections of deliberative and epideictic rhetoric in Menander's texts and in the fourth century more generally.

9. An additional piece of evidence of Libanius' passion for free speaking can be found in a short *progymnasmatic* exercise, an encomium of the Homeric character Thersites, maligned by Odysseus for speaking up against Agamemnon and thus an early prototype of the *parrhēsiastes* (*Encomium*).

10. This position contrasts sharply with the stance of Dio Chrysostom in Oration 7 (see chapter 2).

11. Woods has written about this phenomenon and its gendered potential by drawing on the autobiography of St. Augustine.

12. A word search I performed in Perseus, the online compendium of classical literature hosted by Tufts University, turned up almost five hundred references to *barus*. The *LSJ* entry for the term is available here: http://www.perseus.tufts.edu/hopper/text?doc=Perseus%3Atext%3A1999.04.0057%3Aentry%3Dbaru%2Fs (accessed 17 May 2019).

13. Wendy Brown takes a Foucauldian approach in *States of Injury*, arguing that a political truth derived from "wounded attachments" is at risk of

reinscribing structures of domination. Gerard Hauser's recent book *Prisoners of Conscience* features many suffering political subjects; however, these rhetors derive their agency not from the suffering but by virtue of using their imprisonment as a locus of political conscience and resistance (see, for example, 59, 67, 170 passim).

8. Conclusion: Refractions of Empire

1. See Terada for a meditation on addressability in the era of *pax Americana*. She contrasts the self-immolation of Mohamed Bouazizi with the incident in which an Iraqi journalist, Muntadhar al-Zaidi, threw his shoes at George W. Bush in December 2008.

2. In making this claim, I appear to be overlooking the vigorous theoretical efforts of rhetoric and communications scholars who have challenged the theoretical grounds—possessive individualism, humanism, liberal democracy, and referential linguistics, among others—on which rational free speech is based. The phenomenon I point to here is a gap between those theories and the discourses and postures most often chosen for teaching and for political participation. For a lively entry into the debate between advocates of rhetorical agency and those of various "post" theories (postmodernism, poststructuralism, posthumanism, etc.), see Lundberg and Gunn.

3. See essays in the recently published collection, *Unruly Rhetorics*, for insights into the current proliferation of performative political discourses (Alexander et al.).

4. See Jameson on a new flourishing of utopia "as a political slogan and a politically energizing perspective" projected through various literary and cinematic forms in the current era (*Archaeologies* xii).

WORKS CITED AND CONSULTED

Ackerman, John, and David Coogan, editors. *The Public Work of Rhetoric*. U of South Carolina P, 2010.

Aeschylus. *Agamemnon*. Translated by Peter Meineck, Hackett Publishing, 1998.

Agamben, Giorgio. *Homo Sacer: Sovereign Power and Bare Life*. Translated by Daniel Heller-Roazen, Stanford UP, 1998.

———. *State of Exception*. Translated by Kevin Attell, U of Chicago P, 2005.

Agapitos, Panagiotis A. "Narrative, Rhetoric, and 'Drama' Rediscovered: Scholars and Poets in Byzantium Interpret Heliodoros." Hunter, *Studies*, pp. 125–56.

Ahl, Frederick. "The Art of Safe Criticism in Greece and Rome." *American Journal of Philology*, vol. 105, no. 2, Summer 1984, pp. 174–208.

Alcaeus. Fragment 6. *Greek Lyric I. Sappho and Alcaeus*. Edited and translated by David A. Campbell. Loeb Classical Library 142. Harvard UP, 1982. p. 239.

Alcock, Susan E. *Graecia Capta: The Landscapes of Roman Greece*. Cambridge UP, 1993.

Alexander, Jonathan, et al., editors. *Unruly Rhetorics*. U of Pittsburgh P, 2018.

Ammianus Marcellinus. *The Roman History of Ammianus Marcellinus during the Reigns of the Emperors Constantius, Julian, Jovianus, Valentinian, and Valens*. Translated by C. D. Yonge, G. Bell and Sons, 1911. *Project Gutenberg*, gutenberg.org/ebooks/28587.

Anderson, Graham. *Ancient Fiction: The Novel in the Graeco-Roman World*. Barnes and Noble, 1984.

———. *Philostratus: Biography and Belles Lettres in the Third Century* A.D. Croom Helm, 1986.

———. *The Second Sophistic: A Cultural Phenomenon in the Roman Empire*. Routledge, 1993.

Ando, Clifford. *Imperial Ideology and Provincial Loyalty in the Roman Empire*. U of California P, 2000.

Arendt, Hannah. *The Human Condition*. U of Chicago P, 1958.

Aristides, Aelius. Oration 19. *A Letter to the Emperors concerning Smyrna*. Behr, vol. 2, pp. 10-13.

———. Oration 18. *A Monody for Smyrna*. Behr, vol. 2, pp. 7-9.

———. Oration 26. *Regarding Rome*. Behr, vol. 2., pp. 71–97.

———. Oration 2. *To Plato: In Defense of Oratory*. Behr, vol. 1, pp. 78–150.

———. *Roman Oration*. Oliver, pp. 895–907.

Aristotle. *Movement of Animals*. *Aristotle*, translated by A. L. Peck and E. S. Forster, vol. 12, Loeb Classical Library 323, Harvard UP, 1937, pp. 440–79.

———. *On Rhetoric: A Theory of Civic Discourse*. 2nd ed. Translated by George A. Kennedy, Oxford UP, 2007.

———. *On the Soul*. *Aristotle*, translated by W. S. Hett, vol. 8., Loeb Classical Library 288, Harvard UP, 1957, pp. 8–206.

Atwill, Janet M. *Rhetoric Reclaimed: Aristotle and the Liberal Arts Tradition*. Cornell UP, 1998.

Atwill, Janet M., and Josie Portz. "Identity and Difference in Aelius Aristides' 'Regarding Sarapis.'" *Advances in the History of Rhetoric*, vol. 22, no. 2, 2019, pp. 179-93.

Aune, James Arnt. *Rhetoric and Marxism*. Westview, 1994.

Ballif, Michelle, and Michael G. Moran, editors. *Classical Rhetorics and Rhetoricians: Critical Studies and Sources*. Praeger, 2005.

Bann, Stephen. "Philostratus and the *Narcissus* of Caravaggio." Bowie and Elsner, pp. 342–55.

Beard, Mary, and John Henderson. *Classical Art: From Greece to Rome*. Oxford UP, 2001.

Becker, Andrew Sprague. "Reading Poetry through a Distant Lens: Ecphrasis, Ancient Greek Rhetoricians, and the Pseudo-Hesiodic 'Shield of Herakles.'" *American Journal of Philology*, vol. 113, no. 1, Spring 1992, pp. 5–24.

Behr, Charles Allison. *Aelius Aristides and the Sacred Tales*. A. M. Hakkert, 1968.

———, translator. *P. Aelius Aristides. The Complete Works*. 2 vols. Brill, 1981 (vol. 2), 1986 (vol. 1).

Benediktson, D. Thomas. *Literature and the Visual Arts in Ancient Greece and Rome*. U of Oklahoma P, 2000.

Benjamin, Bret. "Making the Case: *Bamako* and the Problem of Anti-imperial Art." *The Megarhetorics of Global Development*, edited by Rebecca Dingo and J. Blake Scott, U of Pittsburgh P, 2012, pp. 199–232.

Berry, Edmund. "Dio Chrysostom the Moral Philosopher." *Greece and Rome*, vol. 30, Apr. 1983, pp. 70–80.

Bhabha, Homi. *The Location of Culture*. Routledge, 1994.

Billault, Alain. *L'univers de Philostrate*. Latomus, 2000.

Birley, Anthony R. *Septimius Severus: The African Emperor*. B. T. Batsford, 1988.

Borger, Julian, and Michael White. "US Public Backs Bush to Go It Alone." *The Guardian*, 11 Feb. 2003.

Bourdieu, Pierre. *Outline of a Theory of Practice*. Translated by Richard Nice, Cambridge UP, 1977.

Bowersock, G. W. *Greek Sophists in the Roman Empire*. Oxford UP, 1969.

Bowie, E. L. "Greeks and Their Past in the Second Sophistic." *Past and Present*, vol. 46, Feb. 1970, pp. 3–41.

Bowie, Ewen. "Literary Milieux." Whitmarsh, *Cambridge Companion*, pp. 17–38.

———. "Philostratus: The Life of a Sophist." Bowie and Elsner, pp. 19–32.

Bowie, Ewen, and Jaś Elsner, editors. *Philostratus*. Cambridge UP, 2009.

Bradbury, Scott. "Constantine and the Problem of Anti-pagan Legislation in the Fourth Century." *Classical Philology*, vol. 89, no. 2, Apr. 1994, pp. 129–39.

———. "Julian's Pagan Revival and the Decline of Blood Sacrifice." *Phoenix*, vol. 49, no. 4, Winter 1994, pp. 331–56.

Brown, Eric. *Stoic Cosmopolitanism*. Cambridge UP, forthcoming.

Brown, Peter. *Power and Persuasion in Late Antiquity: Toward a Christian Empire*. U of Wisconsin P, 1992.

Brown, Susanna Shelby. *Late Carthaginian Child Sacrifice and Sacrificial Monuments in Their Mediterranean Context*. JSOT/ASOR Monograph Series 3, 1991.

Brown, Wendy. *States of Injury: Power and Freedom in Late Modernity*. Princeton UP, 1995.

Brunt, P. A. "Aspects of the Social Thought of Dio Chrysostom and of the Stoics." *Proceedings of the Cambridge Philological Society*, vol. 19, 1973, pp. 9–34.

———. *Roman Imperial Themes*. Clarendon Press, 1990.

———. "Stoicism and the Principate." *Papers of the British School at Rome*, vol. 43, 1975, pp. 7–35.

Bryson, Norman. "Philostratus and the Imaginary Museum." Goldhill and Osborne, pp. 255–83.

Burke, Kenneth. *A Grammar of Motives*. U of California P, 1945.

———. *The Philosophy of Literary Form*. Rev. ed., Vintage Books, 1957.

———. *A Rhetoric of Motives*. U of California P, 1950.

Burkert, Walter. *Greek Religion: Archaic and Classical*. Translated by John Raffan, Basil Blackwell, 1985.

"Bush Says He Is Undeterred by Weekend Protests against War," *The New York Times*, 18 Feb. 2003.

Butler, Judith. *Antigone's Claim: Kinship between Life and Death*. Columbia UP, 2002.

Cameron, Alan. *The Last Pagans of Rome*. Oxford UP, 2011.

Carruthers, Mary. *The Book of Memory: A Study of Memory in Medieval Culture*. Cambridge UP, 1990.

Carson, Anne. "Simonides Painter." *Innovations of Antiquity*, edited by Ralph Hexter and Daniel Seldon, Routledge, 1992, pp. 51–64.

Cassin, Barbara. *L'effet sophistique*. Gallimard, 1995.

———. *Sophistical Practice: Toward a Consistent Relativism*. Fordham UP, 2014.

———. "Time of Deliberation and Space of Power: Athens and Rome, the First Conflict." *Javnost—The Public*, vol. 12, no. 4, 2006, pp. 39–44.

Cassius Dio. *Dio's Roman History*, vol. 6: *Books 51–55*. Translated by Earnest Cary, Loeb Classical Library 86, Harvard UP, 1917.

Cheng, Anne Anlin. *The Melancholy of Race: Psychoanalysis, Assimilation, and Hidden Grief*. Oxford UP, 2001.

Cicero. *On Invention*. Translated by H. M. Hubbell, Loeb Classical Library 386, Harvard UP, 1949.

———. *On Duties*. Translated by Walter Miller, Loeb Classical Library 30, Harvard UP, 1913.

———. *On the Orator*. Translated by E. W. Sutton and H. Rackham, Loeb Classical Library 348–49, Harvard UP, 1942. 2 vols.

Clark, Suzanne. "Julia Kristeva: Rhetorica and the Woman as Stranger." Lunsford, pp. 305–18.

Cloud, Dana. "The Irony Bribe and Reality Television: Investment and Detachment in *The Bachelor*." *Critical Studies in Media Communication*, vol. 27, no. 5, 2010, pp. 413–37.

Conley, Thomas M. *Rhetoric in the European Tradition*. Longman, 1990.

Connolly, Joy. *The State of Speech: Rhetoric and Political Thought in Ancient Rome*. Princeton UP, 2007.

———. *Vile Eloquence: Performance and Identity in Greco-Roman Rhetoric*. 1997. U of Pennsylvania, PhD dissertation.

———. "Virile Tongues: Rhetoric and Masculinity." *A Companion to Roman Rhetoric*, edited by William J. Dominik and Jon Hall, Wiley-Blackwell, 2007, pp. 83–97.

Crawford, M. H. "Greek Intellectuals and the Roman Aristocracy in the First Century B.C." Garnsey and Whittaker, pp. 193–207.

Crewe, Jonathan. "Believing the Impossible: *Aethiopika* and Critical Romance." *Modern Philology*, vol. 106, no. 4, 2009, pp. 601–16.

Cribiore, Raffaella. *Libanius the Sophist: Rhetoric, Reality, and Religion in the Fourth Century*. Cornell UP, 2013.

———. *The School of Libanius in Late Antique Antioch*. Princeton UP, 2007.

Crowley, Sharon, and Debra Hawhee. *Ancient Rhetorics for Contemporary Students*. 5th ed., Pearson, 2009.

Davis, D. Diane, and Victor J. Vitanza. "Diogenes of Sinope." Ballif and Moran, pp. 132–36.

Dawson, Doyne. *Cities of the Gods: Communist Utopias in Greek Thought*. Oxford UP, 1992.

Demetrius. *On Style*. *Aristotle*, translated by Doreen C. Innes, based on W. Rhys Roberts, vol. 23, Loeb Classical Library 199, Harvard UP, 1995, pp. 307–521.

Desideri, Paolo. "City and Country in Dio." Swain, *Dio Chrysostom*, pp. 93–107.

Detienne, Marcel. "Culinary Practices and the Spirit of Sacrifice." *The Cuisine of Sacrifice among the Greeks*, edited by Marcel Detienne and Jean-Pierre Vernant, translated by Paula Wissing, U of Chicago P, 1989, pp. 1–20.

Dio Chrysostom. *Seventh Discourse*, or *Euboean Discourse*. Translated by J. W. Cohoon, vol. 1, Loeb Classical Library 257, Harvard UP, 1932, pp. 285–373.

———. *Thirteenth Discourse: In Athens, about His Banishment*. Translated by J. W. Cohoon, vol. 2, Loeb Classical Library 339, Harvard UP, 1939, pp. 89–122.

Dionysius of Halicarnassus. Book 7.70–73. *The Roman Antiquities*, translated by Earnest Cary, vol. 4, Loeb Classical Library 364, Harvard UP, 1943, pp. 356–81. 7 vols.

Dowden, Ken. "Pouvoir Divin, Discours Humain chez Héliodore" *Discours et Débats dans l'ancien Roman*, edited by Bernard Pouderon and Jocelyne Peigney, Maison de l'Orient et de la Méditerranée, 2006, pp. 249–61.

Downey, Glanville. *Ancient Antioch*. Princeton UP, 1963.

———, translator. "Libanius' Oration in Praise of Antioch (Oration 11)." *Proceedings of the American Philosophical Society*, vol. 103, no. 5, Oct. 1959, pp. 652–86.

Dubel, Sandrine. "Colour in Philostratus' *Imagines*." Bowie and Elsner, pp. 309–21.

duBois, Page. *History, Rhetorical Description, and the Epic: From Homer to Spenser*. D. S. Brewer, 1982.

———. *A Million and One Gods: The Persistence of Polytheism*. Harvard UP, 2014.

Edwards, Catherine, and Greg Woolf. "Cosmopolis: Rome as World City." *Rome the Cosmopolis*, edited by Catherine Edwards and Greg Woolf, Cambridge UP, 2003, pp. 1–20.

Ehrbar, Ned. "'Julius Caesar' Star Opens Up about Controversial Shakespeare in the Park Production." *CBS News*, 26 June 2017, cbsnews.com/news/julius-caesar-shakespeare-in-the-park-corey-stoll/.

Elsner, Jaś. "A Protean Corpus." Bowie and Elsner, pp. 2–18.

Epictetus. *The Discourses as Reported by Arrian*. Translated by W. A. Oldfather, vol. 1, William Heinemann, 1961.

Erskine, Andrew. "Polybius among the Romans: Life in the Cyclops' Cave." Smith and Yarrow, pp. 17–32.

———. *Roman Imperialism*. Edinburgh UP, 2010.

Euripides. *Hippolytus*. *Euripides*, edited and translated by David Kovacs, vol. 2, Loeb Classical Library 484, Harvard UP, 1995.

———. *Iphigenia at Aulis*. *Euripides*, edited and translated by David Kovacs, vol. 6, Loeb Classical Library 495, Harvard UP, 2003.

Fairbanks, Arthur. Introduction. *Imagines, Philostratus; Descriptions, Callistratus*, translated by Fairbanks, William Heinemann, 1931, pp. xv–xxxii.

Fields, Nic, and Peter Dennis. *The Walls of Rome*. Osprey Publishing, 2008.

Fleming, David. "Rhetoric as a Course of Study." *College English*, vol. 61, no. 2, Nov. 1998, pp. 169–91.

Foerster, Richard, editor. "Libanii Oratio 11, Antiochikos." *Opera*, by Libanius, vol. 1, Teubner, 1903–27. Hildescheim, 1963, pp. 437–535.

Foster, John Bellamy. "The Rediscovery of Imperialism." *Monthly Review*, vol. 54, no. 6, Nov. 2002, pp. 1–16.

Foucault, Michel. *The Care of the Self*. *The History of Sexuality*. Translated by Robert Hurley, vol. 3, Pantheon, 1986.

———. *The Courage of Truth: Lectures at the Collège de France, 1983–1984*. Translated by Graham Burchell, Picador, 2011.

———. *Fearless Speech*. Edited by Joseph Pearson, Semiotext(e), 2001.

———. *The Government of Self and Others: Lectures at the Collège de France, 1982–1983*. Translated by Graham Burchell, Picador, 2011.

———. *Hermeneutics of the Subject: Lectures at the Collège de France, 1981–1982*. Translated by Graham Bruchell, Picador, 2005.

Fowler, D. P. "Narrate and Describe: The Problem of Ekphrasis." *Journal of Roman Studies*, vol. 81, 1991, pp. 25–35.

Fowler, Ryan C., and Alberto J. Quiroga Puertas. "A Prolegomena to the Third Sophistic." *Plato in the Third Sophistic*, edited by Fowler, De Gruyter, 2015, pp. 1–30.

Fraser, Nancy. "Rethinking the Public Sphere: A Contribution to the Critique of Actually Existing Democracy." *Habermas and the Public Sphere*, edited by Craig Calhoun, MIT P, 1992, pp. 109–42.

Freedland, Jonathan. "The Worst Wing." Review of *Plan of Attack*, by Bob Woodward, *The Guardian*, 7 May 2004.

Futre Pinheiro, Marília P. "Heliodorus, the *Ethiopian Story*." *A Companion to the Ancient Novel*, edited by Edmund P. Cueva and Shannon N. Byrne, Wiley & Sons, 2014, pp. 76–97.

Gage, John. Introduction. *Goethe on Art*, selected, edited, and translated by Gage, U of California P, 1980.

Garnsey, P. D. A., and C. R. Whittaker, editors. *Imperialism in the Ancient World*. Cambridge UP, 1978.

Garnsey, Peter. "Roman Citizenship and Roman Law in the Late Empire." *Approaching Late Antiquity: The Transformation from Early to Late Empire*, edited by Simon Swain and Mark Edwards, Oxford UP, 2004, pp. 133–55.

Garrett, Mary M. "Chinese Rhetoric." *Encyclopedia of Rhetoric*, edited by Thomas Sloane, Oxford UP, 2001, pp. 89–92.

Gasco, Fernando. "The Meeting between Aelius Aristides and Marcus Aurelius in Smyrna." *American Journal of Philology*, vol. 110, no. 3, Autumn 1989, pp. 471–78.

Genette, Gérard. *Figures of Literary Discourse*. Translated by Alan Sheridan, Columbia UP, 1984.

Gera, Deborah Levine. *Warrior Women: The Anonymous* Tractatus De Mulieribus. Brill, 1997.

Gibbon, Edward. *The History of the Decline and Fall of the Roman Empire*. Edited by J. B. Bury, Fred de Fau, 1906. 12 vols.

Gibson, Craig A. "Better Living through Prose Composition? Moral and

Compositional Pedagogy in Ancient Greek and Roman Progymnasmata." *Rhetorica*, vol. 32, no. 1, Dec. 2014, pp. 1–30.

———, translator. *Libanius's* Progymnasmata: *Model Exercises in Greek Prose Composition and Rhetoric*. Society of Biblical Literature, 2008.

Gleason, Maud W. "Greek Cities under Roman Rule." Potter, *Companion*, pp. 228–49.

———. *Making Men: Sophists and Self-Presentation in Ancient Rome*. Princeton UP, 1995.

Goethe, Johann Wolfgang von. *Goethe on Art*, selected, edited, and translated by John Gage, U of California P, 1980.

Goldhill, Simon, editor. *Being Greek under Rome: Cultural Identity, the Second Sophistic and the Development of Empire*. Cambridge UP, 2001.

———. "Introduction. Setting an Agenda: 'Everything is Greece to the Wise.'" Goldhill, *Being Greek*, pp. 1–25.

———. "Rhetoric and the Second Sophistic." *The Cambridge Companion to Ancient Rhetoric*, edited by Erik Gunderson, Cambridge UP, 2009, pp. 228–41.

———. "What Is Ekphrasis For?" *Classical Philology*, vol. 102, no. 1, 2007, pp. 1–19.

Goldhill, Simon, and Robin Osborne, editors. *Art and Text in Ancient Greek Culture*. Cambridge UP, 1994.

Goldsworthy, Adrian. "Imperial Women." *How Rome Fell: Death of a Superpower*. Yale UP, 2009, pp. 70–85.

Gorgias. *Encomium of Helen*. Translated by Brian R. Donovan, 1999. https://faculty.bemidjistate.edu/bdonovan/helen.html. Accessed 30 July 2019.

Habermas, Jürgen. *The Structural Transformation of the Public Sphere: An Inquiry into a Category of Bourgeois Society*. Translated by Thomas Burger, MIT P, 1991.

Hadas, Moses, editor. *Complete Works of Tacitus*. Translated by Alfred John Church and William Jackson Brodribb, Modern Library, 1942.

Hägg, Tomas. *The Novel in Antiquity*. U of California P, 1983.

Hagstrum, Jean H. *The Sister Arts: The Tradition of Literary Pictorialism and English Poetry from Dryden to Gray*. U of Chicago P, 1958.

Hamid, Mohsin. *Exit West*. Riverhead Books, 2017.

"Hans Ulrich Obrist: The Art of Curation." *The Guardian*, 23 Mar. 2014, www.theguardian.com/artanddesign/2014/mar/23/hans-ulrich-obrist-art-curator. Accessed 16 May 2019.

Hardt, Michael, and Antonio Negri. *Empire*. Harvard UP, 2000.

Hariman, Robert. "Political Parody and Public Culture." *Quarterly Journal of Speech*, vol. 94, no. 3, 2008, pp. 247–72.

———. *Political Style: The Artistry of Power.* U of Chicago P, 1995.

Hariman, Robert, and John Lucaites. *The Public Image: Photography and Civic Spectatorship.* U of Chicago, 2016.

Harris, William, and Brooke Holmes, editors. *Aelius Aristides between Greece, Rome, and the Gods.* Brill, 2008.

Hartnett, Stephen John, and Laura Ann Stengrim. *Globalization and Empire: The U.S. Invasion of Iraq, Free Markets, and the Twilight of Democracy.* U of Alabama P, 2006.

Hauser, Gerard A. *Prisoners of Conscience: Moral Vernaculars of Political Agency.* U of South Carolina P, 2012.

———. *Vernacular Voices: The Rhetoric of Publics and Public Spheres.* U of South Carolina P, 1999.

Hawhee, Debra. *Bodily Arts: Rhetoric and Athletics in Ancient Greece.* U of Texas P, 2004.

———. "Looking into Aristotle's Eyes: Toward a Theory of Rhetorical Vision." *Advances in the History of Rhetoric*, vol. 14, no. 2, 2011, pp. 139–65.

Haynes, Katharine. *Fashioning the Feminine in the Greek Novel.* Routledge, 2003.

Heffernan, James A. W. *Museum of Words. The Poetics of Ekphrasis from Homer to Ashbery.* U of Chicago P, 1991.

Héliodor. *Les Éthiopiques (Théagéne et Chariclée).* Paris, 1935–43. 2nd ed., edited R. M. Rattenbury and T. W. Lumb, Budé, 1960. 3 vols.

Heliodorus. "An Ethiopian Story." Translated by J. R. Morgan. Reardon, pp. 349–588.

Henderson, Ian. "The Second Sophistic and Non-elite Speakers." *Perception of the Second Sophistic and Its Times*, edited by Thomas Schmidt and Pascale Fleury, U of Toronto P, 2011.

Henderson, John. "From Megalopolis to Cosmopolis: Polybius, or There and Back Again." Goldhill, *Being Greek*, pp. 29–49.

Herodian. *History of the Roman Empire from the Death of Aurelius to the Accession of Gordian III.* Translated by Edward C. Echols, U of California P, 1961.

Highet, G. "The Huntsman and the Castaway." *Greek, Roman, and Byzantine Studies*, vol. 14, 1973, pp. 35–40. Reprinted in Ball, Robert J., editor. *The Classical Papers of Gilbert Highet*, Columbia UP, 1983, pp. 58–62.

Hilton, J. L. "The *Sphragis* of Heliodoros, Genealogy in the *Aithiopika*, and Julian's 'Hymn to King Helios.'" *Ágora*, vol. 14, 2012, pp. 195–218.

Holmes, Brooke. "Aelius Aristides' Illegible Body." Harris and Holmes, pp. 81–113.

Holzberg, Niklas. *The Ancient Novel: An Introduction.* Translated by Christine Jackson-Holzberg, Routledge, 1995.

Homer. *Iliad.* Translated by Robert Fagles, Viking, 1990.

———. *Iliad.* Translated by Richard Lattimore, U of Chicago P, 1961.

———. *Odyssey.* Translated by Emily Wilson, W. W. Norton, 2018.

Hopkins, Keith. "The Political Economy of the Roman Empire." *The Dynamics of Ancient Empires: State Power from Assyria to Byzantium*, edited by Ian Morris and Walter Scheidel, Oxford UP, 2009, pp. 178–204.

Horace. *The Epistles of Horace.* Translated by David Ferry, Farrar, Straus and Giroux, 2001.

———. *Satires. Epistles. The Art of Poetry.* Translated by H. Rushton Fairclough. Loeb Classical Library 194, Harvard UP, 1926.

Hunter, Richard. "The *Aithiopika* of Heliodorus: Beyond Interpretation?" Hunter, *Studies*, pp. 40–59.

———. Preface. Hunter, *Studies*, p. iv.

———, editor. *Studies in Heliodorus.* Supplementary Volume 21, Cambridge Philological Society, 1998.

Ignatieff, Michael. "The Burden." *New York Times Magazine*, 5 Jan. 2003, pp. 22–27, 50, 53–54.

Inglis, David, and Roland Robertson. "From Republican Virtue to Global Imaginary: Changing Visions of the Historian Polybius." *History of the Human Sciences*, vol. 19, no. 1, 2006, pp. 1–18.

Innes, Doreen, et al., editors. *Ethics and Rhetoric: Classical Essays for Donald Russell on His Seventy-Fifth Birthday.* Clarenden Press, 1995.

Isocrates. *Panegyricus. Isocrates*, translated by George Norlin, vol. 1, Loeb Classical Library 209, Harvard UP, 1928, pp. 116–241.

Jameson, Fredric. *Archaeologies of the Future: The Desire Called Utopia and Other Science Fictions.* Verso, 2007.

———. *The Political Unconscious: Narrative as a Socially Symbolic Act.* Cornell UP, 1982.

Jarratt, Susan C. "Historiographical Trauma: The Case of Polybius." *Emotional Trauma in Greece and Rome: Representations and Reactions*, edited by Andromache Karanika and Vassiliki Panoussi, Routledge, forthcoming.

———. "Libanius' Antioch: A Rhetorical Construction of the Greek (Cosmo) Polis." *Polis and Cosmopolis: Problems of the Global Era*, edited by K. Boudouris, vol. 1, Ionia Publications, 2003, pp. 107–18.

———. *Rereading the Sophists: Classical Rhetoric Refigured.* Southern Illinois UP, 1991.

———. "Sappho's Memory." *Rhetoric Society Quarterly,* vol. 32, no. 1, Winter 2002, pp. 11–43.

———. "Untimely Historiography? Foucault's 'Greco-Latin Trip.'" *Rhetoric Society Quarterly,* vol. 44, no. 3, 2014, pp. 220–33.

Jones, A. H. M. *The Greek City from Alexander to Justinian.* Oxford UP, 1940.

Jones, Christopher P. "Apollonius of Tyana in Late Antiquity." *Greek Literature in Late Antiquity: Dynamism, Didacticism, Classicism,* edited by Scott Fitzgerald Johnson, Ashgate, 2006, pp. 49–64.

———. *Culture and Society in Lucian.* Harvard UP, 1986.

———. Review of *Dione di Prusa: Un Intellettuale Greco Nell'Impero Romano,* by Paolo Desideri. *Phoenix,* vol. 34, no. 2, 1980, pp. 170–73.

———. *The Roman World of Dio Chrysostom.* Cambridge UP, 1978.

Jones, Jonathan. "Make America Decay Again: Thomas Cole and Ed Ruscha Review." *The Guardian,* 8 June 2018.

Julian. Oration 4. *Hymn to King Helios. The Works of the Emperor Julian,* translated by Wilmer Cave Wright, vol. 1, Loeb Classical Library 13, Harvard UP, 1913, pp. 352–435.

———. *Misopogon, or, Beard-Hater. The Works of the Emperor Julian,* translated by Wilmer Cave Wright, vol. 2, Loeb Classical Library 29, Harvard UP, 1913, pp. 420–511.

Kagan, Donald, et al. *Rebuilding America's Defenses: Strategy, Forces and Resources for a New Century.* Project for the New American Century, 2000.

Karadimas, Dimitrios. *Sextus Empiricus against Aelius Aristides: The Conflict Between Philosophy and Rhetoric in the Second Century* A.D. Lund UP, 1996.

Kastley, James L. *Rethinking the Rhetorical Tradition: From Plato to Postmodernism.* Yale UP, 1997.

Kennedy, George A. *Classical Rhetoric and Its Christian and Secular Tradition from Ancient to Modern Times.* U of North Carolina P, 1980.

———, translator. *Invention and Method: Two Rhetorical Treatises from the Hermogenic Corpus.* Society of Biblical Literature, 2005.

———. *A New History of Classical Rhetoric.* Princeton UP, 1994.

———, translator. *Progymnasmata: Greek Textbooks of Prose Composition and Rhetoric.* Society of Biblical Literature, 2003.

Kennerly, Michele. "*Sermo* and Stoic Sociality in Cicero's *De Officiis.*" *Rhetorica,* vol. 28, no. 2, Spring 2010, pp. 119–37.

Konstan, David. *The Emotions of the Ancient Greeks: Studies in Aristotle and Classical Literature.* U of Toronto P, 2006.

———. *Sexual Symmetry: Love in the Ancient Novel and Related Genres.* Princeton UP, 1993.

Krieger, Murray. *Ekphrasis: The Illusion of the Natural Sign.* Johns Hopkins UP, 1992.

Laird, Andrew. "Approaching Style and Rhetoric." Whitmarsh, *Cambridge Companion*, pp. 201–17.

Lamp, Kathleen S. *A City of Marble: The Rhetoric of Augustan Rome.* U of South Carolina P, 2003.

Laplanche, Jean, and Jean-Bertrand Pontalis. "Phantasy." *The Language of Psychoanalysis*, translated by Donald Nicholson-Smith, W. W. Norton, 1973, pp. 281–85.

Leach, Eleanor Winsor. *The Social Life of Painting in Ancient Rome and on the Bay of Naples.* Cambridge UP, 2004.

Lefebvre, Henri. *The Production of Space.* Translated by Donald Nicholson-Smith, Basil Blackwell, 1991.

Leontis, Artemis. *Topographies of Hellenism: Mapping the Homeland.* Cornell UP, 1995.

Lessing, Gotthold Ephraim. *Laokoön: An Essay upon the Limits of Painting and Poetry.* Translated by Ellen Frothingham, Boston, 1887.

Lévêque, Pierre. *Aurea Catena Homeri: Une Étude sur L'Allégorie Grecque.* Annales Littéraires de L'Université de Besançon, vol. 27, Les Belles Lettres, 1959.

Levick, Barbara. *Julia Domna: Syrian Empress.* Routledge, 2007.

Levine, Donald N. *Greater Ethiopia: The Evolution of a Multiethnic Society.* 2nd ed., U of Chicago P, 2000.

Lévy, Carlos. "From Politics to Philosophy and Theology: Some Remarks about Foucault's Interpretation of *Parrêsia* in Two Recently Published Seminars." *Philosophy and Rhetoric*, vol. 42, no. 4, 2009, pp. 313–25.

Libanius. *Encomium of Thersites.* Gibson, pp. 229–36.

———. Oration 1. *The Autobiography. Autobiography and Selected Letters*, translated by A. F. Norman, vol. 1, Loeb Classical Library 478, Harvard UP, 1992, pp. 51–337.

———. Oration 2. *To Those Who Call Him Tiresome. Libanius: Selected Orations*, translated by A. F. Norman, vol. 2, Loeb Classical Library 452, Harvard UP, 1977, pp. 11–51.

———. Oration 11. *The Antiochikos: In Praise of Antioch. Antioch as a Centre of Hellenic Culture as Observed by Libanius*, translated by A. F. Norman, Liverpool UP, 2000, pp. 3–65.

———. Oration 18. *Funeral Oration over Julian. Libanius: Selected Orations*, vol. 1: *The Julianic Orations*, translated by A. F. Norman, Loeb Classical Library 451, Harvard UP, 1987, pp. 279–487.

Liddell, H. G., and R. Scott, compilers. *Greek–English Lexicon, with a Revised Supplement*. 9th ed., revised and augmented by Sir Henry Stuart Jones et al., Clarendon Press, 1996.

Lipson, Carol, and Roberta A. Binkley, editors. *Ancient Non-Greek Rhetorics*. Parlor Press, 2009.

Long, A. A. *Hellenistic Philosophy*. 2nd ed., U of California P, 1986.

Longinus. *On the Sublime*. Edited and translated by W. Rhys Roberts, Cambridge UP, 1899.

Loraux, Nicole. *The Invention of Athens: The Funeral Oration in the Classical City*. Translated by Alan Sheridan, Harvard UP, 1986.

LSJ (*see* Liddell, H. G., and R. Scott, compilers).

Lucian. *On Sacrifices*. Translated by A. M. Harmon, vol. 3, Loeb Classical Library 130, Harvard UP, 1921, pp. 153–72.

Lundberg, Christian, and Joshua Gunn. "'Ouija Board, Are There Any Communications?' Agency, Ontotheology, and the Death of the Humanist Subject, or, Continuing the ARS Conversation." *Rhetoric Society Quarterly*, vol. 35, no. 4, 2005, pp. 83–105.

Lunsford, Andrea A. "On Reclaiming Rhetorica." Lunsford, *Reclaiming*, pp. 3–8.

———, editor. *Reclaiming Rhetorica: Women in the Rhetorical Tradition*. U of Pittsburgh P, 1995.

Lysias. "Against Eratosthenes." Saunders, pp. 43–59.

Ma, John. "Public Speech and Community in the *Euboicus*." Swain, *Dio Chrysostom*, pp. 108–24.

Malosse, Pierre-Louis. "Libanius' Orations." Van Hoof, pp. 81–106.

Mao, LuMing. "Searching for the Way: Between the Whats and Wheres of Chinese Rhetoric." *College English*, vol. 72, no. 4, 2010, pp. 329–49.

Mattingly, David J., editor. *Dialogues in Roman Imperialism: Power, Discourse, and Discrepant Experience in the Roman Empire*. Supplementary Series Number 23, Journal of Roman Archaeology, 1997.

———. *Imperialism, Power, and Identity: Experiencing the Roman Empire*. Princeton UP, 2010.

Mayor, Adrienne. *The Poison King: The Life and Legend of Mithradates, Rome's Deadliest Enemy.* Princeton UP, 2009.

Menander. *Menander Rhetor.* Translated by D. A. Russell and N. G. Wilson, Oxford UP, 1981.

Mendelsohn, Daniel. "Theatres of War." *The New Yorker,* 12 Jan. 2004, pp. 79–84.

Miles, Margaret M. *Art as Plunder: The Ancient Origins of Debate about Cultural Property.* Cambridge UP, 2008.

Millar, Fergus. *Emperor in the Roman World.* Bloomsbury Publishing, 1992.

———. "Empire and City, Augustus to Julian: Obligations, Excuses and Status." *Journal of Roman Studies*, vol. 73, 1983, pp. 76–96.

Miller, Carolyn R. "Should We Name the Tools? Concealing and Revealing the Art of Rhetoric." Ackerman and Coogan, pp. 19–38.

Miller, Patricia Cox. *Dreams in Late Antiquity.* Princeton UP, 1997.

Mitchell, W. J. T. *Picture Theory: Essays on Verbal and Visual Representation.* U of Chicago P, 1994.

Moles, J. L. "The Career and Conversion of Dio Chrysostom." *Journal of Hellenic Studies*, vol. 98, 1978, pp. 79–100.

———. "Dio Chrysostom, Greece, and Rome." Innes et al., pp. 177–92.

Morales, Helen. *Vision and Narrative in Achilles Tatius'* Leucippe and Clitophon. Cambridge UP, 2004.

Morgan, J. P. Introduction. Heliodorus, *An Ethiopian Story.* Reardon, pp. 349–53.

Murray, Oswyn, and Simon Price, editors. *The Greek City from Homer to Alexander.* Clarendon Press, 1990.

Newby, Zahra. "Absorption and Erudition in Philostratus' *Imagines.*" Bowie and Elsner, pp. 322–42.

———. "Art at the Crossroads? Themes and Styles in Severan Art." Swain et al., pp. 201–49.

Newman, Sara J. *Aristotle and Style.* Edwin Mellen Press, 2005.

Nicolet, Claude. "The *Res Gestae* of Augustus: Announcing the Conquest of the World." *Space, Geography, and Politics in the Early Roman Empire,* U of Michigan P, 1991, pp. 15- 27.

Nietzsche, Friedrich. "The Uses and Disadvantages of History for Life." *Untimely Meditations*, translated by R. J. Hollingdale, Cambridge UP, 1983, pp. 57–124.

Nimis, Steven A. "Memory and Description in the Ancient Novel." *Arethusa,* vol. 31, no. 1, Winter 1998, pp. 99–122.

Nock, Arthur Darby. "The Praises of Antioch." *Journal of Egyptian Archaeology*, vol. 40, 1954, pp. 76–82.

Norman, A. F., "General Introduction." *Antioch as a Centre of Hellenic Culture as Observed by Libanius*, by Libanius, Liverpool UP, 2000, pp. xi–xviii.

———. Introduction. Libanius, *Autobiography*, pp. 7–43.

———. Introduction. Libanius, Oration 2, pp. 2–9.

———. "The Life of Libanius." Libanius, Oration 18, pp. xxxix–xlv.

Nussbaum, Martha C. *The Therapy of Desire: Theory and Practice in Hellenistic Ethics*. Princeton UP, 1994.

Ober, Josiah. *Mass and Elite in Democratic Athens: Rhetoric, Ideology, and the Power of the People*. Princeton UP, 2009.

O'Gorman, Ned. "Aristotle's *Phantasia* in the *Rhetoric*: *Lexis*, Appearance, and the Epideictic Function of Discourse." *Philosophy and Rhetoric*, vol. 38, no. 1, 2005, pp. 16–40.

Oliver, James H. "The Ruling Power. A Study of the Roman Empire in the Second Century after Christ through the Roman Oration of Aelius Aristides." *Transactions of the American Philological Society*, vol. 43, no. 4, 1953, pp. 871–982.

O'Neill, Paul. "The Curatorial Turn: From Practice to Discourse." *Issues in Curating Contemporary Art and Performance*, edited by Judith Rugg and Michèle Sedgwick, Intellect Books, 2007, pp. 13–29.

Oudot, Estelle. "Aelius Aristides." Richter and Johnson, pp. 255–72.

———. "Regarder Rome, Percevoir Athènes: Remarques sur le Vocabulaire de la Vision dans les Éloges de Villes chez Aelius Aristide." *Couleurs et Vision dans L'Antiquité Classique*, edited by Laurence Villard, Publications de L'Université de Rouen, 2002, pp. 179–93.

Peradotto, John, and J. P. Sullivan, editors. *Women in the Ancient World: The Arethusa Papers*. SUNY P, 1984.

Pernot, Laurent. "Aelius Aristides and Rome." Harris and Holmes, pp. 173–202.

———. "Chariclée la Sirène." *Études de Littérature Ancienne*, vol. 4, 1992, pp. 43–51.

———. *Epideictic Rhetoric: Questioning the Stakes of Ancient Praise*. U of Texas P, 2015.

———. "Greek 'Figured Speech' on Imperial Rome." *Advances in the History of Rhetoric*, vol. 18, no. 2, 2015, pp. 131–46.

———. *L'Art du Sous-Entendu: Histoire, Théorie, Mode d'emploi*. Fayard, 2018.

———. Review of *Menander: A Rhetor in Context*, by Malcolm Heath. *Rhetorical Review*, vol. 5, no. 1, Feb. 2007, pp. 7–10.

———. *Rhetoric in Antiquity*. Translated by W. E. Higgins, Catholic U of America P, 2005.

———. *La rhétorique de l'éloge dans le monde grécoromain*. Collection d'Études Augustiniennes, série antiquité 136, Institut d'Études Augustiniennes, 1993. 2 vols.

———. "La Rhétorique de l'Empire ou comment la rhétorique grecque a inventé l'Empire romain." *Rhetorica*, vol. 16, no. 2, Spring 1998, pp. 131–48.

———. "The Third Sophistic: A New Concept in the History of Rhetoric." International Society for the History of Rhetoric, 28 July 2017, London. Paper.

Philostratus [the Elder]. *Imagines*. Translated by Arthur Fairbanks, Loeb Classical Library 256, Harvard UP, Loeb Classical Library, 1960, pp. 1–271.

———. "Letter 73: To Julia Augusta." *Letters of Alciphron, Aelian, and Philostratus*, translated by A. R. Benner and Francis H. Fobes, Loeb Classical Library 383, Harvard UP, 1949, pp. 541–45.

———. *The Life of Apollonius of Tyana*. Translated by Christopher P. Jones, Loeb Classical Library 16–17, Harvard UP, 2005. 2 vols.

———. *Lives of the Sophists. Philostratus and Eunapius: Lives of the Philosophers and Sophists*, translated by Wilmer C. Wright, Loeb Classical Library 134, Harvard UP, 1968, pp. 2–315.

Plato. *The Sophist*, translated by Harold North Fowler, vol. 7, Loeb Classical Library 123, Harvard UP, 1921.

Platt, Verity. "Virtual Visions: *Phantasia* and the Perception of the Divine in *The Life of Apollonius of Tyana*." Bowie and Elsner, pp. 131–54.

Plett, Heinrich F. *Enargeia in Classical Antiquity and the Early Modern Age: The Aesthetics of Evidence*. Brill, 2012.

Plutarch. *Moralia*, vol. IV. "Were the Athenians More Famous in War or in Wisdom?" Translated by F. C. Babbitt. Loeb Classical Library 305, Harvard UP, 1936, pp. 489–527.

Polybius. *The Rise of the Roman Empire*. Translated by Ian Scott-Kilvert, Penguin, 1979.

Porter, James I. "Ideals and Ruins. Pausanias, Longinus, and the Second Sophistic." *Pausanias: Travel and Memory in Roman Greece*, edited by Susan E. Alcock et al., Oxford UP, 2001, pp. 63–92.

Potter, David S. "The Unity of the Roman Empire." *From the Tetrarchs to the Theodosians: Later Roman History and Culture, 284–450 CE*, edited by Scott McGill et al., Cambridge UP, 2010, pp. 13–32.

———, editor. *A Companion to the Roman Empire.* Blackwell, 2006.

Poulakos, Takis. *Speaking for the Polis: Isocrates' Rhetorical Education.* U of South Carolina P, 1997.

Pullman, George. "Dio (Chrysostom) Cocceianus." Ballif and Moran, pp. 128–31.

Quandahl, Ellen, and Susan C. Jarratt. "'To Recall Him . . . Will Be a Subject of Lamentation': Anna Comnena as Rhetorical Historiographer." *Rhetorica*, vol. 26, no. 3, 2008, pp. 301–35.

Quintilian. *The Orator's Education.* Translated by Donald Russell, Loeb Classical Library 124–27, 494, Harvard UP, 2002. 5 vols.

Quiroga Puertas, Alberto J. "From Sophistopolis to Episcopolis: The Case for a Third Sophistic." *Journal for Late Antique Religion and Culture*, vol. 1, 2007, pp. 31–42.

Reardon, B. P., editor. *Collected Ancient Greek Novels.* U of California P, 1989.

Reynolds, Nedra. *Geographies of Writing: Inhabiting Places and Encountering Difference.* Southern Illinois UP, 2004.

Richlin, Amy. "Retrosexuality: Sex in the Second Sophistic." Richter and Johnson, pp. 115–38.

Richter, Daniel S., and William A. Johnson, editors. *The Oxford Handbook of the Second Sophistic.* Oxford UP, 2017.

Rives, James. "Human Sacrifice among Pagans and Christians." *Journal of Roman Studies*, vol. 85, 1995, pp. 65–85.

Robbins, Bruce, editor. *The Phantom Public Sphere.* U of Minnesota P, 1993.

Roberts, Jennifer Tolbert. *Athens on Trial: The Antidemocratic Tradition in Western Thought.* Princeton UP, 1994.

Romano, Susan. "The Historical Catalina Hernández: Inhabiting the *Topoi* of Feminist Historiography." *Rhetoric Society Quarterly*, vol. 37, 2007, pp. 453–80.

Rorty, Richard. "The Historiography of Philosophy: Four Genres." *Philosophy in History: Essays in the Historiography of Philosophy.* Cambridge UP, 1984, pp. 49–76.

Rose, Peter W. "Cicero and the Rhetoric of Imperialism: Putting the Politics Back into Political Rhetoric." *Rhetorica*, vol. 13, no. 4, Autumn 1995, pp. 359–99.

———. "Divorcing Ideology from Marxism and Marxism from Ideology: Some Problems." *Arethusa*, vol. 39, no. 1, Winter 2006, pp. 101–36.

———. "The Plural Voices of Thersites." *Arethusa*, vol. 21, 1988, pp. 5–25.

———. *Sons of Gods, Children of Earth: Ideology and Literary Form in Ancient Greece*. Cornell UP, 1992.

———. "Theorizing Athenian Imperialism and the Athenian State." *Contextualizing Classics: Ideology, Performance, Dialogue; Essays in Honor of John J. Peradotto*, edited by Thomas M. Falkner et al., Rowman & Littlefield, 1999, pp. 19–39.

Rosenmeyer, Thomas G. "Gorgias, Aeschylus, and *Apatē*." *American Journal of Philology*, vol. 76, no. 3, 1955, pp. 225–60.

Royster, Jacqueline Jones, and Gesa E. Kirsch. *Feminist Rhetorical Practices: New Horizons for Rhetoric, Composition, and Literacy Studies*. Southern Illinois UP, 2012.

Russell, D. A. *Greek Declamation*. Cambridge UP, 1983.

Russell, D. A., and N. G. Wilson. "Introduction: Epideictic Practice and Theory." *Menander Rhetor*, translated by Russell and Wilson, Oxford UP, 1981, pp. xi–xxxiv.

Said, Edward W. *Culture and Imperialism*. Vintage Books, 1993.

———. *Orientalism*. Vintage, 1978.

Saintsbury, George. *A History of Criticism and Literary Taste in Europe from the Earliest Texts to the Present Day*. Vol. 1, William Blackwood, 1900.

Salmeri, Giovanni. "Dio, Rome, and the Civic Life of Asia Minor." Swain, *Dio Chrysostom*, pp. 53–92.

Sanders, Mark. *Complicities: The Intellectual and Apartheid*. U of Natal P, 2002.

Sandy, Gerald N. *Heliodorus*. Twayne, 1982.

Saunders, A. N. W. *Greek Political Oratory*, Penguin, 1978.

———. Introduction. Saunders, pp. 7–27.

Schiavone, Aldo. *The End of the Past: Ancient Rome and the Modern West*. Translated by Margery J. Schneider, Harvard UP, 2002.

Schofield, Malcolm. *The Stoic Idea of the City*. U of Chicago P, 1999.

Scott, Grant F. "The Rhetoric of Dilation: Ekphrasis and Ideology." *Words and Image*, vol. 7, Oct.–Dec. 1991, pp. 301–10.

Scott, Janny. "The Story of Obama, Written by Obama." *The New York Times*, 18 May 2008.

Scott, Joan Wallach. "Deconstructing Equality-versus-Difference: Or, the Uses of Poststructuralist Theory for Feminism." *Feminist Studies*, vol. 33, 1988, pp. 38–47.

Shaffer, Diana. "*Ekphrasis* and the Rhetoric of Viewing in Philostratus's

Imaginary Museum." *Philosophy and Rhetoric*, vol. 31, no. 4, 1998, pp. 303–16.

Small, Jocelyn Penny. *Wax Tablets of the Mind: Cognitive Studies of Memory and Literacy in Classical Antiquity*. Routledge, 1997.

Smith, Christopher, and Liv Mariah Yarrow, editors. *Imperialism, Cultural Politics, and Polybius*. Oxford UP, 2012.

Smith, John H. *The Spirit and Its Letter: Traces of Rhetoric in Hegel's Philosophy of* Bildung. Cornell UP, 1988.

Smith, Neil. "Space and Substance in Geography." *Envisioning Human Geography*, edited by Paul Cloke et al., Routledge, 2004, pp. 112–29.

Sophocles, *Antigone*. Translated by Hugh Lloyd-Jones, vol. 2, Loeb Classical Library 21, Harvard UP, 1994.

Spivak, Gayatri Chakravorty. "Can the Subaltern Speak?" *Marxism and the Interpretation of Culture*, edited by Cary Nelson and Lawrence Grossberg, U of Illinois P, 1988, pp. 271–313.

Steel, Ronald. *Pax Americana*. Viking, 1967.

Stroumsa, Guy G. *The End of Sacrifice: Religious Transformations in Late Antiquity*. Translated by Susan Emanuel, U of Chicago P, 2009.

Suetonius. *The Twelve Caesars*. Translated by Robert Graves, Penguin, 1957.

Swain, Simon, editor. *Dio Chrysostom: Politics, Letters, and Philosophy*. Oxford UP, 2000.

———. *Hellenism and Empire. Language, Classicism, and Power in the Greek World, AD 50–250*. Clarendon Press, 1996.

Swain, Simon et al., editors. *Severan Culture*. Cambridge UP, 2007.

Tacitus. *A Dialogue on Oratory*. Hadas, pp. 735–69.

———. *The Life of Gnaeus Julius Agricola*. Hadas, 677–706.

Terada, Rei. "Speaking to No One." *Journal of Contemporary Thought*, vol. 39, Summer 2014, pp. 75–93.

Thalmann, W. G. "Thersites: Comedy, Scapegoats, and Heroic Ideology in the *Iliad*." *Transactions of the American Philological Association*, vol. 118, 1988, pp. 1–28.

Thucydides. *Book II*. Edited by E. C. Marchant, Bristol Classical Press, 1978.

———. *History of the Peloponnesian War*. Translated by Rex Warner, Penguin, 1954.

Trapp, M. B., translator. *Maximus of Tyre: The Philosophical Orations*. Clarendon Press, 1997.

———. "Sense of Place in the Orations of Dio Chrysostom." Innes, et al., pp. 163–76.

Van Hoof, Lieve, editor. *Libanius: A Critical Introduction.* Cambridge UP, 2014.

———. "Introduction: Libanius' Life and *Lives* of Libanius." Van Hoof, pp. 7–38.

Vannier, François. "Aelius Aristide et la domination romaine d'après le discours 'A Rome.'" *Dialogues d'histoire ancienne*, vol. 2, no. 1, 1976, pp. 497–506.

Walbank, F. W. *Polybius.* U of California P, 1972.

Walker, Jeffrey. *The Genuine Teachers of This Art: Rhetorical Education in Antiquity.* U of South Carolina P, 2011.

———. *Rhetoric and Poetics in Antiquity.* Oxford UP, 2000.

———. "These Things I Have Not Betrayed: Michael Psellos' Encomium of His Mother as a Defense of Rhetoric." *Rhetorica*, vol. 22, 2004, pp. 49–101.

Wallace-Hadrill, Andrew. *Rome's Cultural Revolution.* Cambridge UP, 2008.

Walzer, Arthur. "*Parrêsia*, Foucault, and the Classical Rhetorical Tradition." *Rhetoric Society Quarterly*, vol. 43, no. 1, Winter 2013, pp. 1–21.

Warner, Michael. "The Mass Public and the Mass Subject." Robbins, pp. 234–56.

———. *Publics and Counterpublics.* Zone Books, 2005.

———. "Queer Theory and Anti-normativity." University of California, Irvine, 14 May 2013. Paper.

Watson, Gerard. *Phantasia in Classical Thought.* Galway UP, 1988.

Watts, Edward. "The Historical Context: The Rhetorical Use of Suffering in Libanius' *Monodies, Letters* and *Autobiography.*" Van Hoof, pp. 39–58.

Webb, Ruth. *Ekphrasis, Imagination and Persuasion in Ancient Rhetorical Theory and Practice.* Ashgate, 2009.

———. "Greek Grammatical Glosses and Scholia: The Form and Function of a Late Byzantine Commentary." *Medieval and Renaissance Scholarship: Proceedings of the Second European Science Foundation Workshop on the Classical Tradition in the Middle Ages and the Renaissance*, edited by Nicholas Mann and Birger Munk Olsen, Brill, 1997, pp. 1–18.

Wells, Colin. *The Roman Empire.* 2nd ed., Harvard UP, 1992.

Wells, Susan. *Sweet Reason: Rhetoric and the Discourses of Modernity.* U of Chicago P, 1996.

Westin, Monica. "Aristotle's Rhetorical *Energeia:* An Extended Note." *Advances in the History of Rhetoric*, vol. 20, 2017, pp. 252–61.

Whitmarsh, Tim. "The Birth of a Prodigy: Heliodorus and the Genealogy of Hellenism." Hunter, *Studies*, pp. 93–124.

———, editor. *The Cambridge Companion to the Greek and Roman Novel.* Cambridge UP, 2008.

——— "'Greece Is the World': Exile and Identity in the Second Sophistic." Goldhill, *Being Greek*, pp. 269–305.

———. *Greek Literature and the Roman Empire: The Politics of Imitation.* Oxford UP, 2001.

———. Introduction. Whitmarsh, *Cambridge Companion*, pp. 1–14.

———. "Performing Heroics: Language, Landscape and Identity in Philostratus' *Heroicus*." Bowie and Elsner, pp. 205–29.

———. "Prose Literature and the Severan Dynasty." Swain et al., pp. 29–51.

———. "Reading Power in Roman Greece: The *Paideia* of Dio Chrysostom." *Pedagogy and Power: Rhetorics of Classical Learning*, edited by Yun Lee Too and Niall Livingstone, Cambridge UP, 1998, pp. 192–213.

———. *The Second Sophistic.* Oxford UP, 2005.

Wiemer, Hans-Ulrich. "Emperors and Empire in Libanius." Van Hoof, pp. 187–219.

Williams, Craig A. *Roman Homosexuality.* 2nd ed., Oxford UP, 2010.

Williams, John. "Liveright to Publish Nelson Mandela's Letters from Prison." *The New York Times*, 27 June 2017.

Williams, Patricia J. "Pax Americana." *The Nation*, 1 Oct. 2001.

Winkler, John. "The Mendacity of Kalisiris and the Narrative Strategy of Heliodorus' *Aethiopika*." *Yale Classical Studies*, vol. 27, 1986, pp. 93–158.

Woods, Marjorie Curry. *Weeping for Dido: Classics in the Medieval Classroom.* Princeton UP, 2019.

Woodward, Bob. *Plan of Attack.* Simon & Schuster, 2004.

Woolf, Greg. "Becoming Roman, Staying Greek: Culture, Identity and the Civilizing Process in the Roman East." *Proceedings of the Cambridge Philological Society*, no. 40, 1994, pp. 116–43.

———."Roman Peace." *War and Society in the Roman World*, edited by John Rich and Graham Shipley, Routledge, 1993, pp. 171-94.

Yahr, Emily. "How 'Indecision 2000' Changed Everything for Jon Stewart and 'The Daily Show.'" *The Washington Post*, 5 Aug. 2015.

Yates, Frances A. *The Art of Memory.* U of Chicago, 1966.

Yunis, Harvey. "Eros in Plato's *Phaedrus* and the Shape of Greek Rhetoric." *Arion*, vol. 13, no. 1, 2005, pp. 101–25.

Zedler, Beatrice H. "Julia Domna." *History of Women Philosophers*, edited by Mary Ellen Waithe, vol 1., Martinus Nijhoff, 1987, pp. 117–38.
Zeitlin, Froma I. "The Artful Eye: Vision, Ecphrasis and Spectacle in Euripidean Theatre." Goldhill and Osborne, pp. 138–96.
———. "Playing the Other: Theater, Theatricality, and the Feminine in Greek Drama." *Representations*, vol. 11, 1985, pp. 63–94.
———. "Religion." Whitmarsh, *Cambridge Companion*, pp. 91–108.
———. "Visions and Revisions of Homer." Goldhill, *Being Greek*, pp. 195–266.
Žižek, Slavoj. *The Sublime Object of Ideology*. Verso, 1989.

Index

Page numbers in italics indicate illustrations.

Susan C. Jarratt is a professor emerita of comparative literature at the University of California, Irvine. She is the author of *Rereading the Sophists: Classical Rhetoric Refigured* and recently coedited *Unruly Rhetorics: Protest, Persuasion, and Publics.* She served as the editor of *Rhetoric Society Quarterly* from 2016 to 2019.